Leni Riefenstahl

Leni Riefenstahl

The Seduction of Genius

RAINER ROTHER

Translated by Martin H. Bott

continuum
LONDON • NEW YORK

Continuum

The Tower Building	370 Lexington Avenue
11 York Road	New York
London SE1 7NX	NY 10017–65–03

First published in German by Henschel, Berlin 2000 as *Leni Riefenstahl Die Verführung des Talents.*

British Library Cataloguing-in-Publication Data
A catalogue record for this book is available from the British Library.

ISBN 0-8264-6101-8 (hardback)

Typeset by YHT Ltd, London
Printed and bound in Great Britain by
MPG Books Ltd, Bodmin, Cornwall

Contents

Translator's Preface

Some of Leni Riefenstahl's films were released in English-language versions which differed from the original in certain respects. To avoid confusion, the original German titles are used here, although a 'courtesy translation' is provided on the first mention of each film (and in the Filmography). Reference is also made to English-language versions where relevant. Translations of the dialogue or captions are my own.

Similarly, for the sake of authenticity, I have translated all other German quotations myself, even where published English translations of the text in question are available. The German sources are therefore listed in the Bibliography (which also specifies the archival sources used). Where English translations of important material exist – Riefenstahl's memoirs are the most notable example – this is made clear on the first mention in the text or notes. Readers should note, however, that *Sieve of Time*, the translation of Riefenstahl's memoirs published in the United Kingdom by Quartet Books, omits some sections of the original text.

Courtesy translations for the titles of German articles and books cited in the text or notes are supplied wherever their meaning is relevant.

Quotations from texts written in English are, of course, from the original and cited accordingly.

I am indebted to Rainer Rother for his friendly and remarkably rapid responses to my queries during the closing stages of my work on his book, and to Pilar for her invaluable help and encouragement.

Martin H. Bott
Zürich, April 2002

Acknowledgements

This book could not have been written without various kinds of help and advice from institutions, colleagues and friends. I would like to thank them all.

The Friedrich-Wilhelm-Murnau-Stiftung enabled me to view films; I am particularly grateful to Gudrun Weiss and the Munich Filmmuseum, the Deutsches Filminstitut, the Stiftung Deutsche Kinemathek and the Bundesarchiv-Filmarchiv, where I was able to view copies from the collections.

I also received tremendous support whilst researching texts and photographs, in particular from Claudia Dillmann and Rüdiger Koschnitzky (Deutsches Filminstitut), Hans-Michael Bock and the CineGraph team (Hamburgisches Centrum für Filmforschung), Elke Schieber (Filmmuseum Potsdam), Hans Helmut Prinzler, Frau Orluc, Eva Orbanz and Wolfgang Jacobsen (Stiftung Deutsche Kinemathek), Karl Griep, Helmut Morsbach, Martina Werth-Mühl and Evelyn Hampicke (Bundesarchiv-Filmarchiv), Stefan Drössler, Gerhard Ullmann and Klaus Volkmer (Filmmuseum München), Irmgard Bartel (Friedrich-Ebert-Stiftung), Loy Arnold and Mark Grünthal (Transit-Film), Dr Franz-Josef Kos and Herr Dr von Boeselager (German Foreign Ministry), Kapitänleutnant Dirk Steffen (Militärgeschichtliches Forschungsamt Potsdam), Herr Hinze and Frau Heidemann (the Bauer Verlag's archive), Herr Dr Luchterhand (Landesarchiv Berlin), Herr Dr Gschaid (Bayerisches Hauptstaatsarchiv), Jan-Walther Hennig and Bernd Michael Finke (NDR), Herr Knuth and Dr Michael Crone (Hessischer Rundfunk), Herr Person (Südwestrundfunk), Walter Roller (Deutsches Rundfunkarchiv), Dr. Jürgen Zimmer (Kunstbibliothek SMPK).

I would like to thank Hans Brecht, Hans Jürgen Panitz and Andreas Schlüter for their readiness to discuss matters with me and their friendly support for the project.

I am indebted for advice and material to Rolf Aurich, Eva-Margarethe Baumann, Hans-Jürgen Brandt, Joachim C. Fest, Jeanpaul Goergen, Erika Gregor, Hans Jessen, Nicola Klein, Martin Koerber, Claudia Lenssen, Hanno Loewy, Martin Loiperdinger, Theo Matthies, Carsten Meyer, Ralf Schenk, Gerhard Schoenberner, Eberhard Spiess, Kerstin Stutterheim, Sonja Trautmann, Angelika Wachs, Barbara Wenner and Merten Worthmann. I am very grateful to David Welch and David Culbert for supporting the idea of an English translation. David Culbert was also most generous in making available photographs from his own collection for this edition. Finally I would like to thank all the staff at the archives and collections where I undertook research, who were always ready to offer me friendly assistance.

Most of all, it was Catherine who repeatedly encouraged me and demonstrated unflagging patience. Without her, this book would never have been completed.

CHAPTER ONE

Introduction: The Problem with Leni Riefenstahl

When the *Frankfurter Allgemeine Zeitung*'s magazine asked Leni Riefenstahl to specify her main character trait, she chose strength of will.[1] Nobody could argue with the ninety-one-year-old's self-assessment: her career provides ample evidence of her determination. Yet this was a characteristic she was forced to conceal for much of her career. If she thought that bursting into tears was the only way forward in a particular situation, she would do just that. Sometimes there really was no alternative: strength of will was regarded as unfeminine in the period during which she was defying the odds by making her way in the male domain of filmmaking. The way she overcame all obstacles, battling against almost exclusively male colleagues and rivals, is certainly a conspicuous aspect of her career. It was an impressive demonstration of strength; her refusal to allow herself to be distracted from her own aims was remarkable, as was her capacity to endure all kinds of strain.

The second aspect of her career concerns the ambitions which Riefenstahl went to such lengths to pursue. According to her memoirs, she never actually wanted to become an actress and she directed her first film without any particular desire to be a director. She claims that Hitler compelled her to make the Party Rally films, that she agreed reluctantly to direct *Olympia* and only made *Tiefland* (The Lowlands) because her *Penthesilea* project seemed inappropriate during the war. Can she really have fought so hard, so tenaciously and so long for projects she would have preferred to avoid altogether? Strong-willed though she was, she represents herself as remarkably indecisive.

Riefenstahl's work and her success at getting her own way are evidence of her capabilities. It is evidence that remains provocative even today. The large exhibition dedicated to twentieth-century art in Germany ('Das XX. Jahrhundert. 100 Jahre Kunst in Deutschland') at Berlin's Altes Museum was a striking example of how Riefenstahl's work has been viewed in recent times. One room was dedicated to Nazi art. Only a few examples of the plastic arts were included, such as *Prometheus* (1937) by Arno Breker, *Menschenpaar* (1936) by Georg Kolbe and Adolf Ziegler's *Vier Elemente* (1936). In the middle of the room stood a 'KdF Wagen' ('Strength through Joy' car – Hitler's term for the original Beetle), a symbol of the populist variety of National Socialist modernism. Large reproductions from the advertising brochure that accompanied the 'Deutschland-Ausstellung' (the Germany Exhibition in Berlin, 1936), designed by Bauhaus disciple Herbert Bayer, and four video projections completed the display. Leni Riefenstahl, and above all her *Olympia* film, dominated the videos. There were scenes taken from the prologue, the various sporting events including the famous high-diving collage, and finally the 'Cathedral of Light'. She was also represented indirectly: the intercut documentaries about Breker and Thorak, by Arnold Fanck and Hans Cürlis, were made by Riefenstahl's production company.[2] The other two examples – a film about the Nazis' ritualistic service of remembrance on 9 November 1937 and a compilation of wartime weekly newsreels – also conspicuously reflected the influence of Riefenstahl's work.

Hanging opposite the *Olympia* projection were four screen-prints by Andy Warhol (versions of *Reflected* and *Stadium*, both 1982) which take up the motif of the 'Cathedral of Light' designed by Albert Speer for the Nazis' show-piece, mass-participation events. It was *Olympia* which imprinted that image on people's collective memory. It is unlikely that any other artist active under the Nazi regime could be shown to have such continuing relevance. Significantly, the exhibition in Berlin traced responses to her work from the 1930s to the 1980s, from 'Nazi art' to Pop Art. It treated Riefenstahl's work as something very special. It might be described, somewhat controversially, as the only form of Nazi art without a parasitic indebtedness either to avant-garde models such as Bauhaus or modern sculpture or, by contrast, to supposedly antique or classical models (like the work of Breker and Ziegler). Rather, it possessed its own, integral strength, enabling it to become a model itself – or at least a source of inspiration – to modern artistic movements such as Pop Art. Clearly, such a claim is more than a little problematic in terms of cultural discourse, for it implies that all Nazi art was bad and kitschy unless it was by Riefenstahl. Nevertheless, that view of her work remains widespread, albeit largely unspoken. In the 1990s, for example, it inspired several artists to turn their attention to Riefenstahl as a person. At the same time, her films and photographs acquired a resonance as legitimate aesthetic quotations.

Posthumous artistic fame rarely happens because of the discovery of a hitherto unrecognized genius. Usually it is the confirmation of a talent that even contemporaries considered significant. The talent therefore received recognition – but was also subject to envy and resentment. According to Walter Benjamin, there is a criterion for distinguishing moderate talents from the real geniuses. This is in fact a delicate distinction, given that both were celebrated alike by their contemporaries. Benjamin claims that there is a 'real structure of "greatness" among the great authors, who are "great" because their influence is historic but who did not, conversely, have historic influence on account of their power as authors'.[3] This conclusion obviously hovers on the brink of tautology, as it does not define historic 'greatness' on the basis of a specific quality in the works. There is something intellectually unsatisfying about the claim that Shakespeare was a great writer because his works remain so influential even today. It would be more satisfying to suggest that he was a great writer because he was 'the first' to develop something, or developed it 'more rigorously' than anyone else, or better still because he was the 'only one' to develop it. That, indeed, is the argument favoured by aesthetes. For Benjamin, however, such an argument is simply a way of evading the paradox. True geniuses, after all, can remain unsung indefinitely, perhaps because their works have actually disappeared or perhaps because, despite being tremendously innovative, they were also tremendously obscure and fail to attract attention even today because of the lack of a continuous trail leading back to them. Unsung 'greatness', however, is impossible.

That which we consider 'great' is always that which is familiar and established: the repertoire. 'In theoretical terms, however, the main axiom of this new mysticism should be: "A work is not celebrated because it is great; rather, it is great because it is celebrated." '[4]

Benjamin's outline of a theory for posthumous fame is materialistic in a very literal, almost primitive sense. If 'greatness' is considered to mean historic influence, then the enduring talents really are significant. That does not mean, however, that everything 'significant' also endures. Yet Benjamin's unexpectedly robust materialism does offer some consolation absent from the idiosyncratic claims of spiritual hierarchies. He does not define 'greatness' as a mystery, but as a relatively stable currency.

It is in this sense that Leni Riefenstahl's 'greatness' emerges. Riefenstahl was, for example, considered worthy of a television documentary lasting more than three hours (and broadcast at peak viewing time). A modern choreographer generally described as 'provocative' saw Riefenstahl as her kind of subject. A band more or less synonymous with 'Deutsch-rock' used footage Riefenstahl had produced (back in 1936/38!) in a music video.[5] Exhibitions honoured her artistic work in Tokyo, Milan, Rome and Potsdam. She was invited as a special guest at *Time* magazine's 100th aniversary. This is evidence enough to prove that Riefenstahl is, in the terms of popular culture, a cult artist if ever there was one. Her burgeoning influence is clear to see – not just in sports films or even in the way the image of sport in general has been sexualized, not just in quotations such as those in *Star Wars* or even in an animated film such as *The Lion King*,[6] and not just in the aesthetics of advertising. The truth is that her considerable influence is no longer founded only on her undeniably ingenious inventions as an artist: her own biography is now also a factor. For decades she has persistently advanced her own explanation of herself, and in the public perception that explanation has become as significant as the works themselves. Both Johann Kresnik's work of dance theatre (in the central figure's monologue) and Thea Dorn's radio play[7] draw on Riefenstahl's memoirs. Leni Riefenstahl's apologia for her own life turned her into a 'figure of art' worthy of as much attention as her works of art. In recent years, there have been several announcements of plans to make a film of her life, and Jodie Foster now appears to be going ahead with this project.[8]

The mere idea of making a film about Riefenstahl's life is evidence of a change in her public image. Formerly a non-person, she has grown in popularity because of, not despite, the cliché of the 'Nazi filmmaker'. This transformation has been achieved by a particular version of the public construction called Leni Riefenstahl, a version founded on the persona rather than the person, on a vague conception of her work rather than close analysis of it. Such a construction is born of a discourse that is closely bound to powerful stories and forceful individuals. Both as a person and as a legend, Leni Riefenstahl certainly fits the bill. It would be hard to conceive of a 'more powerful' story.

Recently, therefore, a new myth of Leni Riefenstahl has arisen. Its public appeal – involving a moderate form of outrage – is beyond doubt. Towards the end of the 1990s this 'persona' acquired a unique kind of aura. Even within her lifetime, she began to enter the phase of posthumous fame.

The aesthetic provocation in Riefenstahl's work is now perceived more generally and more clearly. This, allied to the way her life story has been used to create new fictions, has created an additional stratum of significance above that of the moral and political provocation arising from her life and work, which dominated people's view of her for so long. Riefenstahl has, however, not yet become a completely uncontroversial symbol, as the political protests against the exhibition of her photographs in a Hamburg gallery in 1997 showed.[9] She remains the representative figure she always was, but other aspects of that 'persona' have emerged. It is hardly surprising that this should be regarded as (at least) problematic in political terms.[10] Nevertheless, the link between the symbolic, demonized image of Riefenstahl and her career remains to be reconstructed.

The symbolic figure of the 'Nazi filmmaker' was evidently grist to the mill of those seeking to shift blame and make recriminations. There is certainly a 'Riefenstahl problem', but even today there is also a problem *with* Leni Riefenstahl. Moral judgements are an essential ingredient in the debate surrounding the work (which is exemplary and exceptional in equal measure) and its director. That is an inescapable consequence of the extent to which both the work and the person profited from, and contributed to, National Socialism. The problem *with* Leni Riefenstahl only emerged after

1945 and cannot be understood in purely moral categories – partly because it involves the reasons for the fact that no other person whose career blossomed under Nazi rule has attracted the kind of persistent criticism endured by Leni Riefenstahl. Of course, the director is not an innocent victim of boycotts and character assassination: her behaviour until the end of the war generated all the ammunition needed by her later critics. Her justifications, moreover, were precisely what made some of the criticism possible and necessary. Yet the intensity with which her critics clung and continue to cling to the demonic image of her cannot be explained only by Riefenstahl's strategy of keeping quiet about awkward events and insisting that she bore no personal responsibility. She can, after all, claim never to have been a member of the NSDAP (National Socialist German Workers – or Nazi – Party), never to have committed a crime and not to have vilified minorities in her films. She acquired her share of the blame through tacit connivance, suppression and not wanting to know – like so many other Germans.

It was probably inevitable that one of the consequences of the way West Germany went about legitimizing itself – the Federal Republic's famous 'fundamental consensus', which was at once antimilitarist, antifascist and anticommunist – should be the construction of symbolic demons to promote stabilization. In political practice, West Germany had no choice but to rely on the cooperation of many officials and functionaries in the economy, the press and the world of culture. Their cooperation largely reflected the fact that the democratic sovereign was identical with the people that had failed to rise up against dictatorship and mass murder. Even at the time, there must have been a suspicion that if, in retrospect, all Germans except a few war criminals were to be treated as somehow equal, there must necessarily be some exceptions within that group: individuals who were implicated in ways that were difficult to determine and who had not been declared guilty in law. Other people must surely have known all about the things which 'we could not have known' – people with more power, influence or fame; people like Leni Riefenstahl.

The public debate in post-war Germany thus started to use her as a 'case' and to cite the conflicting aspects of that case whenever it seemed appropriate. The alternative approaches to Leni Riefenstahl are well established: she was a great genius or a mere talent; an obsessive artist or a barefaced propagandist; the supreme ingénue or a calculating profiteer. There is no foreseeable end to this circle of interpretations, and it is certain that Leni Riefenstahl herself will never say anything that might suggest a new possibility. For a long time now, she has done no more than repeat her own statements, which form a unified version of events – tightly sealed even against verifiable facts. For a long time, therefore, society continued to find the 'case' of the public 'persona', Leni Riefenstahl, provocative. It was as if she possessed some particularly emotive quality. Two equally entrenched, bitterly hostile points of view shared only their mutual insistence that they were opposed in every respect. The only place they ever met was in a court of law.

There is no analogy for the way Riefenstahl's work has been received. To term it problematic is perhaps an understatement. West Germany's evaluation even of Veit Harlan, director of the virulently anti-Semitic film *Jud Süss*, was rather discerning (and certainly not apologetic) compared with its appraisal of Leni Riefenstahl. That is true to an even greater extent of other Nazi propagandists, who did not confine themselves to work on film. The tendency to declare Riefenstahl either a total genius or a mere propagandist for National Socialism seems almost a reflex reaction, and it has been very slow to develop and change. Indeed, perhaps that very process might enable us to understand more precisely the construction of Leni Riefenstahl's public persona.

That is the goal of this book, which deals with Riefenstahl's work and the way it is bound up with Nazi propaganda and the subsequent public debate. Although this approach involves tracing the course of Riefenstahl's life and analysing many statements made in her memoirs and interviews (for these contributed to the construction of her image), the book is not intended to be a biography. After 1945, Leni Riefenstahl always defended her 'whole life'. In her justification she forged a consistent view of her work and her public role. Everything had to interrelate without contradictions, and ultimately it was vital that everything could be represented as entirely private. Similarly, her critics were and are intent on reconciling the life with the work and with the person. They, however, have drawn negative conclusions about the person on the basis of the work. This book attempts to avoid such alternatives.

Part One

THE TALENT

CHAPTER TWO

Beginnings

Leni Riefenstahl considered herself capable of anything and everything. One section of her memoirs, when she quotes from a letter to a girlhood friend, seems almost charmingly naïve now. In the letter she mentions articles she has written but not submitted, plans for novellas, work on material for a film ('but I am keeping it to myself, since I want to play the main role in it myself one day') and the development of 'something to do with aeroplanes, because of the impending dawn of civil aviation'.[1]

Other people took a different view of her abilities. Her father thought her incapable of dancing. Arnold Fanck thought her incapable of acting. The film industry thought her incapable of playing demanding roles, not to mention directing films herself. Stalwart Nazi Party members thought her incapable of making the Party Rally film. Such scepticism explains why her desire to prove herself was such a feature of her career. Hitler and – to begin with, at least – Goebbels were patrons who recognized her abilities instead of doubting them. Perhaps it is no wonder that she was unable to resist them.

Overcompensation

Leni Riefenstahl's career was marked by an excess of motivation. She always felt a compulsion to make grand entrances and tackle the toughest problems first. When she took to the stage, it was never in a supporting role. Right from the start, she was there at the centre of the action. She always demanded one hundred per cent, be it as a dancer, an actress, a director or a photographer. Her ambition rebelled against the narrow bounds which the women of her time were expected to respect. She was characterized by tremendous confidence in her own abilities, an unusual self-assurance which left her undaunted by immense and unexpected challenges. Yet the cautionary memories from her childhood were also important:

> I never wanted to depend on anyone in my life. When I saw the treatment my mother sometimes received from my father – he could stamp his feet like an elephant if he was unable to undo a button because of the starched collar of his shirt – I swore to myself that in later life I would never let anyone else take the wheel. I would always make my own decisions.[2]

Leni Riefenstahl knew exactly what she wanted, and she also knew exactly what kind of life she did not want to lead. Her career therefore could not begin otherwise than as an eruption, as a struggle against her father's will. She had to aim as high as possible from the very start.

This urge was to remain a decisive influence in later years. Her achievement is not the result of a long, cumulative process of development, still less of being properly taught her various professions. Her debuts were outbursts, heroic demonstrations of her abilities or even mere stopgaps; but she always felt the need to begin with an all-out effort in order to justify her career decisions. It is probably fair to say that the only chance she had was to overtrump everyone with proof of what she could do. This lent her career its exceptional character. Looking back, she was never able to identify an interlude during which she had been able gradually to test her skills. She made up for her lack of experience and education with demonstrative self-confidence and the desire to be a star from the very start.

In Riefenstahl's definition, a career does not denote a process, a slow struggle for recognition. Rather, it involves a series of stages linked by a paradoxical logic: a brilliant beginning, an acclaimed continuation and a hard-fought finale. Leni Riefenstahl's performances were the results of unexpected chances and sudden moments of insight. Her motto was 'learning by doing'. Her ability to grasp things quickly and her physical agility lent her so much assurance that she soon felt she had mastered each new subject. She then, of course, felt an almost overpowering urge to go on and demonstrate her own skills.

According to her memoirs, this was the case even at the start of her brief career as a dancer. She writes that her first public performance was when she stood in for the 'already very well-known' Anita Berber, who had been taken ill at short notice.[3] Despite all the quarrels with her father, she managed to get her way and shortly afterwards she embarked on the first of her careers. She remembers it as a thoroughly successful beginning. Having just turned twenty-one, she danced her own programme for the first time. Within a few months – between October 1923 and approximately May 1924 – she undertook a tour which allegedly included seventy performances, mainly in Germany but also in Austria, Switzerland and Czechoslovakia. Soon afterwards, whilst unable to dance for a considerable period due to a knee injury, she decided she wanted to play a part in a Fanck film. Her wish was fulfilled: Leni Riefenstahl began her film career with a leading role in *Der heilige Berg* (The Holy Mountain, 1925). She imposed her stylistic will even on the first film she made as a director, in *Das blaue Licht* (The Blue Light, 1932), demonstrating that she felt no hesitation or insecurity about the medium. In 1933 her first documentary, *Sieg des Glaubens* (Victory of Faith), defined a new kind of film which soon came to be regarded as the prototype of National Socialist cinematic art. Similarly, as a photographer – in her photo-reportages, the books of photographs about the Nuba and the later underwater pictures – she presented herself as the finished article even in her first publications. In retrospect, this gives the impression of an astonishing series of incomparable 'debuts'.

There is a popular belief that winners can be recognized right from the start, and it is undeniable that Leni Riefenstahl made a superlative start to each new stage in her extraordinary career. Her total of five brilliant beginnings must surely constitute a record.[4]

The First Performance

Leni Riefenstahl took to the stage for her first solo dance recital on 23 October 1923 as a performer of her own making. Though significantly influenced by teachers and other great dancers, Riefenstahl was fundamentally an original. She danced her programme to music by, among others, Chopin, Grieg, Gluck, Brahms and Schubert. The twenty-one-year-old debutant was responsible for all the choreographies, which had titles such as *Die drei Tänze des Eros* (The Three Dances of Eros), *Tanzmärchen* (Dance Fairy-Tale), *Lyrische Tänze* (Lyric Dances), *Sommer* (Summer) and *Traumblüte* (Dream Blossom). Within the still relatively recent tradition of expressive dance, she freed herself from classical models and sought her individual style of dance. The fact that this style was occasionally reminiscent of the great dancers of the age, above all Mary Wigman and Niddy Impekoven, was hardly surprising. Critics noted the similarities and sometimes quibbled about them.

The young artist did not just impose her personal style on the dances: she also designed the costumes. She was fond of fluid robes or tight leotards for her solo numbers. They were mostly of a single colour in order to set her off more clearly from the similarly plain stage set. It was quite clear from the dancer's stage presence that she had developed her own language within the art form. Her dancing had nothing to do with codified step sequences.

The way her first career developed is typical in many ways of her progress thereafter. In later years too, she repeatedly shunned the established paths when setting off on a new project and preferred to rely on personal contacts and friendships rather than on the production plans of anonymous studios. As she prepared her first performances, the young dancer doubtless received support from her then admirer, Harry Sokal, and her mother. It is unclear whether she also used an agent to represent her during the six-month tour. She did, however, succeed in creating an extraordinary stir in Munich and Berlin even with her first entirely independent programmes. The press reviews were not just very positive, but also very numerous for a debutant. In fact there were so many that, even at this early stage, reviewers at the performances alluded to the fuss the press made of her. Dealing with the media was always to be one of her particular talents. She was quick to recognize, and henceforth to exploit, the value of a good public relations campaign.

In the context of Riefenstahl's work as a whole, her engagements up to May 1924 amount to no more than a brief prelude, seemingly insignificant compared to her subsequent achievements. Yet those few months were in fact of central importance to her. The public acknowledgement of her creativity as an artist was her refutation of her father's doubts. In asserting herself against his will and proving herself a genuine talent, she created herself as an artist. Not only did she quickly master the workings of a business that she, an outsider, had resolved to conquer; she also defined her own 'image' for the first time. The latter is probably best illustrated by the photograph used both for her publicity brochure of 1924 and her advertisement for 'Amor Skin' cream of 1928. The picture shows her in a long, white robe, with her big, earnest eyes directed at the camera and her short hair flat against her scalp. This Leni Riefenstahl – the serious young woman filled with a sense of mission – became her first public persona.

In retrospect her career as a dancer also proved important for another reason. None of her subsequent careers quite succeeded without the help of others. Later, there would always be a story to build on. As a dancer, Leni Riefenstahl had no story whatsoever. That perhaps explains why she later told the tale in simplified terms, purged of opposition and criticism. The narrative construction was intended to portray a talent which was fully formed from the start and which earned immediate, unqualified acclaim.

The first dance recital in Munich therefore acquires a certain significance in the construction of Riefenstahl's biography. It made a moderate impact, with two Munich newspapers registering the debut. Apparently, it was intended as a dress rehearsal for the impending performance in Berlin and was organized by Harry Sokal, who hired the Tonhalle concert hall for just one dollar.[5] It was the era of galloping inflation: the *Münchener Zeitung* newspaper containing the report of Riefenstahl's performance cost 300 million marks, and by the next day the price had gone up to 500 million marks. On 26 October 1923 the reviewer wrote:

> Leni Riefenstahl brings with her to the stage many of the important prerequisites for success, such as beautiful looks and an evidently unorthodox temperament. This enables her to hold the attention of her audience to the end. But [she] spoils her own prospects of achieving truly great art by

remaining in the region of sentimentality. She sprawls, for example, when she should be majestically expressing herself and purifying her sensuality into the highest artistic *form*. For the same reason, her movements sometimes let her down; the risk of . . . sensationalism is a consequence of her temperament. If, however, she were to use her passion as the starting point rather than the final statement of her art (without belittling it in the least) and worked on her technical skills, she might yet become something special. Let us hope that success does not get in her way.[6]

The *Münchener Neuesten Nachrichten* had also sent a reviewer to the debutante's performance. He took a similar point of view in his report:

Leni Riefenstahl, a pupil of Jutta Klamt, is a young dancer whom nature has blessed with beauty and stature. Her first dance recital at the Tonhalle indicated what she is capable of. It took the form of a musical, graceful display of athleticism, without any particular audacity but with some original touches. By choosing Schubert's Unfinished Symphony, the young artist had set herself a task to which, within herself, she was not yet completely equal. The dramatic element remained a mere suggestion, whilst the lyrical element always seemed much more creative. Even the 'Dances of Eros', for all the beauty of the contours in certain passages, never quite lived up to their very ambitious title. They were pretty arabesques around a set motif. However, the dancing of this beautiful, supple figure contained nothing to undermine the positive overall impression: no importunate sham, no cheap showiness. On the contrary, the artist's whole manner, like her sound choice of costumes, demonstrated a sure, cultivated taste.[7]

The two Munich critics did not see the performance as a perfect first attempt, and they noted moments which were flawed or betrayed uncertainty. Ultimately, however, they did suggest that the young dancer possessed remarkable talent. Like later critics, they were unable to resist allusions to her beautiful face and figure, but they also identified some of the debutante's other qualities:

naturalness, a gift for lyricism, a refusal to resort to showy effects, a sure sense of style. On the other hand, they agreed that she was guilty of a certain over-eagerness: her technique and experience as a dancer were not yet completely equal to her ambition. The reviews of her performance in Munich were benevolent, moderately critical descriptions of a *talent* at the moment of its debut. They constituted, by any standards, a positive response to a nascent career.

The way Riefenstahl later described the 'first performance' – this first opportunity for her artistic vocation to prove itself – differs markedly from the published opinions of her contemporaries. The legend she created was of an inspired genius and a perfect debut.

She offers a convincing and colourful description of her own feelings concerning the audience:

> The hall was barely one third full. I was unknown. The few people who did attend had probably received free tickets from the concert organizers. I was not bothered by the emptiness of the hall. I was happy to be able to dance in front of an audience. I did not suffer any stage fright. On the contrary: I could hardly wait to get on stage. Even my first dance, 'Studie nach einer Gavotte' was greeted by considerable applause; by my third dance I was forced to give an encore, and then the applause grew and grew until, during the last dances, the members of my audience came forward and demanded encores. I carried on dancing until my exhaustion forced me to stop.[8]

More problematic is her attempt to draw on contemporary reviews to prove what an overwhelming success her performance was. Immediately after her euphoric recollections of the evening, there follows a passage from the *Münchener Neuesten Nachrichten* – clearly intended as evidence of the enthusiastic response from audience and critics alike. To give the impression of unqualified praise, however, she has to resort to some creative quoting. Not only did the newspaper article she used actually relate to her second performance (in December 1923), she also misrepresented the tone of the piece.[9] The critic did indeed remark on the 'large and grateful audience' and praised the young artist because this time she subordinated 'her eagerness to her ability'. Nevertheless, he regarded Leni Riefenstahl as 'nothing less than problematic':

> *She takes after Wiesenthal.* Her domain is that of normality and
> naturalness. Everything else comes across as unspontaneous,
> calculated or formulaic, even if the innate beauty of the
> moving form sometimes makes it easy to overlook this. The
> proud, bold opening march of the Caucasian suite is a typical
> product of the Mary Wigman school. Unfortunately, its
> bellicose power is watered down by femininity: a dainty
> Amazon! Even the Oriental fantasy dance – despite exhibiting
> the sprung power of a body under complete control – is not
> really the forte of *a dancer blessed with natural talent, whose
> truest successes will always arise from forceful, authentic dancing
> such as in the 'Valse caprice' and in the summery concluding dance,
> when she becomes a surging, circling delight, as natural as a
> swaying poppy or a nodding cornflower.* The Munich audience,
> with its long-standing tradition of discernment in dance,
> instinctively understood this. It demanded encores of pre-
> cisely those dances.

The young dancer doubtless sent the publicity brochure
(containing press reactions up to 29 April 1924) to theatres and
journalists when she was preparing a comeback after her injury.[10]
Understandably, it omitted negative opinions and even nuances. It
is striking, however, that the memoirs should, so many years later,
employ the same strategy.

An Intimation of New Grandeur in Dance

Riefenstahl's description of the rest of her career as a dancer also
reflects her insistence on the legend of consummate success, of
unwavering applause from audience and critics alike. That is the
only possible explanation for the way she misrepresented the
thrust of Fred Hildebrandt's review in the *Berliner Tageblatt*. Once
again, the publicity brochure and the memoirs quote the same
excerpts, and once again the editing is manipulative. Both the
brochure and the memoirs used only the passages marked here in
italics. The rest of the text was suppressed.

This very beautiful girl, who received a tumultuous response from the daily press when she began her career in the Blüthnersall, in the Kammerspielen, in the Deutsches Theater in Berlin, in Munich, Cologne, Innsbruck and Prague, is doubtless fighting fervently for a place beside the three who enjoy serious reputations: Impekoven, Wigman and Gert. And when one sees this tall, perfectly developed creature standing amid the music, one has an intimation that dance might achieve a grandeur which none of the three was able to carry and uphold – not in Mary's heroic stroke of the gong, not in Niddy's sweet fiddling, not in Valeska's terrible drum-beat: the grandeur of the dancer who reappears every thousand years, the perfect, powerful grace, the unparalleled beauty, the divine image. But then this young woman begins to unfold her body; the idea wilts, the brilliance fades, the tone flattens; a wonderful sham now occupies the stage – expansive, certainly, and with a thirst for rhythm and a nostalgia for music. Unfortunately, her expansiveness fails to enliven the space, the rhythm withers in the face of her thirst, and her nostalgia sits on the music like a straitjacket. It is the élan, the thirst and the yearning of a foolish, moonstruck maiden. ... Nevertheless: this is no careless beauty tripping her way up the intricate paths towards art. In this dancing there is an insane will to escape such chains of the enchanted body; a humble individual is groping around in the darkness; a human being is wrestling with the angel. Thus, a spectacle which might easily provoke anger in fact leaves one feeling sad – regretful that such superficial perfection is not blessed with the inner gift, the grandeur of genius, the daemonic flame.[11]

Riefenstahl's selectivity turns a review that is mainly about a great but disappointed hope into a hymn of praise. The tactic says a great deal about Riefenstahl's need for recognition.[12] Modern assessments of Riefenstahl's dancing, which have to rely entirely on the contemporary commentaries and the scenes in *Der heilige Berg*, are necessarily tentative – but there is no doubt that at the time the young talent was thought almost unanimously to possess remarkable potential. It is all the more surprising that the memoirs should seek to exaggerate such a consensus.

There were relatively few thoroughly negative reviews. Most

were basically favourable, whilst some were uncritically enthusiastic. The *Vorwärts* critic, John Schikowski, underwent an
instructive change of attitude. At the first dance recital in Berlin
he was particularly severe on the second part of the programme:
'All in all: a very strong artistic temperament achieving perfection
within her field. That field, however, is extremely limited. For
higher things, the most important ingredient is missing: the soul.'
On hearing from Munich that this very section had been greeted
there with enthusiasm, he decided to attend Riefenstahl's second
performance and review his opinion. He experienced 'a revelation.
Virgin territory!' and summed up:

> Here bubbled the longed-for spring, here flowed the Fountain
> of Youth. It may not yet be powerful enough to brim over and
> carry all before it, but it is set on its course, clear and
> confident. If (despite the dazzling popular successes and
> disconcerting press furore) her serious sense of artistic
> purpose remains vigilant and effective, I am convinced that
> this young Berliner is capable of fulfilling our hopes for the
> future of dance: of delivering a new spirit and stylistic
> grandeur.[13]

Schikowski's point of view seemed entirely reasonable, and his
relatively objective evaluation appeared superior to the more
effusive, less distanced reviews.[14] The obvious reasons for the
extraordinary reception Riefenstahl's dance recitals received were
her youth and beauty. The critics tended to concentrate on her
physical attractiveness, largely irrespective of any aesthetic
appraisal of her performance. It would appear that her beauty,
'which is doubly delightful in view of how scarce it has become
among dancers',[15] distracted some critics from weaknesses in the
performance. Even those who considered her a mere 'variety show
attraction' rather than the stuff of two-hour matinees at least found
her 'young' and 'pretty';[16] those who felt that the shape of her
dancing was overly influenced by the music never neglected to
mention 'the slim, youthful, beautiful dancer'.[17] The reviewers
admired her beautiful, flexible build[18] and thought her body
seemed 'chiselled from marble, perfectly proportioned, beautifully
groomed and evenly honed',[19] or 'perfectly formed in every
respect'.[20] In short, although the dancer – who was indeed very

young – failed to earn unanimous praise for her art, she did earn it for her physique. Her youth, beauty and slenderness were exactly what people wanted; her artistic abilities could not quite live up to the same ideal.

It was the sensational-seeming alliance between the 'lovely girl wonder'[21] and the artificial form of dance which made the most lasting impression. A kind of unreformed, naïve sexism manifested itself in such descriptions. Schikowski began his first review with the words: 'If her name ended in "ini" or "enko", one would say she is hot-blooded and racy. Since her name is Leni Riefenstahl, one contents oneself with calling her spirited.'[22] The *Deutsche Zeitung Bohemia* was more direct, describing her as 'a stunning, hot-blooded Berliner'.[23] It is hardly surprising that she took a rather aloof view of such pieces, even if, as she was doubtless aware, her youthful attractiveness played no small part in the explosive start to her career. In any case, that career seemed to have truly taken off. Her seventy performances in eight months represented a performance every third day, often separated by long train journeys. She even appeared at hotels,[24] as if loath to miss any opportunity. In retrospect the tour, which was halted only by a knee injury, comes across as a protracted attempt to prove that she really could be a successful dancer.

It could hardly have diminished Riefenstahl's reputation if her memoirs had dwelt a little more on the difficulties she faced as a debutante. In fact this part of her life was no more than a short episode. All that could reasonably be expected of any young dancer at such an early stage is that she should gradually win over the critics and the public; unless, of course, the dancer in question is a genius. That is what the memoirs were intended to suggest. They were designed to consolidate a claim that Riefenstahl was particularly keen to defend after 1945: that she had been a 'star' long before Hitler came along. Her retrospective need to justify herself led her, even sixty years on, to portray her debut as a kind of glorious firework.

The fame of Leni Riefenstahl the dancer has long since faded. Dance, in her own view, was her original vocation, but none of her achievements as a dancer secured her a lasting reputation. Her 'greatness' arose from films which are inconveniently notorious for their propaganda qualities. For that reason, Riefenstahl describes the start of her career as the revelation of a virtual genius, rather than as the emergence of the notable talent she was destined to remain.

Her First Leading Role

Leni Riefenstahl has often described her move into cinema as a classic moment of revelation. Indeed, this is one of the invariable elements in her autobiographical writings.[25] She tells of a powerful, spontaneous fascination which overwhelmed her when she saw a poster advertising *Berg des Schicksals* (Mountain of Destiny, directed by Arnold Fanck, 1923/24), and which became even more intense when she saw the film itself. The episode seems convincing, if only because her subsequent actions were so improbable.

Her decision to take a role as an actress, moreover in a *Bergfilm* (mountain film), was far from logical. It was all the more perverse in view of her knee injury, which was as big an impediment to activities such as skiing and mountain climbing as it was to dancing. Nevertheless, the new world of the mountains and this very unusual film genre so impressed her that she did not hesitate. Her aim was quite clear, and could hardly have been more surprising when seen against the background of her life up to that point: Leni Riefenstahl wanted to act in a Fanck film. The circumstances were not in her favour, but in the end nothing could prevent her from achieving her goal.

When he came to write his reminiscences, Arnold Fanck was lost for words of his own to describe a turn of events which was as unexpected for him in the context of his career as it was for Riefenstahl in the context of hers. Instead, he quoted at length from Riefenstahl's account.[26]

In one respect, however, the change of direction might be seen as a way out for her. With the knee injury threatening to put an end to her career as a dancer at such an early stage, the film represented an alternative opportunity. Moreover, she was evidently not a complete novice to the medium.[27] Her memoirs suggest that she could have made a comeback as a dancer in 1925/26, but she took a more sceptical view in her first book of reminiscences, *Kampf in Schnee und Eis* (A Struggle in Snow and Ice).[28]

As well as her first small role in a film, her career as a dancer also apparently earned her an invitation from Erich Pommer to take the leading role in *Pietro der Korsar* (Pietro the Corsair, directed by Arthur Robison, 1924/25) – for the 'fabulous fee of 30,000 marks': 'What attracted me was that it involved playing a dancer'; she 'could not completely resist the temptation and did a screen test', but finally, 'after a difficult struggle with my conscience', she refused the offer.[29] Allegedly, she actually made an appearance in another role, but this has been impossible to verify. Various writers credit her with a part in *Wege zu Kraft und Schönheit* (Ways to Strength and Beauty, directed by Wilhelm Prager, 1924/25; the shorter British version of 1932 was entitled *Back to Nature*), specifically as one of the scantily clad slave girls serving a Roman noblewoman in the scene called 'Das Römische Bad' (The Roman Baths).[30]

Riefenstahl's first significant role in a film was in *Der heilige Berg*; and her debut appearance was worthy of a star. There is a close-up of her face in the first scene. This shot, however, awakens expectations which the actress was never actually called upon to fulfil – and which perhaps exceeded her capabilities in any case. She does not, in fact, go on to 'carry' the film. She herself is not to blame; in Arnold Fanck's films the actors and actresses all have to compete for attention with the mountains, the sky and the sporting competitions. The first caption makes that point in programmatic terms:

> The eminent sportspeople involved in the film *Der heilige Berg* request the audience not to mistake their performances for photographic tricks – in which they would never consent to participate. All the exterior shots really were made in the mountains – indeed, in the most beautiful parts of the Alps – in the course of a year's work. Top German, Norwegian and Austrian skiers participated in the great ski race. The script for the timeless, placeless story set in the mountains is based on the real experiences of a 20 year life in the high mountains.

The cast list in the film's opening credits reflects the director's priorities. It includes one 'actress' – Frida Richards – and 'the sportspeople'. In that list, Riefenstahl's name appears above Luis Trenker, Ernst Petersen and Hannes and Friedrich Schneider. For Fanck, the list of sportspeople was a role of honour; Riefenstahl had earned her inclusion. She had learned to ski and climb, and had paid for the principle of the film with injuries to her person. The characteristic pathos of authenticity required that the actors really did go before the cameras and perform the feats demanded by the script. In this respect their physical agility might be compared with that of certain American film stars such as the western heroes or the comic genius, Buster Keaton.[31]

In *Der heilige Berg*, Riefenstahl is a star within a certain context. The first image, following the main title, shows the 'holy mountain', a massif looming beyond a lake in hazy light. The beginning of the film confronts 'the woman' with 'the mountain', introducing an almost mystical figure and a mythical landscape. The close-up shows Riefenstahl's perfectly made-up face with a relaxed expression. Her eyes are closed, while her prominent lips and eyebrows appear as geometric, symmetrical lines. This is a cool, stylized icon of beauty, and seems to have more to do with transfiguration than with seduction.[32] It is the beauty of an entirely non-sensual ideal, and the whole film goes on to oscillate between its insistence on authenticity and the construction of a narration dominated by polar opposites.

Leni Riefenstahl introduced a new element into Arnold Fanck's *Bergfilme* – and into his life. That element was the self-confident woman,[33] otherwise virtually invisible in his world. Unlike Hertha von Walther, who played the female lead in Fanck's previous film *Berg des Schicksals*, Riefenstahl did not allow herself to be robbed of her independence. Her characters assert themselves among the men – just as the actress herself did – and she casts her spell over two of them. The dancer Diotima in *Der heilige Berg* was the first such heroine. She was also the first of Riefenstahl's outsiders – marked out by their origins, status and vocation. In the elevated tone typical of the film's captions, we are told: 'There, where the cliff drops steeply and defiantly down to the breakers . . . is her home.' The character's foreignness is related to her anti-realism, which is heavily emphasized. She is introduced as a natural being rather than a social one. The initial shots of Leni Riefenstahl are stark and backlit: she is visible only as a silhouette against the sea and the sky. There are beautiful shots of the sea, which 'is her love'; 'her life, however, is her dancing – the expression of her tempestuous soul'.

The montage links the dancing[34] with the sea, creating a symbiotic relationship between Diotima and the element. In *Tanz an das Meer* (Dance to the Sea), shots of waves breaking high on the quay wall twice follow the dancer throwing her arms aloft. Immediately afterwards, the dancer stands amid the breakers with her arms upstretched: Diotima both commands and worships the element. When the dancer stretches her arms out horizontally in calming gestures, there are attendant shots of gentle surf. The dancer and the element are in harmony, until the final bow which appears to symbolize not just the end of the performance, but also submission to the element.

The second dance introduces a sort of 'vision'. Above the quiet sea, the silhouette of the holy mountain appears in double exposure, followed by a backlit shot of a man standing upon a peak. 'And Diotima dances . . . dances on account of her enraptured longing for the man she saw as if in a dream on the highest summit.' Arnold Fanck loaded the narration with symbolism. Instead of producing a 'boy-meets-girl' story, the encounter is between two elements, two principles – mountain and sea, man and woman. This makes the film top-heavy, for (like other Fanck films) it pays little heed to narrative consistency. The introduction of the 'two friends', who subsequently meet again as rivals for Diotima's affections, is overshadowed by the (extradiegetic) shots of beautiful mountain scenery. Even the central love story fails to develop: 'the friend' (the character played by Luis Trenker has no name in this film) sees photographs of Diotima in the foyer of the Grand Hotel and is immediately gripped, as if by the hand of fate. In fact he leaves the valley after her first dance and climbs to a mountaintop to collect his thoughts.[35] By this point, however, the juxtaposing of close-ups of Trenker and Riefenstahl on the one hand and Riefenstahl and Petersen on the other means that the film has already constructed the triangular relationship, founded on a misunderstanding, which is fundamental to the rest of the story.

The first part of the film was not demanding for Riefenstahl as an actress. The first scene requiring an interpretative presence is after the hotel dance, when she notices the gentian flower left for her by Vigo (Ernst Petersen) and indicates with a nod that he should approach. The intensity of that presence, however, was impaired both by an abrupt and unmistakable reverse angle and by Riefenstahl's unsubtle miming.

Fanck's use of montage to inject emotional significance into the scenes is certainly successful (although there is often a relative lack of dramatic interest). A good example is the way he sets up the relationship between Trenker and Riefenstahl. He uses parallel editing first to juxtapose the 'friend's' ascent with Diotima, who is sitting at the window of her hotel room, and then to set her journey into the mountains alongside his descent. This same episode, however, also offers an example of Riefenstahl's uneven performance as an actress. According to the caption: 'A joyful mountain springtime ascends through the valleys and hills. And joyfully Diotima makes her way towards the peaks.' Unfortunately, Riefenstahl's expression of 'joyfulness' relies entirely on a single, oft-repeated gesture: as she runs out of the building, she stretches her arms out wide. Perhaps her training as a dancer explains the conventionality and exaggerated expressiveness of her gestures. Be that as it may, her weaknesses as an actress are all the more prominent when compared to the performances by the rest of the cast.

As she ascends, Diotima discovers the sea of spring flowers and grazing herds in the valley. She pets a young boy and a lamb and, being an unfamiliar figure, excites the interest of local children and the shepherd. She explores the natural world around her, which becomes harsher as she climbs higher. Diotima's discoveries, however, tend to be mere statements: they do not constitute an experience-driven process, realized in the dramatic action. Here Riefenstahl seems awkward, as if unsure of the options available to her as an actress. She doubtless received little help from her director.

The scene entitled 'Die Begegnung' (The Encounter) is proof of the fact that she was capable of better things. It is, indeed, one of the highlights of the whole film. The 'friend' has entered a hut on his way down. Even before this, he has been shown against the background of the Matterhorn; now the frame composition manifestly relates him to the mountain. The peak can be seen through the window beside Trenker's profile, and again through the doorway when he leaves the hut. This is where Diotima finds him, and she too is filmed against the background of the

Matterhorn. Now, however, the peak appears less distinct and Diotima in effect blocks off the mountain from the viewer as she approaches the camera. This shot, with Riefenstahl framed before the silhouette of the mountain, is loaded with symbolism. When the woman enters the picture she is ranked alongside the mountain peaks as a challenge facing the man. The dialogue captions stress this even more,[36] and Riefenstahl builds up convincing intensity during the scene. She becomes somewhat coquettish, in contrast to Trenker's stoic calm. This suits her character and lends a slightly ironic undertone to the encounter. Fanck, however, immediately buried the irony beneath two time-lapse shots of accumulating cloud formations: an almost heroic image with which to conclude an intimate scene.

There are many similar scenes in which Fanck's wishes and his cinematic style created difficulties for the actors. Inevitably, the love story cannot compete with the intensity of the protracted downhill ski races and ski-jumping competitions, with their many breathtaking camera angles, and still less with the film's dramatic climax. The confrontation between the two men, in which Vigo falls from a rocky outcrop and his friend holds on to him all night before they both die, is certainly the most memorable scene. Even with more experience, Riefenstahl would have found it hard to compete against such a finale. It was, however, not just in *Der heilige Berg* that her acting was uneven. The only one of Fanck's films in which she was consistently convincing was *Die weisse Hölle vom Piz Palü* (for which G. W. Pabst filmed the 'acting scenes'; the two English-language versions were entitled *The White Hell of Piz Palü* and *Prisoners of the Mountain*). His male characters enjoy a much more assured status, so it was predictable that Riefenstahl would eventually have enough of investing so much effort for so little reward as an actress.

Struggles in Snow and Ice

In fact, whenever Riefenstahl stepped before a camera for Fanck she went through torment. The demands he made of her in their first film were harmless in comparison with what was to follow. Even *Der heilige Berg* tested her resilience: she had to allow herself to be engulfed by small-scale avalanches. Later, the lightly dressed actress had to jump into mountain lakes and icy streams and bloodied her feet climbing barefoot on rocky pinnacles (*Der grosse Sprung* (The Great Leap), 1927). During the filming of *Die weisse Hölle vom Piz Palü* (1929) she had to spend night after night on a rock in temperatures below freezing, and even let herself be pulled up a rock face while quantities of snow and chunks of ice pelted down on her. The films were tests of her courage, and she passed them all. She balanced on a slender ladder above a deep glacial crevasse, and she endured her exclusively male colleagues and their obscene jokes whilst filming in a primitively appointed ski-hut (*Stürme über dem Montblanc* (Storms Over Mont Blanc), 1930). Finally, in Greenland (*S.O.S. Eisberg*, 1932/33 (the English-language version, *S.O.S. Iceberg*, is not identical)) she was overcome by colic, from which she had suffered since those nights on Piz Palü. It is hard not to impute a somewhat sadistic streak to director Arnold Fanck – and an appetite for self-chastisement to Leni Riefenstahl.[37]

There is no doubt that she was repeatedly influenced by her need to prove herself to the male establishment. Riefenstahl never gave in meekly. This earned her respect and ensured that she was offered parts which surely no other actress could have played or endured. During all this she was dreaming of other roles.

It was not long before she realized that she was trapped in the 'Fanck circle'. An acting career which had begun amid such fanfare was leading Leni Riefenstahl towards a dead end. After *Der heilige Berg*, she played the female lead in five more of Fanck's films, but in all of them her own performances came a poor third to the other attractions: the opulent set-pieces – involving mountains, avalanches, storms, and glorious sporting and mountaineering achievements – and the dominant roles for male actors. Yet Fanck did need Riefenstahl. Without a female lead, his films would have been condemned to the cinematic sidelines as 'cultural films'. It is understandable that Riefenstahl soon began to doubt that she needed Fanck to the same extent. Under his direction she – compared to the real stars of silent films in the late 1920s (even within Germany) – had become little more than an interesting personality – ideal for skin-cream and ski-boot advertisements . . .

Her roles were not the stuff that real stardom is made of. Their true significance was as the personification of a new kind of woman. Leni Riefenstahl was more of a sporting idol than an erotic icon. This could hardly be enough, in the long term, to satisfy a young woman who had so often demonstrated her exceptional ability to assert her own will. This was not because she had any special desire to acquire an erotic image, but rather because, as a 'sportswoman' she was never considered for more demanding roles. In her first book of reminiscences, published in 1933, she describes her attempts to obtain other parts:

> [The director, Arnold Fanck] knows about my concern and does want to help me. He has made many attempts to get hold of other roles for me, to stop the industry seeing me in such narrow terms and also so that I can work creatively during the long breaks between his films. But he has been unsuccessful, and so have I.[38]

Indeed, until she made her debut as director, Leni Riefenstahl only acted for one director other than Fanck. *Das Schicksal derer von Habsburg – die Tragödie eines Kaiserreiches* (The Fate of the House of Hapsburg – The Tragedy of an Empire, directed by Rudolf Raffé, 1928) provided her with the role of Baroness Vetsera, the Austrian crown prince's lover – a minor part, according to the cast list in the programme notes. It appears that only two short fragments of the original German version, of about eleven minutes' duration (and not featuring Riefenstahl), have survived.[39] At least this is enough evidence to gain a general impression of the style of the film, which was certainly not one of the prestige productions of that year.[40] The direction seems inelegant and clumsy in both scenes and within the context of contemporary filmmaking. Only the wedding night scene betrays a certain sense of direction. Judging by the surviving evidence of the film's aesthetic qualities, the press of the time was fully justified in remaining largely silent about it. The newly restored Italian version, which was recut to give the film a somewhat anti-Hapsburg message, does not evince a particularly impressive performance from Riefenstahl. Riefenstahl's venture beyond the *Bergfilm* genre was certainly no great help to her career, and it is not surprising that she ascribed relatively little significance to the role in her memoirs (the English translation, *Sieve of Time*, omits the relevant chapter altogether).[41]

The characters she played in Fanck's films were not calculated to let her dispel the cliché of the 'sportswoman' through subtle, interpretative performances. In the comic roles – *Der grosse Sprung* and *Der weisse Rausch* (The White Rapture) – she was unable to attempt any sophistication. As she later complained, she was only ever allowed to exclaim: 'Ooh marvellous!' Even so, the films themselves were very successful, and her performance in *Der weisse Rausch*, in which she plays a town-dweller learning to ski, does exhibit a degree of self-mockery. The dramatic roles in *Die weisse Hölle vom Piz Palü, Stürme über dem Montblanc* and *S.O.S. Eisberg* had a greater influence on her reputation. Unlike the comedies, with their elements of slapstick, these films demanded a more carefully conceived performance. In *Die weisse Hölle vom Piz Palü*, at least, Riefenstahl was able to display her talent. This was no doubt largely thanks to Pabst, who – unlike Fanck – was concerned about the credibility of the story and the acting.

In the opening sequence, in which the young couple (Riefenstahl and Ernst Petersen) enter the ski-hut, Riefenstahl's acting is relaxed and unforced. She had rarely had the chance to give such a performance in previous films. The young people's dalliance and their uneasiness when a third person, the mysterious Dr Krafft, appears in the hut are convincingly acted. Moreover, the direction does not disrupt the performances by inserting 'spectacular' shots of the mountain scenery.[42] Riefenstahl was also able to display a degree of ambivalence for the first time. Once again she was the woman in the middle, but this time there was room for her to develop her fascination with the mysterious stranger without being irrevocably committed to 'Mr Right' from the start. The tension also has an erotic edge which complicates the story and lends the film a gripping quality even outside the action-packed scenes.

This challenge was destined to remain an exceptional one for her. In her reminiscences she blames prejudice among the production companies for the film industry's open lack of interest in Leni Riefenstahl the actress. She claims that they saw her as a 'mountain climber and dancer' or a 'mountain climber and not an actress'.[43] In order to act in Fanck's films, she had acquired skills which were now seen as innate talents and which came to stand in her way. Instead of being seen as an actress who could even climb mountains, she was regarded as a mountain climber who also acted a little.

Her next roles were in the same, familiar genre and did not stretch Riefenstahl to the same extent. Her characters were increasingly short of conflicting emotions, becoming simpler and one-dimensional. She had shown that she could do more than just say 'Ooh marvellous!' – but little more was demanded of her. For this reason, *Stürme über dem Montblanc*, which featured wonderful photography and some spectacular moments, was not the next big personal success it seemed to be. In fact it was a step backwards.

That is true even more clearly of *S.O.S. Eisberg*, which boasted perhaps the most elegant exposition of all Fanck's films as well as some outstanding images from Greenland's glaciers. The female lead, however, plays an even lesser part than in the earlier films. Not only are her scenes few and far between, they also contribute very little to the progress of the plot. Even when the airwoman played by Riefenstahl finally manages to emerge from her enforced passivity and fly her aeroplane to Greenland in order to help her husband – who was missing for a long time but has now been found – her crash obliges her to sit tight once again. She, together with the other characters, can only wait for the appearance of the fearless rescuer played by Ernst Udet. Acting so manifestly trivial a role can hardly have been a rewarding experience, especially since Riefenstahl was probably well aware that the film's director would really have preferred to dispense with female characters altogether. In this, her last role for Fanck, Riefenstahl had become a mere sideshow to the extraordinary shots of the natural world and the action scenes, which were added in order to appeal to a wider audience. Her decision to try a change of direction was therefore entirely logical.

CHAPTER THREE

The Film Auteur *Emerges*

None of the significant elements in the *Bergfilm* genre – authentic shots, aesthetic scenery and competition – fitted comfortably with the priorities of contemporary, popular cinema.[1] One of the more remarkable aspects of Riefenstahl's career is that she never worked in a typical studio production. Initially she was unable to interest the major companies in her projects because of her background as a *Bergfilm* specialist; later she was in such a strong position that she did not have to tie herself to the plans of the big studios. This unusual circumstance was to work both for and against her.

Two Interpretations of the Same Story

Leni Riefenstahl had single-mindedly made the most of her time with Fanck to familiarize herself with every aspect of film production.[2] She was well prepared for the new challenge of directing, especially since the circumstances surrounding the making of her film project, *Das blaue Licht*, dictated the use of a small, familiar team. No company wanted to make the film,[3] so it became a venture for enthusiasts. It was a low-budget production, initially financed largely by Riefenstahl herself and then, in its final phase, by Harry Sokal. It depended on the readiness of those involved to work almost without remuneration. The six participants formed a tight-knit group, keen to experiment and uncompromising in the pursuit of ideal solutions. Hans Schneeberger, whose intimacy with Riefenstahl was by now a thing of the past, was in charge of the cameras. Walter Traut, Walter Riml and

Heinz von Jaworsky (who became 'Henry Jaworsky' in America) were, like Schneeberger, veterans of Fanck's films, and Riefenstahl knew them well. She always described the months they spent filming together as a happy time, emphasizing the outstanding team spirit. This was the first time she demonstrated her extraordinary ability to inspire others with her own zeal, determination and enthusiasm. Camera assistant Heinz von Jaworsky later recalled: 'We all just loved what she did.'[4]

The credits for *Das blaue Licht* also reflected the ethos of close cooperation; Riefenstahl, Balázs and Schneeberger headed the list as co-creators of the film. Today it is difficult to assess how much each individual contributed to its overall character.[5] After the war, Riefenstahl played down the role of her collaborators – in the 1951 version she claimed responsibility for 'script, direction and art direction,' whilst crediting Schneeberger with the 'photography' and Balázs with 'collaboration on the script'. The 'collective film'[6] had metamorphosed into an *auteur* film. It can certainly be argued that the director claimed the credit for areas she could hardly have managed alone, but there was never any doubt that *Das blaue Licht* was a 'Riefenstahl film'. The fact that she was largely responsible for its subject matter and its particular style was clear even at the premiere on 14 March 1932.

Leni Riefenstahl's two accounts of how she came to direct her first film were written at very different stages of her life, and their perspectives are strikingly different. In 1933 she is still inspired by her own achievement, still optimistic about her future career. In her memoirs, however, which were published for the first time in 1987, she plays down her ambitions as a young artist. The two versions are adapted to their respective historical and political circumstances to such an extent that the central theme of *both* narratives – the difficulties faced by a woman determined to express her creativity in the film industry – is almost obscured.

In Riefenstahl's first look back on her directorial debut, which she must then have regarded as a mere curtain-raiser to stardom and international recognition, she represents herself as much more active and energetic than she does in her memoirs. In 1933 enthusiasm and ambition are given equal precedence: she boasts that she was occasionally able to deputize for Fanck as director.[7] Her assessment of her film roles is a thoroughly sceptical one:

Have my films given me the kind of satisfaction I used to dream of? I cannot answer that question with an unqualified 'yes'. I am glad to have learned about nature, and I am also glad to be living in this new circle of people. Yet there is a catch to all this, something which has never been aired, but which still bothers me. The fact is that the lengthy production time for these films leaves me unsatisfied as an artist.[8]

After *Stürme über dem Montblanc*, her desire for more satisfaction from her artistic work started to become more insistent.[9] Even if she portrays an inner struggle, an attempt at resistance, her 1933 account reflects her self-confidence and her enormous determination much more clearly than the one written five decades later. In that version, the tone is almost apologetic. No longer does she talk of a wish to impose her own will on a film, but rather – more ashamedly – of her longing 'to create something herself'.[10] In 1933 the dominant note had been satisfaction with her recent demonstration of her qualities as a director. In the memoirs she talks about the dreams from which the idea for the film allegedly emerged, thereby setting up an alternative motivation to her own will. Riefenstahl now presents herself as a mere medium, within which something beyond her own control took place. She defines herself as passive rather than active. 'These images gripped me; they took shape, and one day I wrote everything down – an outline of eighteen pages.'[11] Ultimately, her book *Kampf in Schnee und Eis* suggests that her decision to become a director was based on the knowledge she had been single-mindedly accumulating and characterizes it as the confirmation of her own abilities. In the memoirs, however, the decision is diminished into a mere expediency: 'At this point I had never even thought of taking over the direction myself.'[12]

In the memoirs, chance replaces determination. In her reminiscences of 1933, Riefenstahl claims that she and Hans Schneeberger searched long and hard 'through every valley' to find the Sarntal farmers who contribute so memorably to *Das blaue Licht*. In the memoirs, by contrast, a painter friend is credited with pointing her towards her 'discovery' of the amateur actors. Whereas in the earlier version she dealt confidently with the initially hesitant, unenthusiastic farmers – 'I will not fail to achieve my aim!' – she later hints at an element of uncertainty: 'I am going to photograph them, perhaps that way I will achieve my aim.' In 1933 she gives an instructive description of her reaction when the actress whom she wanted to play the part of Lucia turned her down: 'I am absolutely intent on getting her to take the role at any price, but for the time being I am keeping my determination to myself.' In the memoirs this episode is not mentioned at all.[13]

The earlier self-portrait of the artist as a young, impatient, ambitious genius is more convincing and more appealing than the later version, which represents a sort of tactical retreat and does not fit so well with the director's actual achievements. Irrespective of how she is regarded as a dancer and actress, it is clear that Leni Riefenstahl found her own style in *Das blaue Licht*. At the time it seemed that it must surely point the way for her future career. There was, however, no logical continuation along the lines it defined – a fact which distorted the general perception of her directorial debut after 1945. The Party Rally films overlaid the 'mountain legend' like a tinted pane of glass, affording only a distorted impression of its special character. The criticism of her propaganda films almost completely obscured her earlier achievements.

Das blaue Licht

Riefenstahl's first work as a director is unusual in every respect. A film drawing on elements from fairy-tales, horror films[14] and romantic symbols represented a unique kind of production for 1932. *Das blaue Licht* clearly reflects its maker's determination to impose her stylistic ideas and achieve a consistent overall impression. Financial constraints partly explain the use of amateur actors and the fact that it was filmed almost entirely on location with relatively few shifts of scene, but there were also stylistic reasons. There was nothing dilettante or clumsy about *Das blaue Licht*: despite all the constraints, it became exactly the film Riefenstahl had 'dreamed of'. The unreal, fairy-tale aspect of this 'mountain legend' predominates in a way quite unlike anything to be found in other films of the period.

Even the first few takes make the differences between this film and the *Bergfilme* abundantly clear. The shots of Junta (Leni

Riefenstahl) in front of the waterfall are lent a disconcerting quality by being slightly out of focus, as though they had been filmed through a gauze veil. This is the antithesis of the hard outlines and precision favoured by Arnold Fanck. Riefenstahl strove to achieve certain 'moods' which owe more to painting than photography but, like Fanck, she was relatively uninterested in dramatic and narrative consistency. She was willing to accept that some characters seemed insufficiently rounded: she relied – successfully – on the images. On the other hand, her work does not suffer from the striking lack of proportion in Fanck's films between the progress of the story and the inserted, showpiece sequences.[15] Although *Das blaue Licht* also includes spectacular scenes of waterfalls, cliff-faces and mountaintops, as well as some brilliant mountaineering action, it invests these scenes with a different significance. Fanck's priorities were akin to those of a documentary maker: he wanted to present certain mountains and certain sporting achievements as clearly as possible. His ingenious cameramen helped him in his search for the best, clearest angles, turning their cameras on things that were beautiful and attractive in an essential, entirely pre-filmic sense. Riefenstahl had completely given up this policy in *Das blaue Licht* and tried, by contrast, to construct a beauty and an attraction which did not exist as such outside the film. She did not want to reproduce the mountain world, but rather to use exclusively cinematic means to construct a dream world. Her photographic techniques aimed to alienate nature and change it into an 'inner landscape'. She used filters to shift the balance between black and white elements; clouds of fog and smoke softened the contours. Infrared-sensitive film stock was employed for the first time in a feature film. Schneeberger made virtuoso use of it, transforming sunlight into an extraordinary, unreal-seeming night. Far from making the images appear authentic and familiar, the technological tricks lent them a strange, unsettling quality, further heightened by the motifs borrowed from horror films.

In the exposition, the painter Vigo (Mathias Wieman) arrives in the mountains in a mail-coach. He tries but fails to find out from the resolutely silent coachman whether he has arrived at his destination. The comic undertone to this scene stands in contrast to the pointed lack of regard displayed by the other passengers.

Baffled, Vigo remains behind: a stranger, even an intruder, in this district. Here *Das blaue Licht* is harking back to the genre model of a gradually emergent threat. The traveller in a remote area, observing strange phenomena which he only slowly recognizes as portents of disaster, is a classic narrative device in horror films. Here too there is a 'witch', whom the villagers blame for all their incomprehensible misfortunes: Junta, an attractive young woman who lives outside the village. Yet, just at the moment when the locals make their stand against the outsider, the film turns the horror-film pattern on its head. Instead of joining the battle against the perceived curse, the new arrival attempts to combat the very idea of a curse upon the village. And it is precisely through his 'unbelief', his rationality, that he unwittingly brings about Junta's death. The way the film plays with genre conventions is symptomatic of a reflected, non-naïve attitude towards the story, for which scriptwriter Béla Balázs was perhaps responsible.

Nevertheless, there is a sense in which *Das blaue Licht* may be held to be naïve, a realization of a girlish dream[16] – even if it did not turn out to be as innocent as Riefenstahl later implied when she consistently referred to the central character as a 'girl'[17] and as a symbol for the later part of her own life story.[18] The parallel between the character and her own life, however, does not take account of the film's ambiguity. Both the original framework story and the character of Vigo represent reflected narrative elements;[19] the painter functions within the legend as an *artist*, as a reflective figure, who ruptures the naïvety of the story. For, while Junta may live in a 'dream world', the fact that her world is 'beautiful' (and should be represented as such – the painter makes sketches of that beautiful world) is understood only by Vigo. The narrative attitude is thus modern, not anachronistic, and it has implications for the characters' motivation: the film is not just about the contrast between a dream world and economic rationalism. A second strand in the motivation is the sexual uncertainty which the outsider introduces to the village community. In the first encounter in the film between Junta and the locals, she is confronted by an elderly man, the priest and a group of old women. The looks they give her are unfriendly, as are those she receives in the next scene, as she passes the almost exclusively male guests sitting outside the inn. When she tries to offer the berries she has collected, their reaction is hostile; in the end children taunt her and one of them knocks the basket from her hand.

This scene is constructed on glances, and it defines Junta's position as an outsider. The landlord supplies an explanation: something must be amiss if only 'that damned witch' Junta can climb up to the grotto and not the young men. The latter do not look at Junta in the same way as the older men. Vigo regards her curiously; Tonio (Beni Führer) watches her with fascination as she flees. When his father interrupts his thoughts, Tonio leaves and lies in wait for her. The scene portrays an attempted rape. It is not just the mysterious grotto that so attracts the youths; they want to own the girl as well as the treasure. Junta has, in fact, been outlawed partly because she is so attractive; her role as an outsider has an erotic as well as a mystical significance. From the villagers' point of view, however, she is a threat to wedlock, for Tonio is married to the village beauty, Lucia (Martha Mair).

Junta's attraction results from a double denial: she denies herself to the men as an erotic object and she denies them access to the hidden riches. She alone possesses perfect crystals; the unctuous local trader has to be content with specimens which have been found by chance and which are small or of little value. Junta, however, has no desire to sell her flawless stones. Just as the crystals are symbolic not so much of ideals as of material values,[20] Junta's refusal to sell them is symbolic less of idealism than of independence. She is resolutely independent in another respect as well, for her apparent innocence is not identical with asexuality. When Vigo sets off to seek Junta in the mountains after saving her from the furious villagers, she surreptitiously observes him and attracts his attention by throwing an apple down to him. The patent seduction symbolism[21] reveals the secondary significance of the character: that of a young woman who refuses to play the part of an object, who makes her own choices, who is active rather than passive. When Vigo – already in love with her – moves to her hut for a few days, she invites him to sleep beside her. Wieman acts out Vigo's reaction to this offer unambiguously, and the subsequent scenes also hint at the intimacy between the lovers.[22]

By helping the villagers reach the grotto, Vigo hopes to lift the perceived curse from the village and enable Junta to integrate herself in the community. Yet his action goes beyond mere rationality. In fact he is depriving an independent woman of her power, for her control over the crystals is her potential source of freedom. When she loses the crystals, Junta loses more than just an ideal: she loses her self-determination. As she tries to descend the mountain, she grasps a loose crystal on the cliff and plunges with it to her death.

The film received enthusiastic reviews following its premiere in Germany, but there was also some harsh criticism.[23] In her memoirs, Leni Riefenstahl dwells on the unexpected success of the premiere: 'a triumph beyond my wildest dreams – a sensation. The Berlin critics were falling over themselves to express their enthusiasm. "Das blaue Licht" was fêted as the best film of the year.'[24] In his foreword to Riefenstahl's *Kampf in Schnee und Eis*, however, Paul Ickes described a contradictory reaction, almost in the tone which was to turn *Das blaue Licht* into a kind of King's evidence against the 'Jewish film critics' when it was re-premiered in 1938.[25] Ickes wrote:

> But the same press which was so under the spell of the money-making economy, an attitude by which it trespassed against the spiritual revival of the people, withheld its allegiance from Leni Riefenstahl. The reason was that allegiance depends on understanding, and that no under-standing was possible in this case.[26]

Such sentiments invite one to rank *Das blaue Licht* alongside the later works, to categorize it as a pre-fascist film, as Siegfried Kracauer indeed did.[27]

This teleological view, developed retrospectively, overlooks the fact that *Das blaue Licht* was initially persuasive because of its stylistic qualities, which are far removed from Riefenstahl's subsequent Party Rally films. It also fails to do justice to what is, in effect, the film's self-portrait of a young, attractive and talented woman. Biographical interpretations of the film as an unwitting prophecy of the director's 'destiny' are less convincing than those which simply point out how much Junta and the thirty-year-old director probably had in common. Many men doubtless found Riefenstahl attractive, and she – also like her character in the film – could only preserve her independence by the most precarious means. So long as Junta enjoyed sole control of the crystals she was safe in her position as an outsider. So long as Riefenstahl doggedly asserted herself to defend her exclusive area of creativity, she was her own mistress. When Riefenstahl's career is seen in this light, it appears almost as if she lived in constant fear of suddenly finding herself unable to go her own way, reliant on studios instead of associates – a small cog in a big machine instead of the commotion at the centre.

It is hard to judge whether Riefenstahl ultimately found her own form of expression as a dancer, or whether she could have built on her performance in *Die weisse Hölle vom Piz Palü* as an actress in the long term. It is, however, possible to state with certainty that she found her own style immediately as a director. It is curious, almost incomprehensible, that she did not attempt to capitalize on, and progress from, such a start, instead of accepting the offer of a role in *S.O.S. Eisberg*. There were certainly pragmatic reasons for her decision, such as the substantial fee and the hope that the American version of this Universal production would catapult her to fame in the USA. Moreover, accustomed as she was to working on films in familiar, non-hierarchical teams, she must have been attracted by the idea of joining forces with nearly all her former colleagues on Fanck's expedition to Greenland to film *S.O.S. Eisberg*. No doubt she was also influenced by her appetite for adventure and new experiences.

There was probably one further factor. Riefenstahl always tended to resort to tried and tested means in order to cope with critical situations (later, for example, she would take refuge in the *Tiefland* and *Die roten Teufel* projects). Following *Das blaue Licht*, she seems to have lacked any similarly convincing idea for a film. She did not have the kind of artistic temperament capable of conjuring up successful films in a flash from elegant variations on her own ideas. The material had to fascinate her and provoke an emotional reaction if she was to make the most of her abilities. In fact she was far from being an original storyteller. She did not have the necessary ideas, which is why stories were not fundamental to her projects. Instead, they tended to be founded on ideas for images, on moods and on general structures such as the legend. She seems always to have found work on the script a laborious business, and she had to rely on other people's help. After making her first film as a director, she was left without a new project of her own – and indeed, in 1933 she saw herself more as an actress than as a director in her own right. She would have very much liked to play the title role in *Mademoiselle Docteur*, the story of a famous German spy in World War I,[28] under Frank Wisbar's direction, and when she turned to a project of her own, *Tiefland*, in 1934, she wanted to act the main part herself, with Alfred Abel as co-director.

Leni Riefenstahl's creative uncertainty might therefore have meant a long delay before she achieved another success purely as a director to follow that of *Das blaue Licht* – a coup which surprised all and delighted many of those in the industry. In fact, however, she was gripped by another, completely unexpected fascination, which she went on to pursue in her now familiar, resolute style. This time her fascination was with a man by the name of Adolf Hitler.

Part Two

THE GENIUS OF NAZI FILMMAKING

CHAPTER FOUR

A New Kind of Film: Sieg des Glaubens

On 30 August 1933, Leni Riefenstahl stood on the stage of the Ufa Palast am Zoo cinema in Berlin, receiving the audience's ovation after the premiere of *S.O.S. Eisberg*. It was a situation she had experienced at premieres of earlier films she had made with Fanck, and one which she certainly enjoyed. This time, however, everything had changed, and her premieres at the Ufa Palast am Zoo, Germany's most famous cinema, would never be the same again. 30 August had been a busy working day for Riefenstahl: she had flown to Berlin for the evening from Nuremberg, where she was filming her first Party Rally film. One magazine wrote that the Führer himself had made it possible for her to attend the premiere, 'by putting an aeroplane at her disposal'.[1] It was a flying visit in every sense, for she could not afford to neglect her work in Nuremberg. Even 'a motor vehicle had been made available to the artiste' so that she could also fit in a visit to the broadcasting centre, where she spared '10 minutes for a talk about her experiences in Greenland'. When the premiere finished, after 'a few hours away from her work', the Führer's special aeroplane brought her back to Nuremberg, to the 'Parteitag des Sieges' (Victory Rally). Hitler's assistance enabled Riefenstahl to be fêted for a film which had been produced by Paul Kohner and for which Paul Dessau had written the music – and in which she played a lesser role than in any of the earlier Fanck films. Before long the producer, by then working in the USA, would be denigrated by the Nazis as part of the 'Jewish regime in Hollywood'; the composer had already emigrated to

France by the time of the premiere. It can only be assumed that Riefenstahl did not want to notice the evil irony of the occasion.[2]

That evening, 30 August 1933, was the last time Leni Riefenstahl stood before an audience at a premiere as an actress. When she returned to the Ufa Palast am Zoo four months later, she stepped on stage as a film director. She had made her film in circumstances which no industry could ever have arranged.

Behind the Scenes of the First Party Rally Film

The new Nazi regime immediately, and quite openly, made it impossible for Jews, left-wingers and other *personae non gratae* to work in films. For Leni Riefenstahl, however, it brought new opportunities. In her reminiscences she describes her first meeting with Hitler in terms which betray that she is still moved by the memory. She states that the encounter took place the day before her departure for Greenland to film *S.O.S. Eisberg*, which means it must have been in May 1932.[3]

In the months following her return she saw a great deal of Goebbels,[4] whom she was later to describe as her bitterest enemy. In the early months, however, she met him frequently and went on a picnic with him and Hitler to Heiligendamm. She also visited the propaganda minister there on 17 May 1933 – just a week after the infamous book burning – to talk again with him about 'film matters',[5] including a project of particular interest. The minister noted: 'Afternoon. Leni Riefenstahl: she tells me about her plans. I suggest a Hitler film. She is very enthusiastic.'[6] This idea really does seem to have fallen on fertile ground, for by 14 June 1933, Riefenstahl has apparently spoken to Hitler: 'now she is starting to make her film.'[7]

The projected 'Hitler film' appears to have developed informally into the Party Rally film *Sieg des Glaubens*, which was made a few months later.[8] This led to a dispute about how long Riefenstahl had to prepare the Party Rally film. Did she have just a few days, as she claims,[9] or several months? Underlying the superficial dispute there is another question: how early and to what extent was the director involved in Nazi propaganda? Until the 1980s, *Sieg des Glaubens* was thought to have been lost, so Leni Riefenstahl's least known film remained a matter for speculation. When a nearly complete version of it came to light – only the credits and the opening moments were missing – it became clear that the film was not as insignificant as its director maintained. In fact, it is a most successful piece of propaganda, which displays some striking formal qualities. There is further evidence for this assessment in the first roll of film, which has now also been found.[10]

In the light of the controversy concerning *Sieg des Glaubens*, Riefenstahl significantly shifted her position. She played down the political and aesthetic relevance of her own film, describing it as incomplete, truncated and a 'modest film'.[11] The critics, on the other hand, were convinced that her contribution to the production had been substantial, and they were also impressed by the film's political efficacy and formal innovation. It is tempting to posit a correlation: the greater the criticism of Riefenstahl, the greater the praise for the style of the film.

There is certainly evidence to suggest that Riefenstahl only received the commission to make the Party Rally film at the last moment. On 11 May 1933 – at almost the same time as Goebbels discussed the 'Hitler film' with Riefenstahl – he 'handed the monopoly on all films made of Party events to the *Hauptabteilung "Film" der Reichspropagandaleitung der NSDAP'*, i.e. to the 'Film' division of the NSDAP's national propaganda administration.[12] If the minister really was already planning to give Riefenstahl artistic responsibility for the Party Rally film, he was thereby contradicting his own policy: granting privileges to the NSDAP Film division in theory, but depriving it of those privileges in practice.

The first official notification of Riefenstahl's role in the Party Rally film appeared on 23 August in the Party journal, the *Nationalsozialistische Parteikorrespondenz*; two days later the film press also referred to the news.[13] The fact that her new function was announced so late does not in itself imply that she only started to work on the project at the same stage,[14] but contemporary press accounts also support Riefenstahl's version of events. The *Licht-Bild-Bühne* reported a conversation with her:

> . . . What she said amounted to the following: I was overjoyed when the honour of this commission was bestowed on me about three days ago. Tomorrow I will travel by car to

Nuremberg to make the necessary preparations for the work awaiting me. Next Wednesday, however, I need to be in Berlin again, as I shall be attending the premiere of my sound-film, *S.O.S. Eisberg*. By Thursday, though, I shall be back in Nuremberg. Filming will then continue until 3 September.[15]

It seems unreasonable to suggest that this (published in 1933) was already part of a long-term campaign to misrepresent the sequence of events.[16] The fact that Riefenstahl left the Nuremberg Rally to attend the premiere of *S.O.S. Eisberg* also suggests that her activities in Nuremberg had been planned at fairly short notice. Moreover, contemporary analyses of *Triumph des Willens* – a film which clearly benefited from more thorough preparation work – mentioned that *Sieg des Glaubens* had been produced in altogether less favourable circumstances.[17]

Only the *Film-Journal*, in a report of 19 November 1933, indicated that Riefenstahl worked on the film over a longer period:

A few weeks before this year's NSDAP Reich Party Rally, the Party's first since the seizure of power, Leni Riefenstahl learned that the Führer wished her to take over the artistic direction of the Reich Party Rally film. The Film division of the Reich propaganda ministry was the body which passed the honour of this appointment on to her. With what pleasure and enthusiasm she followed the call![18]

Although the accounts do not quite tally, it seems likely that Leni Riefenstahl did have to make *Sieg des Glaubens* in a relatively short time, and that she therefore had to rely on improvisation for some sections.

During the preparations and the filming it was impossible to overlook the resistance of the Film division to the surprising nomination of Leni Riefenstahl as 'artistic director'.[19] The dispute over areas of responsibility was inevitable. The film office attempted quite openly to claim authorship for itself. The 'NSDAP Regional Film Office for the North-East' issued a press release (which was correctly identified as such when reprinted in *Licht-Bild-Bühne* and *Kinematograph*,[20] but which the *Film-Kurier* presented in the form of an editorial) focussing on Arnold Raether and his contribution to 'recreating the German film scene'. Much was made of Raether's responsibility for various Party films – *Das junge Deutschland marschiert* (Young Germany on the March, 1932), *Hitlerjugend in den Bergen* (The Hitler Youth in the Mountains, 1932), *Hitler über Deutschland* (Hitler over Germany, 1932) and *Deutschland erwacht* (Germany Awakens, 1933).

> All these films, created by Arnold Raether, conveyed a true picture of real life and real struggle. Everywhere they were shown they were greeted with extraordinary enthusiasm, particularly by young people, and they represented a significant medium for propaganda promoting the people and the ideal. Similarly, the new film – which we may justifiably call *our* film – will also emerge as a valuable instrument for enlightening the public.[21]

Riefenstahl's role shrank in proportion to Raether's success in representing himself as the author of a work which went 'far beyond the framework of the standard film reportage'. In most reports about the Party Rally film during its making, she was either not named at all, or ranked as 'artistic director' below the 'general director': Raether.[22] The captions accompanying photographs of the preparation work underlined this hierarchy.[23] The *Film-Kurier* of 2 September even included a brief biographical article about Raether, complete with a photograph. Two days later, in a report concerning the completion of filming, it noted

> Pg. [Party Member] Arnold Raether had made use of all the available equipment for the great congress . . . If the picture-symphony of the Party Rally, for which Leni Riefenstahl was the artistic consultant, can be brought in all its powerful grandeur before the eyes and hearts of the German people, then the Film division of the Reich propaganda ministry under Pg. *Oberregierungsrat* Arnold Raether will be entitled to take pride in its achievement.[24]

The attitude of the Film division, which was pursuing its own interests with an eye to the privilege of filming Party Rallies, was typical of the attitude of the Party in general. Albert Speer's reminiscences provide an instructive insight:

> During the preparations for the Party Rallies I met a woman

who had impressed me ever since my days as student: Leni Riefenstahl, star or director of well-known mountain and skiing films. Hitler appointed her to make films of the Party Rallies. As the only woman with an official function in the running of the Party Rallies, she was frequently at odds with the Party organization. In the early days, there were occasions on which this almost sparked a revolt against her. She was a self-confident woman who made no bones about compelling this male world to conform to her own purposes, and she had a provocative effect on the political leaders of an organization traditionally hostile towards women. Intrigues were spun and slanderous accusations were brought before Hess in order to topple her. The first Party Rally film, however, convinced even the doubters around Hitler of the director's cinematic skills, and the attacks came to an end.[25]

Riefenstahl's enemies were therefore delighted in 1933 when she was denounced for being 'of Jewish descent'. The rumour emerged at the end of August, just before filming began. An investigation was launched immediately, but its findings cannot have been very encouraging for the anti-Riefenstahl camp. The report was ready on 6 September, and it confirmed that Riefenstahl 'was recorded in the files of the central register office as belonging to the Protestant faith back to her paternal great-grandparents and her maternal grandparents; there is therefore no doubt that she is of Aryan descent.'[26]

A move to allow only long-term NSDAP members to work on Party Rally films[27] also failed. Riefenstahl's status as an outsider represented an obvious shortcoming to those who had been making the documentary films about the NSDAP until then. Whether or not she did lack ideological soundness, the incomer made a lasting and convincing impression with the film itself. The premiere of *Sieg des Glaubens* confirmed that Riefenstahl was capable of fulfilling the hopes invested in her.

Sieg des Glaubens was put together in rather makeshift fashion; but without Riefenstahl realizing it – indeed, she was in no position even to dream of such a thing at the time – the sixty-minute film had taken her a step closer to her future greatness. It was a step with a more profound influence on her subsequent fame than her first film, *Das blaue Licht*, even though the latter was much more impressive in every respect. Leni Riefenstahl had decided on a career. It was one upon which she had probably embarked partly by chance, but not without ambition. She was on the way to becoming the genius of Nazi filmmaking.

A Party Commission: New Quality

The films made of Party Rallies before 1933 lacked real quality. This was doubtless partly because of the inadequate equipment, but also because of a lack of experience and artistic expertise among the cameramen and producers.[28] The decision to entrust Leni Riefenstahl with the first film about a Party Rally after the seizure of power appears to indicate a desire for higher quality in the Party's cinematic self-portraits. Hitler had been impressed by *Das blaue Licht*, and Goebbels saw Leni Riefenstahl as 'the only one of all the stars who understands us'.[29] The only thing that made her appointment surprising, therefore, was the fact that Riefenstahl had no experience whatsoever of documentary films. However, although she herself was a newcomer to the genre, she could count on the support of three professional cameramen in Sepp Allgeier, Franz Weihmayr and Walter Frentz. These men were responsible for the most successful scenes in *Sieg des Glaubens* – the scenes which experimented with ideas which would later be developed further. The scenes included the 'morning atmosphere' in the exposition, the shots of Hitler's entrance to the city and those of the march past by the military units on the market square.

Why did Leni Riefenstahl accept the commission? It is possible that she was simply obeying Hitler's command – or even that she was compelled to do so. Nevertheless, as she herself has stressed, she was a surprising choice. On the other hand, *Sieg des Glaubens* would probably never have been completed without her self-confidence (particularly in the face of new challenges) and her tried and trusted colleagues. Above all, however, she differed significantly from previous makers of Party Rally films in the way she approached the task. Despite all the obstacles facing her, she wanted this film to be her own work. The announcement that the premiere would take place at the end of September[30] was made on the assumption that the film would be another old-style Party Rally film. That date was only four weeks after the event itself: hardly enough time to produce more than a newsreel-type documentary. Riefenstahl and her colleagues – including Herbert Windt, whose music was particularly important to the success of the film – had a different idea of what made a good film, and they pursued it as best they could, even with equipment which must sometimes have seemed inadequate. The topicality of the event was subordinated to the 'forming' of the material. In consequence, the production of the film became a longer process, and the *Film-Kurier* highlighted the sheer amount of work required of the director. It refers to 'the fact that Leni Riefenstahl directed the photography herself', to the sorting of 16,000 metres of spent film, and to the specific, artistic ideal which shaped the film.[31] Taken together, all this redefined the Party Rally film as the work of a film *auteur*.

Even in reports published in advance of the premiere, *Sieg des Glaubens* was heralded as an example of a *new form*:

> The main difficulty lies in creating a fluid sequence out of events which are basically of a repetitive nature: in achieving a heightening effect, in finding transitions: in short, in giving rhythmic form to the great film of this movement.[32]

Sieg des Glaubens was intended to be both rhythmic *and* documentary. Its artistic success therefore depended to a great extent on making march pasts, speeches and inspections interesting to the wider public. Descriptions of the film's quasi-religious quality also appeared before the premiere took place.[33] These two components – the rhythmic form underpinned by music and the elevation of the image of Hitler – were what really constituted the film's new achievements. As its director said, the film was not limited to a chronological sequence, but rather 'possessed a distinct creative concept, which elevates the film far above the category of a reportage and gives it its own, particular form'.[34]

The 'creative concept' aimed to make the film an 'experience' for 'every German'.[35] The idea was to achieve the kind of intensity which audiences would normally have associated with a feature film. *Angriff* (Attack), the Nazi newspaper published by Goebbels in Berlin, had this to say about the premiere:

The movie is not a straightforward acoustic and optical representation of events at the Party Rally. Rather, it is an artistic symphony of the 'Nuremberg 1933' experience, and it is therefore the culmination of all previous NSDAP parades and rallies ... This film is a contemporary document of inestimable value. It documents the transition of the Party into a state. ... Its triumphant coherence, its exemplary photography, its power and scale make this film more than just a documentary: it is a source of strength for the people as a whole.[36]

The film was thus characterized as the culmination not just of the NSDAP's filmmaking to date, but also of the mass rallies themselves. *Sieg des Glaubens* was the first film which the Party praised not only as a report about a Party convention, but also as the cinematic equivalent of that event. It saw the production as a way of restaging the mass-participation experience of Nuremberg as a cinematic experience. Moreover the audience was defined as the 'people as a whole' for the first time. Just as the Party had become the state, the nation in its entirety had entered Hitler's service.

The metaphorical reference to a 'symphony' recurred in several articles about the film.[37] It created an association with Ruttmann's *Berlin – Sinfonie der Grossstadt* (Berlin – Symphony of a Great City) and thereby with a particular tradition of 'cinematic films'.[38] Comparing the film to representative, large-scale formats such as a 'symphony', 'oratorio', 'nativity play' or 'monumental painting' was a way of encouraging the audience to approach it with a suitably reverent attitude. The main priority was neither to make audiences react to the action portrayed in *Sieg des Glaubens* in a certain way, nor to have them regard that action from a set and necessary distance. Rather, the film itself became an event. The premiere was even staged as a state ceremony. In *Sieg des Glaubens*, Leni Riefenstahl had found a model[39] for elevating the event she was filming through 'cinematic art, by using sequences of shots and constructing pictures of enhanced expressivity'.[40]

Stylization and 'Spontaneity'

It is tempting to blame Riefenstahl's later coolness towards *Sieg des Glaubens* purely on the film's political significance.[41] There is, however, also another reason for her dissatisfaction with it. Despite the positive reviews, the film fell far short of her ideal in several respects. None of her other films is as uneven as *Sieg des Glaubens*, which only exhibits her otherwise dominant sense of style in certain sections. The film's imperfections are persuasive evidence that the preparation time really was inadequate. Riefenstahl still lacked complete control over the shooting. She still had to make do with pictures which did not come up to her standards – and was unable completely to obscure this in the editing process. The extraordinary amounts of film which she later shot for her documentary films were, in this respect, a way of ensuring she would never again have to make do with inadequate material.

The opening images of Nuremberg in the morning, filmed by Sepp Allgeier, displayed a striking technical perfection by comparison with many later sections of the film. The fact that the exposition emerged from the editing process with such coherence is certainly due to the abundance of good footage available. Given the prevailing circumstances, *Sieg des Glaubens* may indeed represent a successful experiment,[42] even an original achievement. Those circumstances, however, did not permit the overall unity that Riefenstahl would subsequently pursue with a determination born partly of this initial experience. In the later documentaries, the relationship between stylization and spontaneity was clearly weighted in favour of the former. *Sieg des Glaubens* fell short of stylistic perfection, but it shows how Riefenstahl's decisions as a director were taking her towards a type of film ideally suited to National Socialism's attempts to project its image and which, moreover, became the prototype for Nazi filmmaking.

Unlike the later films, *Sieg des Glaubens* still contains many scenes of documentary film quality, some of which contain unintentionally amusing mishaps.[43] Sometimes these scenes point up the fact that Party Rallies, at least occasionally, succumbed to chance. Some takes, marred by technical deficiencies, reflect the difficulties faced by the filmmakers in recording the event. Such moments enable the film's audience to step back somewhat, either from the pre-filmic reality on the screen, or from the imperfect filmic portrayal. The event's own stylistic deficiencies (which the film documents in a few scenes) and the stylistic deficiencies apparent in the portrayal (caused by the conditions under which filming took place) are the most revealing evidence of the historic situation within which *Sieg des Glaubens* was made. Together they illustrate that the NSDAP still had a long way to go before achieving its later finesse at projecting its image via such events, and that the cameramen faced great difficulties in trying to produce an idealized image of the occasion.

The footage from the town hall and the festival hall is particularly full of poorly composed scenes which did not live up to the film's aspirations. Filming was even harder inside buildings than it was outside. For example, there is only an indistinct and very short shot of Streicher greeting Hitler when the latter enters the festival hall. The shots of Hitler's arrival also leave much to be desired. They include some ill-conceived camera movements: panning appears to begin, only to be aborted. Even the drive into Nuremberg, filmed by Sepp Allgeier from Hitler's car, is undermined by the shakiness of the shots and the corresponding cutaways to the cheering crowds. In other cases, circumstances evidently dictated the choice of inferior camera positions, from which the focus of interest is obscured by the crowd; examples include the shots of Hitler passing through the lines of jubilant spectators to the hotel, or those in which people enter the picture and distract attention from him. Even where they avoided such 'errors' the cameramen sometimes failed to achieve satisfactory composition. The abrupt switches between directions of movement are uncomfortable for an audience accustomed to strictly narrative films. Such switches spoil the hoped-for impact of the film in that they tend to offer the audience only isolated impressions of something which has already happened, rather than involving it in action presented in continuous form.

The ineptitudes and shortcomings of the film may not be excessively numerous, but each such scene produces a moment of irritation and an effect which the film otherwise strives to avoid. When the audience encounters a noticeable technical deficiency, a moment of confusion or is unable to see the object of its interest, its attention shifts to the film itself – as it typically does in documentaries. Such defects highlight the act of portrayal; the action being portrayed is set at a remove.

The chance incidents which occur within the actual event and are caught on camera exert a similar influence. Many scenes in *Sieg des Glaubens* show a pre-filmic reality which eluded the Party Rally directors' effort to stylize the whole occasion. A long shot taken from a very high position shows the crowd attempting to run after Hitler's car during his entrance to the city. Members of the Hitler Youth, some bearing cameras, rush across green spaces in their hurry to reach a suitable vantage point for a snapshot. Their behaviour, of course, was entirely spontaneous – but including such images would have been out of the question in *Triumph des Willens*. The film repeatedly shows people trying to photograph Hitler. Even when they are not trampling the greenery underfoot, they represent a distraction and disrupt the composition of these shots in the film. We even see stewards trying so ostentatiously to restore 'order' that they achieve exactly the opposite effect.

Today, such moments of 'spontaneity' – the noticeable agitation among the waiting Party dignitaries at the start of the second sequence[44] is another example – provide insights into the pre-filmic event, rather than defining the cinematic perception of that event. These scenes are closer to the traditional idea of documentary films. They may be regarded as an index for what was going on in front of the camera, unformed by the filmmakers and their equipment.

Similarly, there are certain scenes in which Hitler's gestures seem to betray considerable internal disquiet (sequence 3): on several occasions the film shows him characteristically stroking back his hair. Another element of documentary interest which is rather counterproductive to the film's intended effect on most audiences is the speech – in the original Italian – by the Italian fascist, Professor Marpicati.[45]

The film's 'documentary' element does not, however, predominate. The stylistic concept behind *Sieg des Glaubens* is evident even in its basic organization. The film generally employs clear fade-outs, and it is arranged into a total of eight sequences.[46] These 'blocks' of action – which are not in strictly chronological order – provided the model when *Triumph des Willens* came to be constructed, and certain scene sequences in *Sieg des Glaubens* also anticipate this, the second Party Rally film.[47] *Sieg des Glaubens* had shown that the rituals of these mass events placed narrow formal limitations upon any attempt to portray them in a way which reflected their ideological significance. Certain camera angles, such as the long shots of the mass reviews, were therefore more or less essential.

There are three conspicuous differences between *Sieg des Glaubens* and *Triumph des Willens*. First, *Sieg des Glaubens* completely lacks the overall unity of the later film. Second, the photography is mediocre in substantial sections of the film. Third, it does not yet focus entirely on Hitler as the vanishing-point of every activity. The 'Führer' is certainly central to *Sieg des Glaubens*, and the film's innovations serve to emphasize his importance.[48] In a sense, however, he remained in the film, as at the Party Rally itself, an integrated figure. This was illustrated, for example, by Rudolf Hess's use of the familiar 'du' form of address when greeting Hitler in his opening speech. In *Sieg des Glaubens* the camera seldom isolates the leader of the NSDAP from his followers, and it shows so much of the setting during his speeches that the effect can even be distracting.[49] He still seems to be part of a group; other members of the Party elite appear more often than in *Triumph des Willens* – particularly Röhm, who is picked out as the second strongman.[50] This tendency is conspicuous even in the way the shots were constructed. In *Sieg des Glaubens* Hitler is almost always seen in relative terms, within a certain space. The shots which are so typical of *Triumph des Willens*, showing Hitler against the backdrop of the sky, filling the picture, are rare in the earlier film.

The differences and similarities between Riefenstahl's first two Party Rally films become particularly clear when their opening sequences are compared. In *Sieg des Glaubens*, the opening consists of three parts: impressions of Nuremberg in the morning, preparations in the city and the march of columns of SA into town. They total approximately eight minutes, and clearly exhibit Riefenstahl's influence; except for the march of the SA, the photography is of a high standard. The three scenes form the prologue, concentrating on the relationship between the city and the event in order to produce a kind of festive mood.[51]

Sieg des Glaubens contains a rough adumbration of the famous opening of *Triumph des Willens*, Hitler's descent from the clouds. As in the later film, the audience first sees only clouds, from which the camera pans down to show Nuremberg from above. The take continues with a very long shot, panning over the city. Although the beginning with the 'cloud formation' may appear clumsy and cheap compared to the spectacular shots in *Triumph des Willens*, the long shot definitely anticipates the point of view which would later be ascribed to the 'eye of the Führer': the same buildings, the same misty atmosphere of a new dawn. Here too, in the 'morning mood' evoked after the initial scene, Riefenstahl found material to which she would subsequently return. In *Triumph des Willens*, however, it corresponds to the second rather than the first sequence, in which the impressions of Nuremberg introduce the images from the tent city. Here *Sieg des Glaubens* is even more clearly the model: in both films the camera tracks left, showing the same house beside the river. *Triumph des Willens* uses three separate takes, of which the middle one represents an almost identical quote from *Sieg des Glaubens* – the difference being that this time the house is adorned with two swastika banners.

Even the famous shot in *Triumph des Willens* of a cat appearing to observe Hitler's passing is adumbrated in *Sieg des Glaubens*. In the first film, however, the cat is watching the SA troops marching to Nuremberg – one of many details betraying the fact that the film was not exclusively dedicated to mythologizing Hitler. Nevertheless, reverence towards Hitler, without which Riefenstahl's engagement would have been unthinkable, is evident in *Sieg des Glaubens* as well. The means by which it illustrates the ardent devotion of the masses towards the 'Führer' are strikingly similar to the tactics employed in *Triumph des Willens*. Both films tend to favour women and children in order to reflect this 'enthusiasm'.[52] This was an expression of Riefenstahl's own fascination with Hitler, and also provided her with the strategy which would enable her to make the next Party Rally film completely *her* Hitler film.

Sieg des Glaubens was imperfect, but it was intended to be a 'great' and glorious film. That ambition is evident in the stylistic devices in its direction. The realization of the ambition was assisted by the orchestrated reception it received. Initially, it was the Nazi press which dictated the notion of Riefenstahl as a genius. It was not an aesthetic judgement, but rather a political prescription.

CHAPTER FIVE

The Auteur *of Nazi Filmmaking*

Leni Riefenstahl's second visit to Nuremberg must have been a very different experience from her first one. This time she was the star; the local *Fränkische Tageszeitung* referred to her general popularity 'which, among most of the SA and PO men at least, is quite frankly largely due to her charming personality'.[1] It is indicative of her new status that this time she took her leave of the city 'at an informal tea-party' in the Grandhotel, where none other than Julius Streicher[2] summarized 'in a most sincere manner, both humorously and seriously, all the difficulties which reveal the true measure of [her] achievement'.

The director herself was in a conciliatory mood, saying:

> . . . She could understand perfectly that many people found it difficult to defer to a woman at an event such as the NSDAP Reich Party Rally, which is first and foremost a men's affair. She was, however, delighted to declare that this time it had gone a thousand times better than it had in the previous year. She therefore hoped with some confidence that if she is given another opportunity to make a Party Rally film things will, of course, go even more smoothly.

That opportunity did indeed arise the following year, although it is not known whether her optimism proved misplaced or not.

Riefenstahl repaid Streicher (dubbed the 'Frankenführer' or 'leader of the Franconians') for his hospitality when he visited Berlin in February 1938. Streicher visited the Ufa and Tobis production companies to express 'his particular interest in German filmmaking'.[3] He was shown the studios in Johannisthal and viewed various documentary films.

> Leni Riefenstahl had come up with a special surprise. She is currently at Tobis putting the finishing touches to her much-awaited Olympia film. The excerpts which were shown from the first part of the Olympia film brought the unforgettable scale, power and drama of the historic Olympics in Berlin back to life again, and made a most tremendous impression.

Triumph des Willens can also be said to have made a tremendous impression. If the Party Rally had been staged in order to convey an ideological message to a mass audience, the film reconstructed that ideological message for an even wider public: cinema audiences. Riefenstahl was extremely successful in this endeavour.[4] She proved her skill in giving form to material which was, in logistical terms, unwieldy. The ritualistic character of the Party Rally gatherings acquired its ultimate significance in unconditional devotion to Hitler: 'Loyalty to the Führer signifies a readiness to die for Germany.'[5] The film consistently focuses on the 'official' events, and uses all the means at its disposal to heighten their impact as much as possible.[6] On the other hand, the film alludes to one major fly in the ointment – the SA's fall from power after the murder of its chief of staff, Ernst Röhm – only because it had to. Nevertheless, despite the film's reticence on the subject, it clearly betrays that there were further (albeit indirect) indications at the Party Rally that murdering opponents from within the Party was legitimate.[7]

Given the historical circumstances, it would have been surprising if *Triumph des Willens* had failed to fulfil its ideological purposes. What is astonishing is that for so long a different kind of project had been envisaged, even after the 'Röhm putsch'. The work's success – if one looks beyond its propaganda role and the support it received from the Party and government – is largely due to its aesthetic form,[8] but initially it was going to take a very different shape. It may seem paradoxical, but political factors prevented *Triumph des Willens* from becoming the film which had originally been planned.

The Story of the 'Movement'

The original plans for *Triumph des Willens* envisaged more than just an improved version of *Sieg des Glaubens*, and probably corresponded to Riefenstahl's own ideas. Hitler entrusted her with the new film in April 1934,[9] and she seems to have begun making preparations in May.[10] There is reason to believe that at this point she would have preferred to continue her career as a feature film actress and director.[11] The book about the Party Rally film suggests that the first cameramen were hired as early as May 1935. Riefenstahl sometimes proceeded in a very vigorous fashion, as shown by her behaviour towards Emil Schünemann, who refused to collaborate on *Triumph des Willens*.[12]

It seems certain that the preparations for *Tiefland* were Leni Riefenstahl's main priority in summer 1934, while Walter Ruttmann was already working on the Party Rally film.[13] The film journals described his assignment.

> Unlike last year's film, the aim is not merely to capture the events in Nuremberg themselves, but rather to make a full-length film, in which the history of the National Socialist freedom movement will be woven around the core of the events in Nuremberg. The task ahead is therefore an onerous responsibility. Shooting for this film has been taking place for weeks already, all over Germany. Director Walter Ruttmann and cameraman Sepp Allgeier have been hired to work in extremely close collaboration.[14]

Licht-Bild-Bühne referred to 'magnificent paintings of what [. . .] the movement has become and what it has created'.[15]

Even after the Party Rally, the plan was still to begin with a cinematic look back at the history of the NSDAP. Ruttmann described his own ideas in *Film-Kurier* in mid-September 1934:

> I therefore suggested creating a film which would not just consist of an artistic report about the events at the Reich Party Rally, but which would go further, offering an ideological representation of the historic facts of the National Socialist movement's story . . . The worker and the farmer, the SA man and the labourer in the Reich Labour Service: the working

people as a whole play the leading part . . . The representation of the history of the movement, the battles and the victories, from the Ruhr and Upper Silesia to the Führer's seizure of power on 30 January 1933, presents us with a series of technical cinematic challenges which will not always be easy to surmount. Enthusiasm for this great, unique project will ensure that we create a document all for one and one for all – for the German people and for its freedom movement.[16]

Some of these intentions are clearly at odds with the cult of Hitler in Riefenstahl's film. According to Ruttmann the focus of the film was to be on the 'movement' rather than the Führer, on the German people rather than Hitler's obedient servants. The look back at the 'time of struggle', however, necessarily evoked memories which were not altogether easy to reconcile with the situation in 1934. In October, reports appeared regarding filming 'for the Reich Party Rally film which is currently being made', providing a more precise indication of the kind of material Ruttmann had shot so far. One scene, for example, was described under the title 'Misery Over Which the Will Triumphed':

Above the piles of debris, above the dirty puddle: amongst all this, the late autumn [wind] blows dust, scraps of paper and withered leaves. Slowly, stooping, with their questing eyes to the ground, people wander through the fields of a city's refuse dump, searching in the hope that there might be something of value, perhaps something edible for their hungry stomachs, in this overburden of used goods . . . Human debris, wrapped in rags, creeps over the hills . . .[17]

Ruttmann seems to have had symbolic editing in mind, for soon after this the film magazine published extracts from the screenplay indicating that Hitler's seizure of power was to be preceded by images from nature: 'The outlined symbolism of the surging sea and the heaving crowd before the moment of supreme delight at the victory is not just cheap, retrospective retouching. That is how the whole of Germany felt about the victory evening.'[18]

In October, Goebbels, Willy Krause (Reich director of film), Viktor Lutze (SA chief of staff), Otto Dietrich (the NSDAP's Reich press chief) and other Nazi dignitaries visited Babelsberg, where the film was being shot: 'Leni Riefenstahl and Walter Ruttmann are directing the shooting in the studio.'[19]

Insofar as it is possible to reconstruct Ruttmann's concept, it seems that he envisaged a heightened, heroic representation of the NSDAP's success story. Leni Riefenstahl would later dismiss Ruttmann's footage as altogether 'useless',[20] but his goal of presenting the 'story of the movement' in the film was not only at odds with Riefenstahl's wishes. The main problem facing Ruttmann's reconstruction was that of how the 'ideological representation of the historic facts' could immortalize the contribution made by thuggish SA troops and the roles of Röhm and others, whilst reconciling all this with the new situation following the purge of the SA and the murder of Hitler's former brothers-in-arms. The original idea was that Ruttmann contribute about a third of the film's overall length.[21] There is a great deal of evidence to suggest that the decision to abandon that idea was linked to Hitler's visit to the cutting room on 6 December 1934.[22] From then on the press has nothing to say regarding either Ruttmann himself or the large amount of material he had shot.[23]

The Party Rally Film – A Historical Document?

Had Ruttmann and Riefenstahl cooperated as originally intended, their film would have been a mixture between a montage film, glorifying the 'movement', and a portrait of the Party Rally, glorifying that event. Only when the decision was taken to dedicate the film to the Rally alone was Riefenstahl installed unequivocally as the sole *auteur*.

She seized this opportunity to make the definitive film about the Nazi cult of the Führer. In doing so, she emphasized the relationship between Hitler, the various sections of the Party and the population of Nuremberg.[24] This, more than anything else, represented her original contribution to Nazi mythology; she used the Party Rally as a chance to highlight the emotional potential which was merely hinted at in *Sieg des Glaubens*. Later Riefenstahl would repeatedly claim, with calculated naivety, that the film was purely a documentary or historical work. This represents a tactical retreat: her claim is intended to minimize her responsibility for the film's aesthetic structure. In fact, of course, simply affirming the documentary nature of the film is relatively meaningless: every decision about what the cameras should or should not record, about the nature of a take, the editing and the music, inevitably implies a particular perspective on the event in the film. That *Triumph des Willens* is a documentary film goes without saying, but that in itself signifies very little. The real questions are: in what way is it documentary, and what does it document?

Simply setting the 'documentary film' against the 'propaganda film' is unhelpful, as they each mean various different things. Like the feature film, the animated film and the film essay, the 'documentary film' is a cinematic genre. These differ in their relationship to the reality before the camera, or they define that reality – the *pre-filmic* world – in different ways.[25] Documentary films can of course also be propaganda films: in this context, 'propaganda' merely denotes a departure from factuality, a representation of a real set of circumstances which seems at least flattering, if not actually distorted. 'Propaganda films' can belong to any of several quite distinct genres, including the feature film *(Jud Süss)* and the newsreel (indeed, the wartime weekly newsreels of the 'Third Reich' are regarded as particularly successful examples).[26]

Riefenstahl's statements represent an intellectually inadequate target for potential objections. They do not offer a thesis capable of sparking meaningful critical comment. Anyone wishing to dispute her suggestion that, notwithstanding all its aesthetic and political qualities, *Triumph des Willens* is a documentary film – that is, a specific cinematic genre – has to resort to making distinctions which cannot be meaningfully justified.[27] Yet seeing Riefenstahl's films purely as propaganda films does not do justice to their uniqueness. They could not have developed so effectively if they had stylized a non-documentary subject.[28] It is true, however, that they document more than the political significance of the Party Rally: they testify to its emotional, even erotic basis.

The Party Rally Narrative

In *From Caligari to Hitler*, Siegfried Kracauer compares the *Bergfilm* genre and *Triumph des Willens*. He refers to 'the majestic cloud displays' in *Stürme über dem Montblanc* and argues:

> That in the opening sequence of the Nazi documentary
> *Triumph of the Will*, of 1936, similar cloud masses surround
> Hitler's airplane on its flight to Nuremberg, reveals the
> ultimate fusion of the mountain cult and the Hitler cult.[29]

In terms of the motifs, this comparison is unconvincing: there is a
conspicuous absence of any specific relationship. In another sense,
however, the *Bergfilm* genre certainly may be regarded as a model:
in the way it accentuates spectacular elements, placing more
weight on presenting them in the most effective fashion than on the
requirements of the narrative. *Triumph des Willens* approached the
documentary film in the same way, privileging spectacle and
entertainment over the 'report'.[30]

In terms of structure, Kracauer's symbolic interpretation would
suggest that Riefenstahl's second Party Rally film had made use of
peculiarities and forms which are characteristic of narrative
cinema. In fact it was inspired by feature films not so much in its
symbols, but rather in the way it was edited. This is evident right
from the start. No audience is likely to miss the invitation to
interpret the initial scenes in *Triumph des Willens* in a particular
way. The captions announce that Hitler is coming to Nuremberg 'to
review the armed forces'. An aeroplane then appears, and there are
various shots of cloud formations. The machine appears above the
city and there are views of what is taking place down below.

The point of all this is crystal clear. Hitler's aeroplane, the view
from the cockpit or other windows of the sky and subsequently of
the city: Hitler is coming to Nuremberg. This is an unusual opening
for a documentary film, as it makes no attempt to declare its
authenticity, to convince the audience that this really is 'Hitler's
aeroplane' and 'Hitler's point of view'. Yet this does not impede
the audience's ability to appreciate and follow the film, for the
opening sequence unmistakably suggests its own interpretation.
This is based not on the conventions of the documentary, but rather
on those of the narrative. *Triumph des Willens* thus begins in a
manner which could be termed classic if it were a feature film, and
it presupposes that the members of the audience will activate a
mode of perception which has been instilled in them by
conventional feature films, thereby making the connections

suggested by the montage (Hitler's review of the armed forces – Hitler's aeroplane – Hitler's point of view from the aeroplane).[31]

Riefenstahl's achievement lay in applying the tools and formal language of the feature film to a documentary film. To that extent, it is perfectly legitimate to discuss the 'leading role' played by Hitler,[32] and even to conclude that Riefenstahl effectively had Hitler at her mercy as his director. It was she who defined his image, she who created the calculated poses. In doing so, she provided the material around which the film itself revolved. The fundamental prerequisite for Riefenstahl's special 'documentary style' was emancipation from the usual limitations imposed on documentary films. Even her polemical remarks concerning the weekly newsreels[33] represented an attempt to address the conditions under which her own work was to be produced, as she was very much aware that 'newsreel style' was not simply the result of inadequate effort on the part of the cameramen. Rather, it reflected the purely practical difficulties of obtaining better camera angles, privileged access and the greatest possible variety of perspectives. Her documentary films typically used a large number of camera teams; she aimed positively to encircle the action if she possibly could.[34]

In a certain sense, *Triumph des Willens* offered Leni Riefenstahl her first opportunity to approach a major occasion – which would last only a week and include many different events[35] – as though she were making a big studio production. Riefenstahl's stylistic ideal was remarkable in two ways. On the one hand, she employed a sequence of cuts modelled on narrative films in an attempt to place the audience in the position of the 'ideal spectator' (who is enabled to identify with the progress of the action or story by formal means). On the other, she was concerned to 'heroize' the action itself.

A good example of the way she worked is the sequence involving Hitler's journey from the airport to the hotel, for which she utilized genuine narrative forms. The sequence ends with an emphatic fade, and includes approximately ninety shots within about five minutes, from the landing of the aeroplane to Hitler's appearance at the hotel window to greet the crowd. The shots are therefore strikingly brief: just over three seconds on average.[36] More remarkable still is the lack of variety in the rhythm: most of the shots last between about one and a half and four seconds. The montage technique is also extremely repetitive: in general it consists of an exchange between shots and counter- or reaction-shots. This form of montage is very artificial in a documentary film, as it assumes that the various 'characters' are gazing fixedly at one another. The fact that nearly all the shots actually used in this sequence[37] were taken by moving cameras (mostly from cars), makes the combinations seem even more dynamic. In her montage, Riefenstahl attempted to add variety to the presentation of the bond constructed by virtual eye contacts between Hitler and the cheering crowds. This she achieved by using as many different camera ranges and angles as possible within the superficially uniform pattern. The hierarchy of the eye contacts, however, never changed: the 'people' are always shown in high-angle shots, Hitler from a low or eye-level angle. Only the long shots depart from this rule, as they sometimes employ extreme high angles. Their function is one of orientation, clarifying the distance already covered.

The shifting points of view in the shot–reaction-shot montage define the relationship between Hitler and the 'people'. The crowd jubilantly expresses its support; Hitler is the recipient. This is of little documentary value, as the virtual eye contacts are un-changing. Nor were they set in a broader context, perhaps by invoking other situations (such as the SS waiting in front of the hotel or the preparations for the column of vehicles). Riefenstahl concentrated entirely on a multifaceted illustration of a single situation: Hitler's journey to the hotel is a chain reaction of ovations; everything relates to him. The reception becomes a triumphal procession.[38]

The influence of narrative conventions is not only obvious in the basic form of the sequence, but also in many details. The first example of a decidedly narrative approach to the finer points of montage comes when the aeroplane lands. First there is a close-up of three cheering women, their hands raised in the Nazi salute. Then Riefenstahl cuts to Hitler, who appears to 'look left' at the end of the short take, before returning to the previous shot. The camera now tracks slightly to the left, which brings more women and children into view. This brief passage is a superb example of dynamic cutting. It assigns the gazes to each other and reinforces the relationship between shot and reaction-shot by having a character (Hitler) and the camera (which follows him) move in the same direction. The privileged object of the gaze also determines the form of the exchange of gazes.

In the first part of the journey, images of the crowds lining the route are alternated with shots of Hitler. The crowd on the 'left' appears each time Hitler turns 'to the left' and vice versa. Once established, this pattern enabled Riefenstahl to put her faith entirely in the montage technique and to introduce some additional levels of significance. She was able to insert a close-up of Hitler's hand, stretched out in a salute, without disrupting the impression of continuity. The motif was a carefully chosen one, for the close-up shows the light striking the palm of Hitler's hand to great effect. The film includes symbolism to do with light elsewhere as well, thereby helping surround its 'central character' with an almost religious aura.[39]

Within the strict, alternating pattern, the preponderance of women and children in the crowd cheering Hitler is striking. Only occasionally does the film show any other kind of onlooker, such as an SA formation standing beside the road and saluting the Führer. Some particularly emphatic moments in the sequence also help promote Hitler as the champion of women and children. This is particularly noteworthy, as the film features few shots – here or elsewhere – of individual members of the crowd, and still fewer in close-up. The exceptions in the opening sequence all involve women or girls, as when Hitler briefly interrupts his journey into the city to receive a bunch of flowers from a woman who has her daughter in her arms. The film does not show Hitler's reaction; instead, it reflects the devotion evident in the reactions of other onlookers. First the camera focuses on a girl, smiling and apparently watching the scene from between two SA stewards; then come two close-ups of laughing girls. After this we return to the shot of the mother with her child as she hands over the bunch of flowers. The episode concludes with a group picture in which four boys and an old lady seem to be observing the presentation.

In this scene the film's subjective approach to the action reaches its first climax. Afterwards, it cuts dynamically from Hitler to shots of a cat which appears to be following him with its gaze, to the 'Gänsemännchen' fountain, and to a statue: the whole of Nurem-

berg seems to be greeting the Führer. The public is divided
between those in uniform (members of the army or an NSDAP
section) and the rest. Those not in uniform are prominent at the
start of the film, but later they vanish almost altogether. Only in the
sequence dedicated to the march past by the Nazi units do they
reappear as extras in order to endorse a ritual of submission, for,
with the review of the Reich Labour Service, a new element enters
the film which will be taken up and subjected to variations. If the
start of the film can be interpreted as the illustration of a love story
with Hitler, the later part replaces this with unilateral commitment
to Hitler. In both relationships he is the central figure; the second
part of the film also uses the tactic of cutting between shot and
reaction-shot to accentuate the point. However, while the love
remains largely passive – fulfilled in its desire 'to see our leader'[40] –
the unilateral commitment has consequences which the rituals of
the Party Rally both articulate and prescribe. The narrative pattern
made it possible for Riefenstahl continually to illustrate the
hierarchy of 'leader' and 'followers' by alternating between high
and low angles; it enabled her to consolidate the ideological basis;
and it allowed her to use cross-cutting to inject some variety to
basically similar sequences of events.

Most of the sequences which follow the opening are also
indebted to the pattern of shot and reaction-shot. In these
sequences Riefenstahl managed to define the relationship between
the Party sections, the 'people' and the 'Führer' as the followers
saw it. There are, however, a few exceptions, above all in the first
half of the film. Once the 'exposition' is over, Hitler tends to vanish
from view again almost as soon as he appears.[41] He is initially
absent from the passages immediately after the arrival scene – from
the army *Zapfenstreich* (tattoo), the impressions of Nuremberg in
the morning, the detailed transfiguration of life in the tented cities
and the arrival of the *Trachtenzüge* (parades in traditional
costumes).[42] He only reappears when he steps out of his hotel to
greet the *Trachtenzüge*. Here Riefenstahl again draws heavily on the
potential of cutting and counter-cutting, taking the opportunity to
stage another love story. Once again the more or less anonymous
fervour of the inhabitants en masse is individualized, both in
anticipation of the Führer's appearance (a young woman, a girl and
two boys) and at the moment of fulfilment (two young women).

Except for one woman, all these individuals appear at least twice, always as a 'reaction-shot' to a shot of Hitler, and all of them represent incarnations of love for the Führer. This is a film in which individuals do not figure;[43] these close-ups are included as evidence of a fervour which has nothing personal about it. The erotic connotations of the shots are patent, but they too evince above all the love of the 'whole people'.

The press drew attention to how many close-up shots there were of the Führer in the film, but after this scene it changes its strategy and makes its audience wait for Hitler. This applies to the speeches in the conference hall, which repeatedly refer to him and invoke him as an authority, and it also applies to the review of the DAF (German Labour Front), during which the film only cross-cuts briefly to Hitler four times during the offering from the 'choir' before he makes his speech. This address begins the rhythm which dominates the montage of the second part of the film, in which long shots of the formations on parade and close-ups of the men are combined with shots of Hitler. Unlike the beginning of the film, with its strict alternation between shots and reaction-shots, here the camera angles are somewhat more objective, in that Hitler is occasionally shown in long shots within the context of the ceremony. Such shots do not, however, undermine the ideological message of the film. On the contrary, they illustrate rituals which revolve around the Führer and highlight them in cinematic terms. These rituals are impersonal and thus distinct from the love story established at the start of the film, but they are also more compelling. The (female) love story is the basis of the affirmation; its significance resides in the way it consolidates the (male) submission to the Führer.

Significantly, the second part of the film only uses shot–reaction-shot montage once more to 'narrate' a love relationship, in the Hitler Youth sequence. Virtual eye contact is constructed between Hitler and the boys, whose facial expressions betray a joyful reverence not exhibited by their adult counterparts. In *Triumph des Willens*, it is the women and boys who love the Führer and the men who are his followers.

This theme is developed extensively in the second part of the film, starting with the various reviews. Both the exceptionally long sequence in which the Nazi organizations and *Wehrmacht* (army) units marched past Hitler at Nuremberg's market square and the closing rally in the Luitpoldhalle (the venue for Party congress) also relate all the action to Hitler. This means that more than two-thirds of the film consists of variations on the same basic situation, in which the Führer receives his Party colleagues' declarations of loyalty. This relationship does not change in any significant sense. Within the same context, the tribute to the fallen and subsequent consecration of the flag provide the outstanding expression of the Nazi cult of the dead.[44] In Ray Müller's television documentary, Riefenstahl still appeared to find these scenes particularly moving. She took pride in, amongst other things, the vertical tracking shots, which were made possible by a lift on one of the three great flagpoles in the Luitpold Arena, and in the massing of the flags for their consecration in the stadium:[45] particularly powerful images which were often quoted in later compilations. Riefenstahl's formal language is inventive and functional; she illustrates the rituals of the Party Rally with consummate sensitivity, patently intent on overwhelming her audience and achieving 'classical' unity.

The only significant exception to the general rule that the participants in the Party Rally are defined only in relation to Hitler is the nocturnal ceremony in honour of the SA. It is the only event represented in *Triumph des Willens* which did not take place *for* Hitler;[46] it is the only part of the film dedicated to an event which was not listed in the official programme for the Party Rally and the only scene which is not related to Hitler at least 'in anticipation'.[47] It shows the SA, which Hitler had stripped of its power just two months earlier, enthusiastically saluting its new leader, Viktor Lutze – successor to the murdered Röhm. The truly spontaneous enthusiasm evident here is quite unlike most of the film's other scenes. It was due not to a triumph, but rather to the achievement of survival. 'The attention paid to the SA in *Triumph des Willens* is bestowed on an organization stripped of power, which was given the task of representing the Party legend in compensation for being condemned to political insignificance.'[48] This very function however, made it impossible to try to portray the 'history of the movement' by means of documentary footage and re-enactments. In one form or another, Ruttmann would have had to reconcile the 'heroic story' with the SA's fall from power. Riefenstahl's concentration on a stylistically heightened portrayal of the events at the Party Rally may have represented a return to familiar territory, a retreat from the more ambitious project – but it proved to be the politically more astute option.[49]

The Film *Auteur*

Despite Riefenstahl's later efforts to present her film in a different light, the political significance of *Triumph des Willens* was never in any doubt. The contemporary press was, in any case, bound to toe the Party line, and any deviations from the general expressions of enthusiasm had to be phrased extremely carefully.[50] Occasionally critics would cautiously attempt to express reservations:

> One passage in particular, the parade of the Party sections, betrays just how easily the film could have turned into a mere repetition of *Sieg des Glaubens*. It is all the more remarkable, then, that this danger was avoided elsewhere in the film.[51]

It appears that the *Deutsche Filmzeitung* was alone in taking a more explicitly critical attitude. It regretted the lack of the 'idyllic, the "National Socialist" [element] *alongside* the official events' and recommended shortening the 'parades of the last third' of the film. It considered that the audience's attention is 'subjected to uniform impressions for rather too long in the last third of the film' – an opinion that seems altogether justified from a modern perspective. This was the only review which came close to genuine criticism of the film, and it was also the only one which – astonishingly – dared make reference to the ideological attempt to come to terms with the 'Röhm Putsch': 'The film particularly highlights the concentrated embodiment of the movement and the state in the person of the Führer, which was so clearly apparent at the Party Rally in the aftermath of the purge of June 30.'[52]

For Riefenstahl, in retrospect, the film's ideological function vanished completely. Instead, she preferred to remember the awards – less the German National Film Prize of 1934/35 than the award for the best documentary film it won at Venice in 1935 and the Gold Medallion at the Paris World Exhibition of 1937.[53] There were also other indications that she had now established herself as an *auteur*. Indeed, according to her she was even her own producer. This claim was particularly important to her after 1945. Every serious investigation, however, has come to the conclusion that the NSDAP should be regarded as the producer of *Triumph des Willens*, as well as of *Sieg des Glaubens* and *Tag der Freiheit*.[54] Ufa regarded Riefenstahl as the 'special representative of the NSDAP', which in September 1935 prohibited *all* showings of film footage of the Party Rally, except for the authorized weekly newsreel reports, until 30 November 1935, in order to ensure its film's exclusivity.[55] The 'Geschäftsstelle des Reichparteitagsfilms' ('Reich Party Rally Film Office') used the official letterhead of the NSDAP Reich leadership, and did so again when *Tag der Freiheit* came to be made.[56]

Leni Riefenstahl's role as an *auteur*-director has to be seen in the context of the huge support she received from the Party, the state and the city of Nuremberg. She could, in a sense, secure the 'industry standard' for her films without being tied down by the production plans and calculations of the big studios. In that sense she was an 'independent' director – an *auteur* of the kind that could only exist in the particular environment of National Socialism. Even if the ideological function of her film is set on one side, she remains the Nazi director par excellence: the regime recognized the ideal image of the 'new Germany' in her films and she could therefore rely on its support. Leni Riefenstahl – uniquely and, it would seem, paradoxically – enjoyed absolute artistic control over films which dovetailed perfectly with the aims of the regime.

She was a film *auteur* on commission, a kind of Nazi counterpoint to the ideal inherent in the *auteur* films of later years: a blueprint, greatly influenced by the traditional artistic concept of the genius, in which the 'personal touch' was indivisible from the 'personal objective'. According to the *auteur* theory, saying something well also means saying something personal. This explains its adherents' abhorrence of everything impersonal and every routine, be it a matter of habit or a consequence of studio practice, and it also explains their rejection of smoothness and perfection. In this context, style is always also personal style, the expression of an individual who wants to do more than just complete a task as a craftsman or technician.

By contrast, Riefenstahl was an *auteur* who always strove above all to make her films interesting. She too wanted to avoid repetition, routine, imprecision – but only in order to complete a task which she saw purely in terms of craftsmanship. She saw herself as the cinematic stylist, whose aim was to give appropriate form to predetermined content (be it a Party Rally or a legend, a sporting event or a popular fiction). The result is perfection without provocation, as if the *auteur* in question were missing only one quality: personality.

Her 'personal style' was unmistakable, but it was also unmistakably split. The documentaries and the feature films each possessed a separate stylistic ideal. They were similar only in the most general sense – for example in the clear choice of motifs and the skilful photography. Riefenstahl took full account of their particular themes in achieving two fundamentally different styles. The documentary films only betrayed the picturesque touch in their expositions. Otherwise they relied on a mode of portrayal which was as realistic as possible, albeit highly stylized. Both *Das blaue Licht* and *Tiefland*, by contrast, were defined by the attempt to achieve a picturesque effect.

As a stylist, Leni Riefenstahl demonstrated her creativity in the way she realized her aims, but her originality depended on having a predetermined task. It is hard (particularly after reading her memoirs) to imagine her as somebody capable of developing new stories or inventive variations on imported patterns.

Tag der Freiheit

The premiere of *Triumph des Willens* turned into another personal triumph for Riefenstahl. The unparalleled press campaign on behalf of the film confirmed her in the role of National Socialism's cinematic genius. She had created a film in which the dictatorship recognized an ideal image of itself, and which – surprisingly – won acclaim not just in fascist Italy but also on a wider international stage, such as at the World Fair of 1937 in Paris. For Riefenstahl, a great deal, if not everything, seemed possible. It seems probable that she had already turned her attention to her most ambitious project – the *Penthesilea* material. In June 1935, she took time off for a mountain tour,[57] but in September she returned to Nuremberg for the Party Rally where, following reintroduction of conscription, displays by the various armed services were a major attraction.[58] The demonstration of military strength was also the focal point of Riefenstahl's *Wehrmacht* film, *Tag der Freiheit*.

As with her first Party Rally film, she later played down the
significance of this work (which was also thought for many years to
have been lost) and spoke of shooting it very rapidly. It is a short
film of only twenty-eight minutes, but from a formal point of view
it is far from a trivial 'finger exercise'. The team making the film
had to find a satisfactory means of capturing the military
manoeuvres which are the main focus for attention. The experience
of making the earlier Party Rally film was reflected in a very
concentrated approach to the work and probably also in some
rigorous preparations. The tried and tested team on location
included cameramen Guzzi Lantschner, Walter Frentz, Hans Ertl,
Kurt Neubert and Willy Zielke. Their names alone argue against a
drop in quality. There are no failed or ill-conceived shots and no
half-hearted perspectives in *Tag der Freiheit*. Peter Kreuder's music
is an effective backing to the images and brilliantly integrates the
sounds of the manoeuvres in the relevant scenes.[59]

Previous experience also contributed to the montage technique
(the film is organized in four sequences). After the opening credits
comes the 'morning atmosphere': soldiers awaken in the camp,
wash, get food and march to the parade ground. The second
sequence is devoted entirely to Hitler's address to the massed
ranks, the longest of any of his speeches in a Riefenstahl film. The
director concentrated on a close-up of Adolf Hitler, who is
photographed against the sky. She then intercut pictures exclusively of the ranks or individual squad leaders, but without
resorting to the technique of 'virtual eye contact' that she had
developed. Shots and reaction-shots are never used to create
relationships between the Führer and his subordinates in this film:
there is only an inspection of the troops and the formations gazing
up at their leader. There is no 'personal' nuance to Hitler's
relationship with the *Wehrmacht*: it is merely the relationship
between a commander-in-chief and his soldiers. The third
sequence features the parade of the various armed services, and
the final one deals with the manoeuvre in which the army and air
force participate. Here, above all, it is noticeable how carefully the
shots were chosen, to create small narrative units dedicated to the
infantry battle, the cavalry advance and the contributions made by
the artillery, tanks and aeroplanes. There is certainly no sign of any
improvisation: the scenes continually engage with one another, a

sure sign of good preparation and detailed consultations between the film crew and the men in charge of the manoeuvres. It would otherwise be hard to explain how the cameramen came to be 'on the spot' on every occasion.

Its brevity and the fact that it concentrates entirely on presenting the *Wehrmacht* make *Tag der Freiheit* a minor film in comparison with *Triumph des Willens*. Within its ideological context, however, it was an effective way of sponsoring enthusiasm for military service. Riefenstahl's somewhat dismissive attitude towards the film cannot be due to its formal qualities. It is more likely to be a response to its theme, which offered a great deal of scope for the glorification of Hitler and none for the portrayal of popular enthusiasm for him. There was little room in *Tag der Freiheit* for Riefenstahl's personal predilections; she was unable to translate her own fascination into the kind of images she favoured. The result was a somewhat more sober kind of film. It represented a good opportunity for the cameramen (of whom Ertl, Lantschner and Frentz went on to become war correspondents) to practise shots of military manoeuvres, but a poor one for the director to illustrate devotion towards the Führer.

While she was in Nuremberg, however, Leni Riefenstahl also filmed scenes which were not intended for the '*Wehrmacht* film', but rather as a stock of material for later use.

> As the *Film-Kurier* has already reported, many cameramen entrusted with special tasks are again working under the direction of Leni Riefenstahl . . . Leni Riefenstahl's footage is, in part, additional footage for the Reich Party Rally archive, which, as is well known, is housed in the Geyerwerke complex and continues to work there. The Führer's speeches naturally receive particular attention.[60]

Supervising the archive cannot have been much of an aesthetic challenge, and the same might be said of shooting the additional footage for it. Thanks to her familiarity with the footage already available, however, Riefenstahl would appear to have been predestined to evaluate and utilize the vast quantity of material. *Tag der Freiheit*, however, remained an unavoidable duty, an intermezzo on the way towards greater things.

CHAPTER SIX

The Best Sports Film of All Time

The Party Rally films, and *Triumph des Willens* in particular, were regarded as quasi-sacred dramas – befitting the Party rallies, which had themselves evolved into ritualized forms. The political significance of the mass-participation events in Nuremberg was primarily demonstrative: everybody involved had an allotted role to play in a choreographed performance. The Party rallies became endorsements of the dictatorship through their aesthetic representation of the masses. In cinematic form they became the ideal celebration of the inspiration which 'the whole German people' was intended to draw from the Führer. *Olympia*, by contrast, celebrates a community spirit in which no such subordination seems apparent: the spirit of happy harmony which 'the German people' perceives between itself and the Führer. The Party Rally films emphasize the duty of creating the 'new Germany'; *Olympia* presents the Führer, the Party and the people in such a way as to create a celebration of that 'new Germany'. The Party Rally films and *Olympia* represent the different sides of the community experience. Both are clearly constructed upon the ruthless exclusion and persecution of those who do not belong: the Jews, the Sinti and Romany gypsies, the leftists, the homosexuals, the weak and the sick and many others. Both kinds of community experience are influenced by this exclusion mechanism, albeit in different ways. The Party Rallies – and the films dedicated to them – contain a definition of the rejected enemy. The Olympic Games, along with the cinematic *Olympia* – conceal the policy of exclusion.[1]

The perfect world of the Games is the KdF ('Strength through Joy' – the Nazis' populist leisure movement) version of the Party Rally and *Olympia* is the KdF version of a Party Rally film.

This helped *Olympia* become emblematic of the zenith of Leni Riefenstahl's career. She had found a focus for her abilities which suited her much better than the rituals of the NSDAP. The massed ranks had become spectators; the main attractions were now athletic competitions. After completing the 'set exercises', Leni Riefenstahl could finally turn to the free programme. She may not always have enjoyed making the Party Rally films, but doing so had paid dividends. *Olympia* was, in a sense, the reward for her own 'triumph of the will'.[2]

Storming to the Summit

It seemed as though she had now made it to the very top and won general recognition. Whilst preparing and shooting the film she enjoyed an unparalleled status. She had hundreds of workers at her disposal, and could even count on the support of the German navy.[3] Hers was the undisputed voice of command: this film amounted to a realization of the Nazi *Führerprinzip* – the cult of the leader (a female one, in this case).

Leni Riefenstahl had become the centre of her own cinematic world, quite independent of the film industry. Her team spent weeks encamped at 'Haus Ruhwald', as if on an expedition within Germany. She took a hand in everything and enjoyed the work. This project was the really big film she had long dreamed of making: *her* film.

Leni Riefenstahl's unceasing activity did attract some malicious comments.[4] There was more than a grain of truth in them, as is evident from the following report from the scene of the shooting. It appeared in the *Film-Kurier*, which did a great deal for the reputation of the film and the director with its numerous preview articles in summer 1936:

> She has allocated seven hours for this important afternoon of the third day, discussed five different takes with each of 34 cameramen, as well as talking to each of them for an extra ten

minutes about material, filters and apertures. Let us work it out: 34 × 5 takes in a five-minute conversation with each cameraman and an encore of ten minutes with each of them. According to my calculations, that makes a total of 510 minutes during the morning and midday for organizing the afternoon . . . eight hours of conversation at an Owen-like pace. No wonder the sparks fly if one of her team is unable to cope. She works and treats her cameramen as if she were possessed.[5]

The second part of the film offers a brief, fortuitous glimpse of the director herself. At the end of the sequence in *Fest der Schönheit* (Festival of Beauty) dedicated to the men's 200-metres breaststroke swimming race, the camera pans slightly to the left from a long shot of the pool. Leni Riefenstahl is visible at the bottom of the picture, gesticulating energetically as she angrily berates an official. The shot lasts only a moment, but it betrays how much stress the director was under. She was determined that every detail of *Olympia* should live up to her dream.

That determination explains the incessant instructions to the cameramen, most of whom were experienced specialists who had themselves developed new methods in order to capture the sporting action in spectacular pictures. It also explains her differences of opinion with the judges, umpires and referees, who naturally considered that guaranteeing the best possible camera-angles was not their main responsibility.[6] If necessary, Riefenstahl evidently fought unashamedly to obtain such angles. In the scenes from the swimming stadium, cameramen are frequently visible directly behind the starting-blocks at both ends of the lane. At the end of the 200-metres breaststroke, Japan's Tetsou Hamuro and Germany's Erwin Sietas are shown at their moment of triumph. The resulting shot is particularly memorable: the final had been terrifically close, and the film shows Hamuro learning of his victory and taking a moment to comprehend his success.

What inspired Riefenstahl's absolute commitment to *Olympia*, which was, after all, another documentary about a large-scale spectacle rather than a feature film? This event offered a much better basis for a gripping film. The competitions themselves guaranteed tension, the athletes provided Riefenstahl with ideal objects for stylizing the human body and the whole occasion was made to measure for projecting an image of Germany as peace-loving nation. Moreover, the whole world was interested in the Olympic Games: it was a golden opportunity for Riefenstahl to demonstrate what she could do with an event which enjoyed support abroad as well as in Germany.

As early as 1936, Leni Riefenstahl contacted Paul Kohner and offered MGM distribution rights to the film.[7] The plan came to nothing, but she was right to speculate on a major international coup: the premieres in various European countries were hugely successful. *Olympia* took Riefenstahl to the height of both her stylistic art and her fame. In her memoirs she goes into great detail about the frustrations involved in the work, the insurmountable obstacles and – inevitably – the intrigues led by Goebbels against the film, but it is clear that she feels very gratified by the success she enjoyed with *Olympia*.

Riefenstahl made more elaborate preparations for *Olympia* than for any previous film. In total, she worked towards and on the film in one way or another for three and a half years. She started her preparations in summer 1935. From spring 1936 she began visiting sporting events with her cameramen to test techniques for shooting the action. Press reports started to appear even at that stage, snowballing into an unparalleled campaign shortly before the Games and during them. When Riefenstahl travelled to Greece in order to shoot the lighting of the Olympic flame and the start of the torch relay, journalists were of course in attendance; the trip turned into a veritable mission. The *Völkische Beobachter* dispatched a special correspondent who accompanied the torch for the whole of its journey. Ernst Jaeger, who also happened to be the Olympia Film GmbH chief press officer, reported for the *Film-Kurier*. The filming of the various events attracted attention from beyond the specialist press.[8] The fuss around the film only started to die down when Riefenstahl shot a few additional scenes and then sections of the prologue in the late summer of 1936.[9] Shooting further additional scenes and synchronizing the sound and music meant further interruptions to the process of viewing the footage and editing it even in 1937. The film received an even grander premiere than any of its predecessors on 20 April 1938 – Hitler's forty-ninth birthday – at the Ufa Palast am Zoo, which had been decorated inside and out for the occasion. Riefenstahl's work on the film was now over, but not her work with the film. In the following months her team produced a total of five foreign versions, and the director travelled to glittering premieres across much of Europe, from Paris to Athens. In November she travelled all the way to the United States. Even after returning from there, this uniquely successful ambassador for German cinema continued her promotional tour until spring 1939.

A Commission

After 1945, Leni Riefenstahl tirelessly insisted that *Olympia* had been commissioned by the IOC, and that she had produced it herself and bore sole artistic responsibility for it. The film received no support from the Party and ultimately had no ideological function.[10] The surviving files give a different picture of the film's production, one which has been repeatedly highlighted since the 1970s.[11] Riefenstahl was undoubtedly the author of the film. The contract between her and the Reich Ministry for Popular Enlightenment and Propaganda specifies that she had 'overall charge' of the film and its direction, and that responsibility for 'the artistic structure and organizational implementation' lay in her hands alone.[12]

   The story of *Olympia* began before the shooting of *Tag der Freiheit*, as one of the entries in the Goebbels diaries shows: 'Fräulein Riefenstahl reports on the preparation work for the Olympia film. She's a smart cookie.'[13] There were public hints about the new project as early as September 1935, when the *Film-Kurier* published an article about Riefenstahl's plans, including the 'Penthesilea' project. The journal stated, however, that first she would undertake another project, similar to the Party Rally films, 'probably for the Olympiad films'.[14] While editing the *Wehrmacht* film, she continued to confer with Goebbels about the Olympia project and various contractual matters,[15] and on 9 December 1935, a company to make the film was founded: Olympia-Film GmbH, whereby 'the shares in the business were held in trust for the Propaganda Ministry by the shareholders Leni Riefenstahl, with RM18,000 and Heinz Riefenstahl with RM2,000.'[16] This suggests that the company was a cover for the Propaganda Ministry:

The Olympiade-Film GmbH is founded on the instigation of the Reich and with funds provided by the Reich. All the funds needed by the company for making the film will also be made available within the Reich budget. The founding of the company is necessary because the Reich does not wish to be seen openly as the maker of the film.[17]

The ministry approved a sum of RM1.5 million from its budget, which also included Riefenstahl's fee of RM250,000. The company was answerable to the Propaganda Ministry, and its financial conduct later gave rise to a dispute.[18] The distribution contract with Tobis also needed approval from the ministry,[19] and the surplus made by the film went to the Reich.

Once *Olympia*, the foreign versions and a few shorter films had been completed, the company's role was over. From the start of 1939, therefore, the Propaganda Ministry pressed for the firm to be liquidated. This eventually happened belatedly in January 1942. The balance sheet giving the final figures was a positive one: production costs amounted to RM2,831,355.41 (including the short films and the dubbed versions), but after taking off all expenses, there was a profit of RM91,123.20. Riefenstahl herself had received a total fee of RM350,000; after the premiere, Goebbels patronizingly noted: 'I hear nothing but unreserved praise. I make Leni Riefenstahl a present of an extra 100,000 Mk.'[20] In a letter of March 1939, Riefenstahl asked the propaganda minister to grant her a monthly fee of RM5,000, backdated to 1 May 1938, as since the film's premiere she had been confronted with tasks 'which were not foreseen when the contract was completed. By this I mean foreign trips made in the interests of publicity and the commercial exploitation of the film, and the trip to America necessary for marketing.' All her trips, she insisted, were 'of a representative nature'. This was certainly true, and the minister approved her idea until February 1939 inclusive, despite his officials' protestations that Riefenstahl's estimate of RM99,000 for her travel expenses could not go unchallenged:

[For] Frau Riefenstahl was reimbursed by Tobis most generously for all her travel expenses. The fact that, on top of this, she always took a set of colleagues with her . . . cannot be represented to us as a necessary expense.[21]

From March 1939, Riefenstahl was entitled to 'a share of 20 per cent of the net profit of the Olympia film'. After all this, it is hardly surprising that a contract of October 1941 between the ministry and Riefenstahl stipulated: 'the Olympia films are the property of the Reich. Riefenstahl GmbH, Berlin, which also holds the negatives in safe keeping, is authorized to undertake the commercial exploitation of the Olympia films and administer them for the Reich.'[22]

The Political Significance of an 'Unpolitical' Film

Today, nobody disputes the formal quality of *Olympia* or its political character. This blend, however, has led to some hostile comment. Some critics have resorted to dismissive epithets; others have employed irony to distance themselves, as it were, from the film. They repeatedly lament the purely 'formalistic' cinematic technique – but they cannot but concede that 'this allegedly documentary film anticipated structures in montage, collage and cutting-room technique which continue to influence the filmmaking of today – not only sports documentaries but also feature films and political reports'.[23] The more weight given to the film's political function, the harder it seems to be to accept its quality.

The formal mastery of most sequences in *Olympia* is partly due to how long many of the crew members had worked together. Almost all the core members of Riefenstahl's previous teams were reassembled. Moreover, the budget was greater than anything previously contemplated for a documentary film; even the original estimate of RM1.5 million would have been enough to finance an opulent feature film.[24] The result possibly even exceeded the expectations, and has yet to be overshadowed: 'By any comparison, *Olympia* remains one of the best, if not the best, sports film ever made.'[25]

Yet *Olympia* continues to create unease, perhaps precisely *because* it documented the Olympic Games in cinematically impressive style, even 'without exaggerated Nazi accents'[26] – whilst also representing Nazi propaganda. If the film were dedicated simply to the depiction of an event which was (in itself) vital to the interests of Nazi propaganda, audiences would long since have come to terms with it. In that case, Riefenstahl could be said to have used the film's cinematic potential to stylize the sporting competitions, but not explicitly on behalf of Nazi propaganda. The whole aim of the Propaganda Ministry, after all, was to avoid anything that might cast a cloud over the image of the 'new Germany'.[27]

When the film was shown, two years after the Games, it fitted the regime's bill; it reported the sporting competitions fairly, did not even favour the German athletes and entirely lived up to the festive atmosphere of 1936. Leni Riefenstahl was not necessarily aware of the campaign to con the rest of the world into believing in this peace-loving, non-xenophobic Germany, although it is hard to believe that she had not noticed certain aspects of it, such as the temporary cessation of anti-Semitic propaganda.[28] Press policy was partly adjusted for tactical reasons when the Olympic Games came to Berlin. Nevertheless, during the same period in which anti-Semitic articles were banned, there were regular, aggressive misrepresentations of the Spanish Civil War. Moreover, no sooner had the Games begun than Germany launched its intervention in Spain by dispatching the 'Condor Legion'.

The latent unease felt by those who see *Olympia* is not the result of watching a political film pretending to be an unpolitical one.[29] Nor is it a consequence of the ultimately insignificant differences between the original version shown at the premiere and the foreign versions.[30] Rather, the unease arises from the assumption that any film welcomed by the Nazis and helpful to their cause must exhibit some form of fascist aesthetic. In identifying certain stylistic and thematic peculiarities as expressions of fascist aesthetics, however, interpreters find themselves tripping over contradictions. Nobody could deny that many aspects of Riefenstahl's work are extremely problematic: her fondness for 'beauty', 'strength' and particularly the male physique; her documentaries' consistent failure to break free of the messages implied in the staging of the event they treated, be it a Party Rally or the Olympics Games; her readiness to underpin that staging with all the cinematic means at her disposal. None of this, however, necessarily produces fascist or Nazi aesthetics. Riefenstahl's films – and this is their prime characteristic

– are based above all on magnitude, significance and beauty; they conspicuously refrain from portraying any seemingly incidental occurrences. As a consequence, they admit of no ambivalences – and certainly no contradictions. They have no room for everyday life or for oddities. These films seek a quality which might be defined as 'typical' – or more specifically, 'typified'. Riefenstahl's concept of art is without irony and humour; her works avoid reflection. Her films therefore share an underlying lifelessness. Her cinematic language may be elegant, ingenious and open to experimentation, but it steadfastly avoids formal provocation. Yet the fascist aspects of Riefenstahl's films do not necessarily conform to the definition of fascist art as, above all, 'a utopian aesthetics – that of physical perfection'.[31]

Olympia is certainly an example of the cult of the human body and it does celebrate beauty and athleticism. But is it problematic because 'the physis, photogenicized to absolute smoothness,' suppresses the 'actual effort'?[32] Or, on the contrary, because it describes and glorifies symbolic sacrifices?[33] Like the Party Rally films, *Olympia* poses the question of what Riefenstahl's films *themselves* contribute to the ideologization of events which are already emphatically ideological in their own right. Only if the Nazi message manifestly influenced the presentation of individual scenes and sequences and the organization of the material is it legitimate to claim that the films made such a contribution. This does apply to *Olympia* in several respects: the prologue and the opening ceremony define the Olympic Games as a homage to Nazi Germany and Hitler himself; the way the German athletes are presented in the first part of the film is calculated to demonstrate the much-vaunted, inviolable bond between the Führer and the people; finally, the German radio reporters' commentaries elucidate the competitions in terms of a battle between the races and the nations. All three formal elements of the film exist alongside the 'unpolitical' and 'impartial' portrayals of the athletes, thus offering an alternative interpretation of the Games.

The commentaries are the most obvious aspect of the way the Nazi stereotype is rendered topical. The marathon commentator tells his audience: 'Finland's forces are determinedly battling to catch up with the leaders. Three runners, one country, one will!' In the 200-metres breaststroke swimming competition, 'the battle between Germany and Japan has broken out!'; in the crawl, 'the fastest swimmers of Europe and America battle against the Japanese frontline'; in the 800-metres race, 'two black runners' line up against 'the strongest representatives of the white race'. The examples are very plain, but relatively infrequent in this form. Linguistic elements, such as the repeated references to athletes by nation rather than name, are doubtless also intended to structure the audience's perception, but they do not achieve dominance over the images.

The images themselves, however, are complemented by more effective strategies for influencing the audience's attitude. The emphasis is on the contest between the nations (as it often is even in modern sports reporting). This constructs links between the athletes and their compatriots among the spectators, supported by the (retrospectively filmed) 'typical' shouts of encouragement in the relevant languages. Seldom is there any 'non-patriotic' applause. On the one hand this inclusion of the crowd provides a fresh note; on the other, it serves to divide the individual national groups.

The editing links the prominent figures of the Nazi Party – Hitler, less often Göring and Goebbels – almost exclusively with the German athletes, but not only with eventual winners. The women's 100-metres relay team, which missed out on almost certain gold by dropping the baton, provides an example of intensive editing; it includes four shots of Hitler without a crowning victory. The exciting duel between Luz Long and Jesse Owens in the men's long jump also lacks the climax of a German triumph.[34] Nevertheless, Hitler is more frequently associated with the successes of German athletes (the hammer, shot-putting and javelin). In this context he is shown in a less distanced, heightened manner than in the Party Rally films: he might even be described as a sports fan, whose enthusiasm, excitement and delight brings out the best in the German athletes. In this film too, however, clear hierarchies underlie the relationship. These are established at the start and are confirmed, for instance, in the Nazi salute from javelin winner Gerhard Stöck (among others) to the Führer's box.

This was an almost private facet to Hitler's image, duly acknowledged by the press,[35] and entirely in tune with the idea the 'peaceful games' were intended to project. Behind the façade,

Souvenir programme for *Sieg des Glaubens* (1933)

Ernst Röhm, SA chief of staff, on his way to welcome the Führer to Nuremberg (*Sieg des Glaubens*)

Hitler and Röhm, the two most powerful Nazi leaders, in a close-up shot (*Sieg des Glaubens*)

SA columns marching into Nuremberg which is decked with swastika flags for the occasion (*Sieg des Glaubens*)

Hitler and Röhm reviewing a march past in Nuremberg market square (*Sieg des Glaubens*)

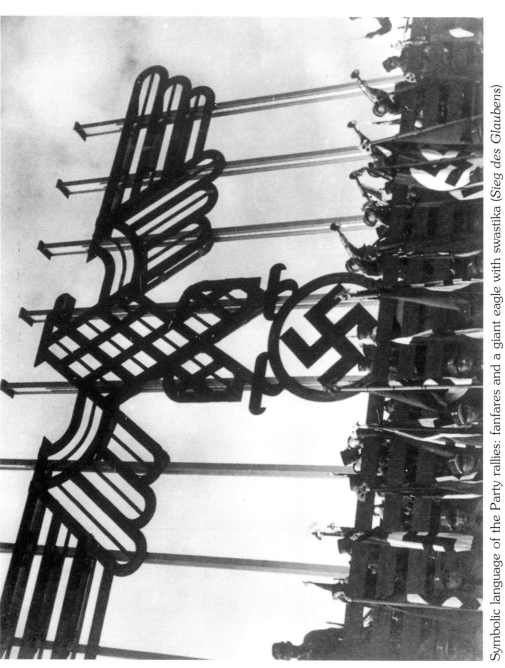

Symbolic language of the Party rallies: fanfares and a giant eagle with swastika (*Sieg des Glaubens*)

Trumpeter from Hitler's personal SS guard signalling the opening of the SA review (*Sieg des Glaubens*)

Stumbling in search of the perfect propaganda ritual: Hitler, stewards and followers in a less well-choreographed moment (*Sieg des Glaubens*)

Leni Riefenstahl apparently arguing with Party officials during the shooting of *Sieg des Glaubens*

Gala premiere for *Sieg des Glaubens* in the prestigious Berlin cinema Ufa-Palast am Zoo

Souvenir programme for *Triumph des Willens* (1935)

The almost endless sea of flags presented to Hitler (*Triumph des Willens*)

The central moment in *Triumph des Willens*: Hitler addressing SA and SS units, to consolidate Party unity after the murder of Röhm and others

Panorama shot taken from the elevator on one of the main flagstaffs (*Triumph des Willens*)

Flags on the march to be presented to the Führer (*Triumph des Willens*)

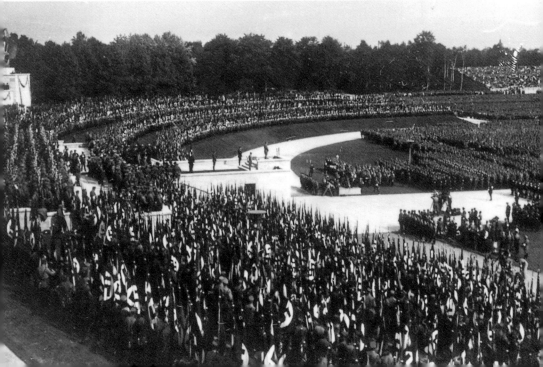

A city of flags: Nuremberg (*Triumph des Willens*)

Hitler Youth drummer announcing the Führer's arrival (*Triumph des Willens*)

The *Reichsarbeitsdienst* (Reich Labour Service) presenting spades as if they were guns (*Triumph des Willens*)

Magnifying effects: Riefenstahl and crew members in SA uniform during the shooting of *Triumph des Willens*

Searching for the most effective angle

With a little help from the Nuremberg fire brigade: to obtain extremely high-angle shots during the reviews, a cameraman is positioned on an extended ladder

The hard work involved in producing an idealized image: kneeling beside Hitler's car during the review

however, *Olympia* does include occasional – at least symbolic – intimations of the reality of Nazi Germany. The shot of the scoreboard with the results of the shot-putting, won by Germany's Hans Woellke, is not accompanied by the national anthem as usual, but rather by the *Horst Wessel Lied*.

The truly 'political' element in *Olympia* is realized by purely cinematic means at the beginning of the first part. The prologue ends with the animated sequence designed by Svend Noldan: the truncated torchbearers' relay. The camera floats over model landscapes: inserts identify the states, there are model capitals, and flags define the nations. 'As the relay reaches the German border, she [Riefenstahl] cuts the swastika symbol on to the *Deutschland* lettering, and then summarizes by means of just four pictorial symbols the significance of this trade mark of Nazi politics.'[36] Further dissolves are used to associate an unspecific (animated) landscape, a real shot of the Olympic Stadium taken from the *Hindenburg* airship, the Olympic bell and finally a close-up of Hitler in profile, before the next cut – to the crowd in the stadium, their arms extended in the Nazi salute.

In a manner altogether characteristic of her stylistic approach, Riefenstahl uses this montage to identify Hitler with the German people. It is an unambiguous, cinematic tribute, which sets up the close-up of Hitler as the culmination of the prologue and the starting point of the Games themselves. The film identifies the Olympic movement as the rebirth of classical antiquity in Arian Germany.[37]

Regarding *Olympia* as a remake of the Party Rally film, *Triumph des Willens*,[38] mainly on account of the way the nations are related ever more clearly to Hitler as they march in, is more justifiable with regard to the formal techniques than in terms of the significance of the two productions. The Party Rally films illustrated rituals of submission, whereas *Olympia* treats the 'leisure aspect' of the Games. In the prologue, Riefenstahl offers a symbolic prehistory for the modern Olympic Games from a Nazi perspective; her clearest political statement in *Olympia* is couched entirely in the language of a filmmaker.

Sports and Suspense

The finest scene in *Olympia*, the high-diving sequence, has a precursor. The comparison between the two is a way of high-lighting Riefenstahl's particular achievement and *Olympia*'s excep-tional status. The earlier film was *Jugend der Welt* (Youth of the World), dedicated to the winter Games in Garmisch-Partenkirchen, and it is most unlikely that Riefenstahl was not familiar with it. Carl Junghans had assembled *Jugend der Welt* from footage he had not been involved in shooting – a similarly difficult situation to the one faced by Riefenstahl when she made *Sieg des Glaubens*.[39]

Junghans ended his film with the ski-jumping filmed by Hans Ertl; half a year later, Ertl was also the cameraman who shot the high diving at the Olympic pool. Ertl's contribution to the closing sequences of the Junghans and Riefenstahl Olympic films was certainly immense. Both sequences seek to achieve the same effect, largely by the same means. In the Junghans montage, the ski-jumpers are filmed against the bright sky in slow motion, following one another in a seemingly endless flow of 'flying people'. The Riefenstahl montage aimed for the same effect: the high divers are also choreographed as 'flying people'; they too are filmed in slow motion against the sky, the last of them as stark silhouettes against the light. In one sense, the final scenes could be described as bravado: they emphasize their spectacular quality and flaunt the cinematic techniques employed. In both cases spatial continuity is irrelevant; the scenes aim to create graphic moments and attempt to create something independent and new – a kind of 'ballet' – from the succession of individual images.

Despite all that they have in common, Riefenstahl's approach comes across as more rounded, and it is presented more compellingly. The idea of cutting three reversed shots (of divers appearing to emerge from the water and land back on the board) into the sequence is just one of the ways in which Riefenstahl's version is more tightly formed. Here, if not before in this film, her training as a dancer made itself felt. Her montage has a choreographic quality, and the high-diving sequence is rightly regarded as the most convincing sequence in *Olympia* in formal terms.

Disquiet surrounding Riefenstahl's work led to post-war

attempts to play down the director's achievement by, for example, highlighting the contribution made by the main cameramen. There can be no doubt of the contribution Riefenstahl's colleagues made to the film's formal quality; the effect of the high-diving sequence is heightened considerably not just by Ertl's camerawork, but by Herbert Windt's music. But it was Riefenstahl who injected rhythm into the sequence. The end of the version directed by Junghans seems mechanical and the images seem to have been lined up next to one another; in Riefenstahl's version, they seem to emerge from within one another. Only in her film can one really speak of a 'ballet' of flyers.[40]

The Junghans film was also important for *Olympia* in another respect. *Jugend der Welt* is not a chronicle. Indeed, it goes so far in its determination to disassociate itself from the newsreels that it does not even mention the winners of the competitions by name – it offers only vague hints by means of flags.[41] Junghans clearly wanted to set his film apart from 'mere' reportage, to the extent that certain disciplines are only presented in staccato form within an extremely 'fast' montage. Walter Gronostay's music contributes to this by adding a dynamic element to the shots. The work's 'avant-gardism' was not to everybody's taste and doubtless prevented it from gaining a wider audience. In fact Junghans did not aim to give the film popular appeal: he saw it more as a chance to try out his editing principles. Hans Weidemann, vice-president of the *Reichsfilmkammer* (Reich Film Chamber), approved his director's desire to experiment.

In *Olympia*, Riefenstahl avoided the extremes which Junghans actively pursued in *Jugend der Welt* (and which he perhaps had to pursue on account of the poor quality of the footage available). As a rule, she identified the medal winners and refrained from representing whole competitions only in the form of montage fragments. Windt's music gives each sporting event a musical theme. The audiences which had found *Jugend der Welt* overly demanding received ample guidance in *Olympia*. The film made allowances for its audiences; concerns about how it would later be received influenced every aspect of its making. The inevitable need to truncate or omit some of the action does not disrupt the flow of the film or disorientate the audience: the consistent aim was an easy-to-follow narrative pattern.

Wherever possible, the individual competitions were edited with an eye to the element of suspense. This led to a paradoxical mushrooming of apparently 'last-gasp' decisive sporting moments. This did not coincide at all with what really happened in the competitions (such as in the men's long jump or the women's javelin). The film was intended to 'grip' its audiences from start to finish. As a result, even the hockey final acquires a drama on the screen which was quite lacking in the stadium, as Germany never had any chance of beating India and eventually succumbed 8-1. This result does not feature in the film.

The Junghans film perhaps showed Leni Riefenstahl some of the things she should not attempt if she wanted to create a successful sports film. In her Party Rally films, on the other hand, she had already demonstrated some of the forms which she re-employed in *Olympia*. Indeed, the latter film is surprisingly close to the original pattern in its basic form. *Olympia* followed the tried and tested method right up to the final scenes and harked back to the same elements: flags, anthems, camera movement. Instead of the swastika flag, the Olympic flag appears; the Olympic hymn replaces the *Horst Wessel Lied*, and the camera's final pan is not directed towards the Party regiments or formations of aeroplanes, but rather towards Speer's 'Cathedral of Light'. In *Olympia*, such gestures are not meant to enlist the people as they were in the earlier films. If there is such a thing as a repertoire of Nazi cinematic language, then Riefenstahl might be said to have used it and quoted from it in this film as a reservoir of symbols. She proved herself a stylist, varying 'heroic' forms and gestures in order to adapt them to the leisure version of the mass-participation events staged by the Nazis.

CHAPTER SEVEN

The Function of the Genius

As an artist and producer in Nazi Germany, Riefenstahl occupied a unique position. In her own way she used her talents to serve the regime, but without making anti-Semitic films or aggressive propaganda as Harlan and others did. She did, however, consent to help with 'little necessities', such as the collections for the *Winterhilfswerk* relief organization or the writing of an article to mark the 'election' in newly annexed Austria.[1] Nevertheless, she was never made a professor, as her fellow directors Harlan, Liebeneiner and Ritter were, nor did she covet a more influential role. The artistic committees, in which Goebbels had intended to give Riefenstahl a position at Tobis, did not survive for long, and she was thus able to avoid any long-term official commitment.[2] She was not a member of any Nazi organization and remained an outsider in the film industry, but she knew how to pursue her projects with charm and persistency. The new system made use of her abilities in its own way, but by the start of the war she could certainly claim to have successfully exploited it to further her career.

Travel Diplomacy

Riefenstahl was almost uniquely qualified to disseminate a positive picture of National Socialism on the international stage, precisely because neither her personality nor her work could be characterized simply as Nazi. The films were marked by a style of their own, whilst the filmmaker was characterized by her winning manner.

She did not come across as a dogged propagandist; wherever she appeared, she made a favourable impression. She had the knack of presenting her work in purely artistic and personal terms, even if it had been commissioned by the Party. She probably really did regard the Party as nothing more than an opportunity to develop her talent. In 1934 her reputation was still insufficient for her to be perceived purely as an 'official figure' on her trip to England, even if some German newspapers implied the contrary in their reports concerning the short lecture tour.

The *Völkischer Beobachter* was pleased to note that 'with her fresh, spontaneous lectures and the lengthy conversations in which she engaged, she did more for Germany's cause among the youth of Europe than many a full-scale attempt to gain understanding abroad',[3] whilst the *Film-Kurier* described her as the 'ambassador for German cinema'.[4] The English press, however, was less impressed: it considered her rather over-enthusiastic in her interviews, which she treated as opportunities to praise the beneficent effect of the state support for filmmaking in Germany and declare extremely positive views on Hitler, and found her personal fascination too ostentatious.[5]

Her European tour with *Olympia* was more successful. In fact it was a triumph without compare in the history of Nazi cinema, and the elaborate press campaign was equally unprecedented. The *Film-Kurier* followed the tour particularly closely, publishing eighty reports relating to *Olympia* between the premiere in Berlin and the visits to Pressburg and Brünn in March 1939, immediately after the splitting of Slovakia and the establishment of the 'Protectorate of Bohemia and Moravia'.[6] That represents an average of one report every four days. The industry journal kept a minute record of when and where the film was shown abroad, and of any monarchs, heads of government or diplomats in the audiences. The tour took Leni Riefenstahl to nineteen capital cities, where the courtesy visits from Germany's envoys and foreign NSDAP sections underlined the official significance of the events. The film itself canvassed for Nazi Germany through its sheer quality, and was helped by Riefenstahl's assurances that it was unpolitical in character.

The first setback occurred on her 'private' trip to the United States, by which she had hoped to round off *Olympia*'s success. Nobody declared interest in distributing the film in America, and the reason for this cool response became clear to her only too soon. The Anti-Nazi League in New York, whose most prominent members included Mayor F. H. La Guardia and Bishop Francis J. McConnell,[7] raised its voice in protest. It saw the director as a symbolic representative of National Socialism and the film as part of a campaign to disseminate the Nazi doctrine in the United States. Despite her 'unpolitical' outlook, Riefenstahl fully comprehended the political nature of the campaign; in her memoirs she lamented that she was unfairly pilloried and robbed of a well-deserved success.

Although writing the book fifty years after her visit, she continues to complain bitterly about the rejection she received in America and shows no sympathy at all for the reasons behind the boycott. These passages are among her most regrettable public comments. They are even more regrettable in the context of her reactions at the time to the 'Kristallnacht' pogroms of 9 November 1938.[8] She has described these events in very similar terms on many other occasions, from her interrogation by the US army after the war to her appearance in Ray Müller's documentary and an interview with *Der Spiegel* magazine in 1997.[9] Her story, however, is false. She had arrived in New York – with three copies of *Olympia* – on 4 November,[10] and certainly seems to have succeeded in making an impression. Some reports adopted a friendly tone, evidently influenced by the famous director's charm and wit.[11] She had time to establish contacts in New York and enjoy the nightlife.

There is no doubt that the reports of the pogroms in Germany – news which, as Riefenstahl said, she did not want to believe – had a lasting influence on the American public. The Nazi crimes and her refusal to acknowledge them were the real reason for the cool welcome Riefenstahl received in the United States. Shortly before her departure, however, when the failure of her mission was abundantly clear, she offered the following explanation:

Although America achieved great successes at the 1936 Olympiade (*sic*), the film with its triumphant athletes is not being shown here because the American film industry, including production and distribution, is controlled by people hostile to modern Germany. They have managed to ensure that Americans will not have the chance to see their own athletes putting the rest of the world in the shade, despite the fact that Olympic Games were a purely sporting event and although the film has been shown everywhere else across the world.[12]

In that comment Riefenstahl manages to avoid mentioning 'Jewish control', but contemporary readers were clearly invited to infer the idea, and were all the more likely to do so in the light of all the other propaganda. It is hardly surprising, then, that after Riefenstahl had returned and made her report, Goebbels should note in his diary: 'In the evening Leni Riefenstahl tells me about her American trip. She gives me an exhaustive account which paints a far from pleasing picture. We have no say there. The Jews reign through terror and boycotts.'[13]

Even in the memoirs, Riefenstahl describes America as though there had been an organized campaign to persecute and suppress alternative opinions. Her continuing refusal, long after 1945, even to consider the boycott against her film as a reasoned political response to a propaganda film is more than just a symptom of her egocentric attitude. Her insistence that her film is 'unpolitical' and that she was immediately questioned about the atrocities of 9 November 1938 when she arrived in New York, is rooted in her determination to cast a favourable light on her role and function within the system – even in the face of unequivocal facts.

Stylized Events and 'Heroic Reportages'

In the contemporary debate concerning cinematic theory, definitions of Riefenstahl's real significance for a 'National Socialist discourse' were related to the question of what a National Socialist film actually was. The new form of documentary film which she had created was considered to offer at least a partial answer. After all, it was not the content of the films, nor even their manifest or subliminal implications which made them ideal, show-piece products of the 'Third Reich' and perfect examples of 'theoretical debate'. Rather, it was their particular 'style'.

Apart from the rapturous reviews which all Riefenstahl's films received during the Nazi dictatorship, the earliest reference to a special style is probably in an article entitled 'The Riefenstahl School. The Absolute Film'. This was an attempt to describe the particular character of the three Party Rally films as typical of a *German cinematic style*.

> What elements does this style consist of? Its starting point is a creative act of photography which is quite without compare. The camera is enabled to capture its single object on film in unusual diversity. This productive kind of camerawork is based on the first examples created by Arnold Fanck – i.e. the Freiburg School – but it is Leni Riefenstahl, helped by Sepp Allgeier, who has developed it most intensively over the last three years. Her reward for such exemplary stylistic forms was the breakthrough – and the victory – she achieved with the first Reich Party Rally film, *Sieg des Glaubens*.[14]

The attempts to define 'genuinely German cinema' may not appear particularly satisfactory, but the aim is clear enough. 'The great merit of this Riefenstahl School is that it has restored a sovereign, independent significance to the absolute film, which is now almost on equal terms with the feature film.'[15] The reference to the 'absolute film' is decisive. No specific definition is offered, but the fact that such films are extolled as the real achievements of the 'new aesthetics' says a great deal about their function within the debate on cinematic aesthetics under National Socialism. They were regarded as an alternative model for the future, in which respect they acquired an almost legitimizing value. By putting forward the credo of the 'creative survey' as 'something quite distinct from the Russian montage technique of the silent film era',[16] the writer is in effect nominating Riefenstahl's films as a response to the demand Goebbels had made in his first, programmatic speech to representatives of the film industry.[17] In other words, the author of that article in *Film-Kurier* saw Leni Riefenstahl as the German answer to Sergei Eisenstein.

The enormous significance of her work for members of the Nazi intelligentsia in defining their basic aesthetic attitudes is evident in the way it was evaluated in the journal *Der deutsche Film*, which was founded in 1936 and published by the *Reichsfilmkammer* until 1943 (its demise was probably due to wartime economy measures). It was the forum for the Nazis' theoretical debate concerning cinema. It demanded an adequate representation of the (professional) everyday life of workers in the 'new era', but also found space to venerate 'German avant-gardists' such as Basse and Ruttmann, and to discuss the 'absolute film'. Its unequivocal Nazi bias meant that it was anti-Semitic, generally xenophobic, and pro-war.[18] In its politics, the journal united robust ideological attitudes with an emphasis on formal qualities; its objective was an aesthetically 'innovative' form of Nazi cinema.

The many references in *Der deutsche Film* to all Riefenstahl's films from *Das blaue Licht* onwards are unambiguous. For the purposes of the arguments advanced in its pages, her work was *the* paradigm for 'National Socialist cinema', and it was also credited with achieving the formal qualities of the Russian revolutionary film. As early as August 1936, in its second issue, the journal featured a preview of *Olympia* (one and a half years before its anticipated release) and a portrait of Riefenstahl, whose 'large-scale reportages' it considered 'a completely *new, monumental form of filmmaking*'. The director had 'communicated the political experience in the form of an artistic experience by transforming the rhythm of the real event into a cinematic rhythm. In doing so she has created a *new artistic genre*.'[19]

The films were thus held up as an example, and continued to be from then on. An (unattributed) essay on the subject of 'Is There a German Camera Style?' finally came up with the authoritative description of the new type of film, a type represented by 'the most German films of recent years, the Reich Party Rally films and the Olympia film. These films have created a completely new cinematic genre: the heroic reportage, a fitting response to the events of our era.'[20]

The phrase 'heroic reportage' was an apt one, as it neatly expressed a certain peculiarity of Riefenstahl's films. They really were 'reportages', in that they did report a major political event. In many ways they were a precursor to modern television reports about similar large-scale events, albeit with the not insignificant difference of the very long delay between the event and the appearance of the reportage.

They were also 'heroic' in the sense formulated in another article in *Der deutsche Film*, concerning *Olympia*. It argued that the film could only succeed in Germany, the 'place where documentary cinema has been nurtured, its stronghold', because it was Germany that had created 'such a broadly conceived, symbolic framework' for the games. This framework 'prepared the way for the re-creating camera by itself elevating the action beyond the sphere of mere sports reporting'. Moreover:

> . . . Here there is already a cinematic tradition of not merely rehashing reality but also manifesting the idea that animates and illuminates that reality. That is not just a cinematic accomplishment. It is the fruit of National Socialism . . . Only where the National Socialist world-view prevails could the great documentary film emerge as an artistic achievement.[21]

Riefenstahl's films were also convenient examples because *Der deutsche Film* was emphatically opposed to 'literary cinema', considering 'the desire to evaluate the film in literary terms' to be misguided.[22] Other contributors insisted on 'cinematic rules' in contradistinction to the 'kind of theatre customary in our feature films',[23] warned of the danger of 'overvaluing purely thematic material'[24] and decreed that 'there can be no doubt that cinema was not invented in order to hark back to the drama and novellas of nineteenth-century literature'.[25]

Such points of view might fairly be described as advanced within the context of the Nazi debate about what was 'cinematic'. They found constant expression in the pages of *Der deutsche Film*, but also appeared elsewhere.[26] Riefenstahl's description of her own work displays a close affinity with this perspective. Without using the phrase 'heroic reportage' itself, she characterizes her filmmaking in analogous terms, particularly in the way she distances her work from the weekly newsreels:

> We were determined to depict moments which would contribute to a cinematic production going beyond the pattern of purely reportage-style newsreel to become a rounded film in its own right, a film which would be captivating not just because of its purely pictorial representations of the magnificent events in Nuremberg, but above all by virtue of its artistic form and the exciting build-up of the action.[27]

She measured documentary films by their effect on the audience, an effect which she associated with the staged, massed rallies, and was fully aware that the message was the top priority: 'The bond between the Führer and the people was of supreme importance; it was consistently the central experience. Showing this, expressing it, is one of the tasks I have set myself.'[28]

Even after completing *Olympia*, she defined her understanding of documentation in terms of the effect the films were intended to produce in those who saw them.[29] Her method of working – effectively encircling each event with her cameras in order not to miss any possible highlights – was, in her view, a creative or artistic endeavour. Its significance lay in the presentation of an ideological message so that 'the spirit of the action, be it the doctrinal content of a Party Rally film or the struggle-and-victory motif of an Olympia film, is brought out through the rhythm and expression of every scene'.[30]

It was thus no accident that *Der deutsche Film*'s perhaps most radical definition of a Nazi film should relate to *Olympia*. It specified the conditions for the 'new' form:

> In an area of culture . . . that has evolved out of a totalitarian constitutional principle, all cultural factors – including those we generally describe as works of art – must ultimately have a specific purpose . . . To sum it up as a formula, one might say: a modern work of art is worthy of the name if it elicits aesthetic effects without itself being of aesthetic origin. It thereby fulfils its purpose . . . Since the seizure of power, we Germans have developed a cinematic style uniquely suited to serving that purpose . . . The two parts of the Olympia film, *Fest der Völker* and *Fest der Schönheit* are a cinematic and artistic feat which it was Germany's honour to achieve.[31]

A small group of energetic theoreticians thus held up the films Riefenstahl made under National Socialism as models for film production in the nation as a whole. They assessed the significance of Riefenstahl's films in relation to the international avant garde and offered fulsome descriptions of their essential uniqueness. In that sense, the director – who so frequently complained of being misunderstood and wrongly pigeonholed after 1945 – was understood more completely and more precisely during National Socialism than she was for a long period after the war. It was not, however, the kind of understanding that would have suited Leni Riefenstahl after 1945.

Studio Facilities for Leni Riefenstahl

By the time *Olympia* was released, Leni Riefenstahl enjoyed the admiration of the film press, of the German state's 'young guard', and of Hitler himself. The esteem in which she was held is evident from a project to provide her with her own filmmaking complex, including a studio and a processing laboratory. It is still unclear whose idea it was; Albert Speer initially played a central part in his capacity as 'Inspector General of Building for the Capital of the Reich' (GBI); later Hitler, Bormann, Göring and various bureaucratic authorities also became involved.

On 8 March 1939, the first discussion with Albert Speer took place. Speer was joined by his close collaborator Willi Schelkes, whilst Walter Traut was present on behalf of Riefenstahl Film. 'According to Traut, Frau Riefenstahl requires a site of about 5,000 sq. m. and would like a street frontage of at least 69 m.'[32] At this point Schelke estimated the construction budget at RM400,000 which, in the context of Speer's overall plans, did not seem to represent a problem. The facility was a minor project in terms of both its size and cost.

Initially the plans involved a site at the southern end of Kronprinzenallee (the northern part of today's Clay-Allee) in the prestigious Berlin district of Dahlem, not far from Riefenstahl's villa on Heydenstrasse. The search for an architect did not take long, and on 24 March 1939, Traut explicitly mentioned the 'Leni Riefenstahl building project' when he wrote to Chief Building Inspector Stephan,[33] noting that 'following the discussion between Fräulein Riefenstahl and Herr *Generalbauinspektor* Speer', an attempt had been made 'to reserve a site of about 140 : 150 m in the plots to the west of Kronprinzenallee'. There was, however, a difficulty:

> It turned out that except for a few plots – which are much too small – the whole of the area made available to date has been reserved as far as the pond to the south of Pücklerstrasse. Please would you therefore be good enough to contact the relevant city and state authorities in order to reserve a construction site 140 m wide and 150 m deep to the south of the area so far made available, adjoining the forest. Since Herr

Dr Petersen has already been commissioned, with Herr *Generalbauinspektor* Speer's agreement, to design the plans for the building – which is to be in the style of a country house (no more than two storeys high) – I would be very grateful if you would treat this as a matter of urgency.[34]

Riefenstahl was familiar with the architect earmarked for the job, Dr Ernst Petersen. He was evidently the same man who appeared alongside her as an actor in *Der heilige Berg*, *Die weisse Hölle vom Piz Palü* and *Stürme über dem Montblanc* and who was later involved in the set construction for *S.O.S. Eisberg*. Petersen had already built Riefenstahl's villa in Dahlem.[35] His plans for the new project were larger in scale, requiring 21,000 square metres. The necessary land was to be obtained as a matter of priority, independently of the existing town planning provisions, in an as yet undisclosed area.

Speer, Riefenstahl and Schelkes debated the new location on 26 May 1939. Riefenstahl suggested 'a site of 150–200 m in the Argentinische Allee' – again in Dahlem and not very far from her home.[36] Five days later they were joined by the architect to view the site; Speer had the sketch map of the area added to the 'Führer folder' in order to discuss it with Hitler at Obersalzberg.[37] From there he reported

... that the Führer has approved Leni Riefenstahl's site. Either the Party or Bormann will act as the official client. Since the building is urgently needed for a new film, the Prussian Construction and Financial Directorate must be instructed to make the site available immediately. The transfer of ownership could take place later. Herr Speer will approach the General Field Marshal with regard to transferring the site without charge.[38]

The project was treated as an endowment for a director who had rendered outstanding services to Nazi Germany, and decisions regarding it were taken at top level. Negotiations for the transfer of the site began without further ado; Schelkes wrote to the president of the Prussian Construction and Financial Directorate:

Since construction of this film facility is an urgent matter and must not be delayed by the transfer procedure, I request that you grant your approval for development before that procedure is completed. The final demarcation of the site must wait until the plans have been finished.[39]

The particular interest the state took in the project is also reflected in Speer's letter to Göring's permanent secretary, Wilhelm Körner:

> At the request of the Führer, a film facility is to be built near the Argentinische Allee. The Party, represented by Reichs-leiter Bormann, is to act as the client during construction and owner of the building. The facility is designed to provide Frau Riefenstahl with the working spaces she has so far lacked. The site in question, which is outlined in red in the attached planning excerpt, belongs to the Prussian state. Because the site will soon be ready, negotiations have already taken place with the Prussian Construction and Financial Directorate, which is prepared to make the site available immediately. Since this is a Party construction project, the Field Marshal has agreed with me to make the transfer without charge. I hereby inform you of this and request that you brief the Construction and Financial Directorate responsible for administration of the site accordingly, so that transfer of the site can be achieved as swiftly as possible.[40]

In the same letter, Speer also mentions the land on which the 'state studios' for the sculptors Arno Breker and Wilhelm Kreis were to be built. For this he was at least ready to pay half the market value.[41] It appears, however, that the state was expected to take over the whole cost of the filmmaking complex. Traut explained in a consultation of 20 July 'that the necessary resources – as the previous discussion made clear – would not be available.'[42] That must be taken as meaning that Riefenstahl Film could and would not make any contribution of its own towards such a project.

The first plans for the buildings were ready at the start of August 1939, and now involved 22,500 square metres and an estimated cost of RM1,844,700.[43] The construction schedule painted a detailed picture of the project; it stipulated, for example, that Riefenstahl's workroom should have a sliding window four metres wide and 2.8 metres high – unmistakably modelled on the one in Hitler's house on Obersalzberg.[44] There were provisions for all the facilities needed to enable Riefenstahl's company to make its films without outside assistance, right up to the post-production stage: cutting rooms, two projection rooms, a dubbing room, several dark rooms, various workrooms, a canteen, kitchen, an air-conditioned basement for the film archive and a common room which could also be used as gymnasium. A film studio (measuring 15 × 30 m at this stage, but ultimately 15 × 70 m) and the processing laboratory were to be housed in separate buildings.

Bormann approved the plan on 12 August 1939,[45] thereby guaranteeing that the Party would indeed finance the project. Formal planning permission was issued with immediate effect at the end of August 1939,[46] but the outbreak of war just three days later caused the start of construction to be postponed indefinitely. Nevertheless, planning work continued regardless and the scale of the project continued to swell. The final site plan of 19 July 1940 allows for a total area of 28,062.2 square metres – 'of which ca. 1,680.00 sq. m. ceded for road expansion. Suggested expansion ca. 11,000 sq. m.' Speer's department continued to work on Riefenstahl's film studio until August 1942, allowing gardeners to use the site only temporarily and on the condition that the tenants be required to vacate it immediately and without compensation when it was required. 'The applicant must obtain the agreement of the Leni Riefenstahl-Film company. The construction project on behalf of that film company has not been abandoned.'[47]

The plans for Riefenstahl's filmmaking complex – her own, made-to-measure state studio – beg the question of how useful the facilities would in fact have been. The technology and space would have been sufficient for the production of small-scale and perhaps medium-scale films. The film studio would have been too small for filming *Penthesilea* or similar, large-scale projects, but after the film had been shot, various other facilities – such as those for editing, dubbing, recording the music, making foreign-language versions and rushes – would have been perfectly adequate. Riefenstahl's experiences of making documentary films clearly influenced the way the complex was to be equipped: she could have used her own facility at Dahlem to undertake all the work she had been forced to commission from the Geyer processing laboratory (or to carry out there in rooms reserved for her use) when she made the Party Rally films and *Olympia*.

It would appear, therefore, that the planned complex was to serve two purposes. First, it would make it possible to use the huge reservoir of 'leftover material' from her earlier films: Riefenstahl would be able to create new films from the two archives relating to the Party Rally and Olympia films, both of which she already managed. Of the twenty short films using the *Olympia* footage which were planned, eight were actually completed by the end of the war – even though Riefenstahl did not have the resources of a private studio complex at her disposal. Second, commissioned films such as those Riefenstahl's company produced for Speer and the 'Organisation Todt' would have helped ensure that the studio's capacity was fully exploited. The *Reichskanzlei* (Reich Chancellery) film (never completed) and Fanck's films about Breker and Thorak were exactly the kinds of film for which the Dahlem complex would have been ideal. The substantial investment which the Party was prepared to make could only have been justified if the facility produced a steady flow of films. The NSDAP would therefore have had a strong interest in guaranteeing that the studio was used to the full – a decidedly favourable circumstance for a medium-sized enterprise during the dictatorship. This would also have made it possible for Riefenstahl to employ valued, trusted colleagues on a long-term basis, and it would have meant that she really was in a position to go it alone with large-scale projects such as *Penthesilea*. The German invasion of Poland put an end to such dreams.

Part Three

DEPRIVED OF POWER

CHAPTER EIGHT

A Partial Retreat: Tiefland

Shortly before the outbreak of World War II, Leni Riefenstahl was probably the most famous woman film director in the world, even though she had not made any feature films since *Das blaue Licht*. Her best-known works were documentaries: a type of film which seldom turned directors into household names. *Olympia*, in particular, had won her the reputation of being an outstanding artist in her field; she was respected as a film *auteur* in a cinematic era otherwise dominated by stars. Leni Riefenstahl had succeeded in transforming herself from an actress into a celebrated director, but in a genre which did not generally have such a high profile as popular, narrative films. Now it was time for her to take the next step by confirming her talent in a feature film to rival her 'heroic reportages'. She clearly regarded her pet project, *Penthesilea*, as the work which would establish her as a director of feature films. It was to be something entirely distinct from the large, state-staged events which she had filmed with such virtuosity. For this project[1] she had set her sights on a new kind of formal language. On the one hand it was to be based on her experience as a filmmaker, partly in elaboration of the style she had developed in the documentary films. On the other hand, she also intended that it should draw on the romantic motifs and the 'expressionist' images in *Das blaue Licht* (inspired by German silent films) and apply them within the narrative genre. *Penthesilea* would, she hoped, represent the pinnacle of her career: 'I regarded all the artistic challenges . . . I faced as steps towards *Penthesilea*.'[2]

A few of the descriptions from the notes she made in 1939, which were not published until much later, imply certain stylistic similarities to the 'heroic reportage':

> Penthesilea must have a distinct kind of bodyguard. Perhaps
> [the bodyguard], unlike all the other Amazons, might wear
> armour. I envisage the Amazon platoons bearing symbolized
> coats of arms – idols – to be carried at the head of the army
> when it attacks.[3]

This recalls the role of the standards in the Party Rally rites. Other
elements were also evidently born of her documentary experiences;
she wanted to render the battle scenes 'in quite different moods'[4] –
just as she injected formal variation into the fundamentally similar
sequences of events at the Party Rallies and the Olympic Games.
Her patent determination on the one hand to stylize both
Penthesilea and Achilles into almost divine beings, and on the
other to show their 'compulsive, wild temperament' and 'cruel and
terrible side'[5] might be interpreted as a response to the element of
monotony in her previous films. The monumental buildings were
to be archaic and as diverse as possible rather than classical.[6]
Insofar as it is possible to judge from the little information
available, it would appear that *Penthesilea* would have been
Riefenstahl's most ambitious film and her most daring experiment
in form. It might even have been the film in which the director –
clearly driven by the desire for greater stylistic consistency –
overcame her aversion to ambivalence.[7]

The outbreak of war made it impossible to go ahead with the
project. It was on such a large scale that it now seemed improbable
that it could be financed, and the planned shoot 'in the Libyan
desert'[8] was out of the question. Moreover, the plot itself was
clearly inappropriate in this new climate: Amazons were emphatically not the kind of female role models now required.

During the early days of the war, Riefenstahl tried to create a
war-reporting team with a few of her cameramen. Apart from
wishing to make herself useful in some way, Riefenstahl was
perhaps also attempting to keep part of her team together and save
the men from alternative forms of service. The details of her
application to become a war reporter are not known, but she did
set off for the front with some of her colleagues immediately after
Germany's invasion of Poland. This is how Erich von Manstein,
then the Chief-of-Staff in the Southern Army Group, later

described her arrival: 'One day a well-known actress and director appeared among us, "following the Führer's trail", as she put it. She was accompanied by a troop of cameramen and claimed that she was to film at the front on Hitler's orders.'[9]

It is undeniable that, after her arrival, Riefenstahl witnessed acts of violence carried out by German soldiers against Polish civilians. The question of whether or not she also saw the ensuing massacre became a matter of dispute between her and the press after the war.[10] In her memoirs, Riefenstahl denies having been a witness to the executions. She suggests that the events in Konskie began with the laying out of dead German soldiers, who she claims had been murdered and mutilated by Polish civilians. This does not tally with the facts, as there was no sign that the soldiers had been maimed and they fell whilst fighting regular Polish troops.[11] Whatever the truth of her experiences, however, they shocked her enough for her to give up uniformed service. A few of her cameramen, such as Walter Frentz, Hans Ertl and Guzzi Lantschner, did later work as war reporters.

A Substitute for the Pet Project

On returning to Berlin, Riefenstahl needed to develop a new project as quickly as possible. She fell back on material she had tried to film as long ago as 1934, when adverse circumstances had intervened and apparently put an end to the idea for good: *Tiefland*.[12] Her decision to revive material with which she had previously worked was a pragmatic one, a stop-gap solution. Had *Tiefland* been made in 1934, between *Sieg des Glaubens* and *Triumph des Willens*, it would have appeared a logical progression in the direction defined by *Das blaue Licht*. When Riefenstahl turned back to the material in 1940, however, she was simply taking refuge amid familiar terrain. It was not the kind of material capable of carrying the ambitions bound up with *Penthesilea*, but in many ways it represented a continuation of her first work as a director. A report written immediately after shooting began noted: 'It is a good idea to imagine Leni Riefenstahl's *Das blaue Licht*. *Tiefland* will build on the style of that film, enriching it with the experience the artist has accumulated while making her great documentaries.'[13]

The film did not finally receive its premiere until 1954, but it was indeed strikingly similar in style to *Das blaue Licht*. Once again, it was the picturesque quality of the cinematic images – not infrequently achieved by using filters,[14] and sometimes by means of artificial fog, gales and thunderstorms – that set the tone. The style of *Tiefland* employs and develops the same atmosphere of unreality which was a feature of *Das blaue Licht*, although this time the impression it makes is discordant. Riefenstahl's directorial debut reflected her conviction that 'realistic' photography was inappropriate in presenting 'fairy-tale' material. At that time she had wanted the visual style of the film to be in tune with the character of the plot. In *Tiefland*, photographic technique was taken a step further. The cameramen came up with shots which possessed an undeniable and inherent visual appeal – a quality almost without compare in German cinema of the time. Even the stills betray how painstakingly each shot was composed. Yet *Tiefland* has nothing of the charm of *Das blaue Licht*. The stylistic agenda appears to overwhelm the material itself, and the impressions made by the images threaten to become dysfunctional. The 'legend' underlying *Das blaue Licht* perhaps justifies or even demands the use of filters and special film stock to 'transform' the reality of the mountain landscape. In *Tiefland*, the pronounced artificiality and the visible effort to compose aesthetically pleasing shots sometimes seem unduly contrived.

Although *Tiefland*'s plot is quite different from that of *Das blaue Licht*,[15] there are dramaturgical similarities between Riefenstahl's two feature films. She herself played the female lead again, and once again her character is an outsider – this time a 'gypsy girl'. This character, even more clearly than the one she played in *Das blaue Licht*, is the object of a battle between two male admirers. Unlike Junta, however, Martha is dependent on the men around her from the start – first on her disreputable travelling companion, then on Don Sebastian. The marquis dresses her up as a lady when he takes her as his lover, but does not allow her to act with any independence. Pedro, whom she finally follows back to the mountains, is the first man who does not suppress her and treat her violently. Yet even in this relationship, she is not her own mistress: it is she who has to give up her former life in order to follow him. Little remains in *Tiefland* of the independent power of the female character in *Das blaue Licht*. Martha is an entirely 'man-made' being: she is never allowed to define herself.

The confrontation between the world of the mountains and the village is also reminiscent of *Das blaue Licht*, except that this time Pedro is set up as an opposite pole to the village community. In Riefenstahl's first feature film, Junta is unquestionably the central figure; the whole story revolves around the issue of her freedom. The later film, by contrast, is built around the conflicts caused by the marquis, conflicts which rage between him and the village community as well as him and Pedro. Martha is merely the prize for the winner in this game. Ultimately, *Tiefland* differs from *Das blaue Licht* in one very significant respect: the plot involves 'a political and social conflict, of the kind which sometimes features in westerns: the farmers are deprived of their water by a cattle magnate'.[16] It is because it is based on this kind of story, quite unlike a legend or fairy-tale, that the film seems so over-stylized.

Das blaue Licht had been a low-budget production, but ample resources were available to Riefenstahl when she came to make her second feature film. Although there were many complications and other factors which caused the shooting to drag on for years, financial problems were not a major obstacle.[17] Shooting took place in Spain, Italy and at Mittenwald, where a whole village was constructed as a film set. A considerable part of the film was made in the studio, for which other large sets were built. This made it possible to exert greater control over the takes and contributed to the thoroughly anti-naturalistic character of the film. Riefenstahl's fondness for memorable faces offered the farmers of the Sarntal another chance to take to the screen, having previously featured in *Das blaue Licht*. In order to add 'southern colour' to the film, the director even used 'gypsy' internees from a camp near Salzburg, and later from the Marzahn camp near Berlin, as extras.[18]

All kinds of hopes and expectations had been bound up with *Penthesilea*, and *Tiefland* was never the kind of film capable of satisfying them. Later, Riefenstahl would say that by 1940 she was 'no longer properly in touch' with the project; she claimed that the photography was the only aspect of it which really interested her; 'I am almost tempted to say that it was my way of fleeing the war'.[19] Nevertheless, she worked as tirelessly as ever on behalf of the film.[20] There were several interruptions, for example when Leni

Riefenstahl was taken ill, when male lead Bernhard Minetti failed to extricate himself from his theatre commitments, when there were delays in obtaining the currency authorization for shooting abroad and when the director's dissatisfaction with a set already in place meant that it had to be reconstructed.

Riefenstahl herself was also beset by personal problems. While shooting the film, she had fallen in love with a first lieutenant in the *Gebirgsjäger* (mountain troops) named Peter Jacob, whom she married in March 1944. Uncertainty about his fate on the eastern front became part of her everyday life. Moreover, her father's death in 1944 was followed almost immediately by that of her beloved brother Heinz. It was not a happy time for her.

Even by the standards of a complex director whose productions were never straightforward, *Tiefland* turned out to be particularly problem-prone. Yet Riefenstahl's persistence and her influential connections always enabled her to find a way forward for the film – although the spiralling costs meant that it no longer made any kind of economic sense. The vital funds for filming in Spain and Italy could be approved only by the Reich's minister for economic affairs – but Walther Funk refused to make the foreign currencies available, on grounds of the wartime economy. On both occasions, Riefenstahl's company, Riefenstahl Film GmbH, successfully appealed to *Reichsleiter* Martin Bormann to intervene, and the production company finally received the monies (350,000 Lire and 240,000 Pesetas: both came on top of the considerable sums which had been paid out already). It therefore cannot be said that *Tiefland* encountered consistent official obstruction. The Ufa management was undoubtedly right when it hinted in 1941 that in fact it was 'a film project which apparently enjoys special support at the highest level'.[21]

The way Bormann justified his interference in affairs for which the economics minister was nominally responsible is instructive. He wrote:

> . . . Riefenstahl Film GmbH was founded with the special support of the Führer, and the Führer has instructed that the costs of the *Tiefland* film, which has been in production for over two years, be borne from the funds managed by me . . . I have shown the documents to the Führer, who has decided

that the currency payments requested by Riefenstahl Film GmbH should be made available if at all possible.[22]

The second time he intervened, Bormann at least offered some consolation to Hans Heinrich Lammers, the Chief of the Reich Chancellery: 'as the Führer stressed today, we can expect the film to earn considerable amounts of foreign currency once it has been completed'.[23] The 'Secretary to the Führer' administered considerable funds; it remains uncertain whether, as he alleged, *Tiefland* was really funded by the NSDAP's *Reichsleitung* (Reich Directorate).[24] Neither is it clear whether Bormann actually did obtain Hitler's personal approval as he claimed in his letters.[25] It is certain that Riefenstahl knew of Bormann's influence by this time, if not before, and that she used his reputation in the middle of 1944 in her dispute with Terra Film about who had the right to use cameraman Albert Benitz. Benitz was under contract to Terra, but Riefenstahl requisitioned him for the last few days of shooting at the Barrandov studios in Prague. She wrote to Max Winkler, who was responsible for the film industry at Reich level:[26] 'Before I inform Herr *Reichsleiter* Bormann of this new threat, I would respectfully like to ask you, Herr Dr Winkler to use your personal influence in order to avoid any such catastrophe.'[27] This unsubtle hint had the desired result, and no recourse to Bormann was necessary: Winkler informed the Reich's superintendent for film (and SS *Obersturmbannführer* (Lt Colonel)) Hans Hinkel, who ordered that Benitz be freed to work for Riefenstahl during the final stage of shooting. This decision to transfer the highly valued cameraman to Riefenstahl Film GmbH highlights just how great the support for Riefenstahl was: it meant that Terra had to abandon a colour film.[28] This was a significant loss, particularly in view of how hard the film industry was finding it to maintain production on the prescribed scale in the face of the limitations imposed by the war. The industry was now completely state-owned, and its struggle to follow increasingly unrealistic guidelines had given rise to a dog-fight for the scanty resources available. Squabbles over specialists not yet under contract, the sparse studio facilities, décor, costumes and licences for filming on particular days became the rule. Riefenstahl would have stood little chance in competition with the Reich's own companies if she had not had recourse to (in effect) a personal lobby.

After the outbreak of war she certainly lost the privileged access to Hitler she had previously enjoyed, and which she occasionally alludes to in her memoirs. Hitler was now concerned almost exclusively with the progress of the war. Like many other petitioners used to achieving their aims by approaching the Führer directly, she now had to rely on Martin Bormann, the increasingly powerful secretary to the Führer. He used his position to control all Hitler's contacts, and frequently made decisions without consulting the Führer at all.

Nevertheless, the exceptional status Riefenstahl had acquired on the strength of her documentaries was still sufficient to guarantee official support for *Tiefland*. She always aimed to give the film every conceivable advantage, but did not succeed in every case: occasionally her persistence came up against immovable obstacles. In such cases, however, it was the war and the associated production problems which were to blame.

Riefenstahl's special position was respected by the Nazi hierarchy right to the end, as was clear from the treatment she received when attempts were made to reduce the number of 'indispensable jobs' in the film industry. The investigations into the 'entourages', in an effort to root out employees whose 'indispensability' could no longer be proved, descended on the studios in batches. In August 1944 another such 'fine-tooth-comb operation' was imminent, and the Reich's deputy superintendent for film, Walter Müller-Goerne, sent an inquiry to Hinkel about whether 'Riefenstahl-Film should also be combed'. Hinkel, who was not noted for his friendly manner, responded by jotting: 'yes (but nicely)'.[29] Riefenstahl naturally tried to keep as many members of her team as possible in their 'indispensable jobs'. Her company employed delaying tactics, and Riefenstahl even sent for her old friend Schneeberger in order to save him from service in the *Volkssturm* home defence force. As late as February 1945, she interceded on behalf of Lisa and Arnold Fanck, who lived in Berlin, under the pretext of needing their help to finish *Tiefland*. On that occasion, however, Hinkel rejected her application.[30]

As *Tiefland* neared completion, every step turned into a battle for resources: obtaining studio facilities in Prague, requisitioning cutters, splicers and sound specialists, organizing the dubbing, and preparing recordings with the musicians of the Vienna

Symphony Orchestra. Riefenstahl's refusal to compromise was as astonishing as the consistent effort by Winkler and Müller-Goerne to satisfy her demands. Every form of support available in the difficult circumstances towards the end of the war was extended to the production. In autumn 1944, shooting was completed in Prague. There also appeared to be a secure basis for the post-production work: various editing specialists were used, and telegraphs were sent as late as April 1945, requesting that Bernhard Minetti and Maria Koppenhöfer travel to Kitzbühel for synchro-nization recordings. Work on *Tiefland* continued almost until the last day of the war.[31]

After the war the French forces of occupation confiscated the film material, and it took years for Riefenstahl to get it back.[32] Most of the post-production work had to be undertaken again from scratch. Riefenstahl complained that some takes had been lost, and edited the material a second time. Herbert Windt wrote new music for the film, and the dialogues were re-dubbed. The film was given its premiere on 11 February 1954 in Stuttgart; it received a distinctly cool reception.[33]

A New Look at Familiar Territory

The international debate concerning Riefenstahl's work did not start properly until 1960, and *Tiefland* received little attention. It was only after 1990 that this began to change, when the film was reinterpreted – surprisingly and controversially – as a subversive, anti-Nazi work. Even Leni Riefenstahl was taken somewhat aback; she had never previously made any attempt to suggest that *Tiefland* was deliberately critical of the Nazi regime. In general, the 'new view' of the film contributed to the reassessment of Riefenstahl as a person which had begun in the 1970s and came to dominate the general conception of her in the 1990s.

The idea that *Tiefland* should be regarded as an anti-Nazi film was formulated first by Helma Sanders-Brahms and subsequently by Robert von Dassanowsky.[34] It involves interpreting the film as a 'film about tyrannicide' and Don Sebastian as an incarnation of Hitler. Martha (played by Riefenstahl) is seen as reflecting the director's own story: her pact with the regime. *Tiefland* thus represents 'Leni coming to terms with the Nazis, and with Hitler: with the criminal whom she served and whose death she desired above all else'.[35] Such an interpretation turns the film into a veiled reckoning with Hitler and also with Riefenstahl's own career as an artist. It implies that, 'at least from 1940' Riefenstahl had felt herself to be in a 'prison made of dependence and abhorrence, of being involved in power whilst having none'. The film was 'a clearly legible, barely coded call for an end to be put to the usurper's reign.'[36]

In fact it is conceivable that one event in particular – the one she witnessed in September 1939 in Konskie, Poland – might have moved Leni Riefenstahl to distance herself from the regime. Yet neither Sanders-Brahms nor Dassanowsky has attempted to trace the attitude they impute to Leni Riefenstahl back to any key experience in her life. Instead, they simply take conclusions from the film and project them on to the director's biography – somewhat unconvincingly. It is the constellation of the main characters in the film which inspires the interpretation. Don Sebastian is Hitler[37] and Martha's relationship with him is based on opportunism (like the documentaries Riefenstahl made for the dictator). Martha is thus faced by a choice between good – in the form of the naïve and blameless Pedro – and evil, embodied by the marquis. The fight between the men becomes an act of 'tyranni-cide'.[38] It is striking how often these commentators use the symbolic constellation of the characters to make deductions about the director's life story: the plot around the characters acquires an autobiographical burden.[39] It becomes an implicit treatment of Riefenstahl's insight into the criminal character of the regime as well as being her way of symbolically disassociating herself from it.[40] This becomes, of course, a problematic interpretation if we take into account Riefenstahl's enthusiastic telegram to Hitler, con-gratulating him for his victory over France – not to mention the use of interned 'gypsies' as extras in the film itself.

Viewing the film as a form of disassociation is surely a questionable approach, given the complete lack of supporting evidence in Riefenstahl's conduct and her own remarks. Is Martha the least simplistic character in the film because she is invested with Riefenstahl's understanding? Is *Tiefland* a parody and criticism of her documentary films? Is it in fact a representation of her own escape from the pact with the devil?[41] Is it really possible to conclude: 'The content of the film clearly shows that she desired the downfall of the Nazis, and wanted possibly to help bring that about with her work'?[42]

Tiefland offers no additional evidence for the anti-Nazi interpretation. The violent character of the marquis does not reflect the terror in German society, and the other characters do not fit the bill at all – they are merely necessary ingredients in an unsophisticated tale. The only suggestive aspect of such an interpretation is the idea of seeing Martha's opportunism as Riefenstahl's representation of her own behaviour, thereby treating the affair between Martha and Don Sebastian as a metaphor for the director's pragmatic decision to collaborate with the dictatorship.

The reassessment of the film begs the question of whether *Tiefland* would also have been an anti-Nazi vehicle had it been made, as originally planned, in 1934. The 'revisionist' interpretation overlooks the development of the project and also the fact that the internal logic of the film's plot is determined not by the fight against the tyrant, but by the rivalry between two men for one woman. Pedro strangles Don Sebastian not because he wants to end the tyranny, but because he wants Martha. It is worth noting that the film does hint at a planned 'tyrannicide', but the resolve to undertake a desperate act against the marquis is not a central element in the plot. The three villagers who go to the mill to seek out Don Sebastian at night, during the storm, have no intention of begging his indulgence yet again: their whole attitude suggests that they want to call him to account. By the time they arrive at the mill, however, the fight between the two rivals, Don Sebastian and Pedro, has already broken out. They do not intervene in the duel, instead allowing Pedro, who has motives of his own, to complete the job.

Tiefland is not a subversive film – but neither is it a 'Nazi' film. The characterization and the plot development have less to do with the regime than they do with genre conventions. The contra-distinction between mountains and lowlands, between the innocence of life close to nature and the corruption of social life is indebted to the *Heimatroman* tradition of novels celebrating a rural idyll. The lowlands to which the film's title refers are, in abstract terms, society itself, populated by figures such as the ambitious mayor, his single-minded daughter and the conspiring, deceitful steward: figures who are nothing if not familiar. The film simply does not deal with a 'tyrannicide'; Riefenstahl concentrates on the story of a woman caught between two strong men. The contrast between the two is so emphatic as to be almost laughable: Don Sebastian is a man of the world whilst Pedro is at home only in the mountains; the aristocrat is a womanizer whilst the shepherd is an innocent; the rich man is quick tempered and base, the poor man is shy and peaceable. Where Don Sebastian deprives the villagers of the water for the fields, Pedro is self-sufficient, depending only on his flock of sheep. The one thing both men have in common, and which explains their erotic appeal, is their physical strength and their willingness to fight. This is more evident in Bernhard Minetti's portrayal of Don Sebastian than it is in newcomer Franz Eichberger's Pedro, characterized principally by his health, smile, dazzling teeth and shining eyes.

Tiefland confined itself to territory which was unproblematic even from a Nazi perspective. The film did not tell of a social revolt, but rather of a deed carried out by an individual. It did not deal with resistance to a tyrant, but with a fight over a woman. It was a mere variation on the typical, melodramatic situation of a woman having to choose between a rich but evil man and his poor but innocent rival.

Leni Riefenstahl was not very fond of *Tiefland*, and particularly not of her own contribution in the role of Martha: 'I cannot recognize myself there, in that film, because it is simply dead.'[43] It is, therefore, unlikely to be brought back to life by an attempt to transform it into a symbolic act of resistance.

CHAPTER NINE

The Return of the Outcast

The allied victory over National Socialism brought to an end the years of war, murder and the arbitrary abuse of power. Leni Riefenstahl, however, felt no relief. In interviews she gave during the post-war years, she did distinguish between the time before and after the war. Yet the two-volume edition of her memoirs is divided differently, into the periods 'before 1945' and 'afterwards'. It was afterwards, from her point of view, that the hard times began. First she was arrested and released by officers of the US Seventh Army in June 1945.[1] Then the French forces of occupation, arriving in the wake of the American troops, seized her company's assets along with her private fortune. Riefenstahl was interrogated again and this time interned for some time. In her memoirs she refers to being 'at the mercy' of the occupying forces; she mentions 'torture' and calls the period 'a sad time'.[2] It certainly was a sad time for much of the German population; above all, it was a time of need. The director's unique brand of egocentrism meant that the sense of being a victim, shared by so many Germans, was particularly pronounced in her case. She felt as though she were living in a kind of dungeon – not just during the period of occupation, but also in the Federal Republic.

Scandalmongers and Court Cases

Leni Riefenstahl began constructing the legend of her life as early as she could. Her version of events starts in the years of plenty: success after success, first as a dancer and actress and then as a director. The period began in the Weimar Republic and continued into the Nazi era, but she did not notice much difference between the two regimes. In her view, the only important distinction was that some Nazis obstructed and boycotted her (Goebbels) or harboured even darker designs (the SA). Then came the lean years, when, as she saw it, she encountered an unremitting barrage of slander and political persecution and was, in effect, banned from working. This personal perspective evolved without taking account of anybody else's experience, and it made Nazi rule seem like a lost paradise compared to the subsequent hell of democracy.

The underlying message in Riefenstahl's representation of her life has never altered. She has repeated it steadfastly, even in her most recent pronouncements. There have, however, been surprising variations in matters of detail. It is as if Leni Riefenstahl's own story had, in her eyes, undergone a sort of ossification. Successive layers of sediment have constructed a rigid skeleton, which, from time to time, she dresses in new clothes.[3] There is no doubt that many false claims were published about her, particularly in the early years after the war. These, unsurprisingly, sprang from the rumours circulating even before 1945 about an affair between her and Hitler.[4] The first of the many law suits Riefenstahl instigated – the famous 'Fifty Trials', all of which she claims to have contested successfully – involved the tabloid magazine *Wochenend*, which published the alleged 'diary of Eva Braun'.[5] In fact the diary was a trashy forgery, complete with allusions to naked dancing in front of Hitler. Further publication was, of course, prevented. Riefenstahl was perfectly entitled to take legal action to protect herself from attempts such as these to misrepresent her in public.

Yet it is not true, as she has encouraged people to assume, that the only stories about her in the post-war press were those based on insinuations and fabrications concerning love affairs between her and top Nazis. There were derisive allusions to the 'Reich crevasse', particularly between 1946 and 1950, and later she was also described as a convinced 'Nazisse' – but these early, speculative attempts to build invented scandals around her were by no means the main focus for media interest in her. The passing, voyeuristic fascination with the private lives of the top Nazis soon subsided. From then on, very few people really cared whether or not Leni Riefenstahl had once been involved with Hitler. It was

Riefenstahl herself who attached significance to the matter, insisting that the rumours were entirely unfounded without needing to be asked. In fact, Riefenstahl's public image was not based on the stereotype of Hitler's lover, but rather on all the evidence indicating not only that she was a propagandist who had enjoyed special privileges as a director, but also that her character was utterly incorrigible. Even if she was not the victim of a concerted press campaign, most of the attention she received was unambiguously negative. Leni Riefenstahl had been a figurehead for Nazi cinema, so she could hardly expect her work – above all the Party Rally films – to be forgotten about in a flash. There may have been unseemly ulterior motives behind some of the criticism she received, but on the whole it was the result of a clear, political rejection of the work itself. This then led to questions concerning the relationship between the director and the state or Party. Moreover, this period – the late 1940s – also saw the publication of early documentary evidence (such as that relating to her intervention in the 'Schünemann affair') which called into question the idea that her career had been dedicated entirely to the pursuit of art.

In the 1950s there was coverage of Leni Riefenstahl's various professional activities and projects in the press, particularly in the West German film magazines. There were no hostile overtones to the reports, and the reviews of *Das blaue Licht* and *Tiefland* were also largely objective. The specialist press made a visible effort to evaluate the aesthetic qualities of her films irrespectively of political considerations.

The failed attempt to make *Die roten Teufel* (The Red Devils) then almost led to Leni Riefenstahl disappearing from even the specialist media. The press did publish reports about any new projects she was planning (such as the remake of *Das blaue Licht* in Britain), but the focus was shifting away from her filmmaking to her other activities. The court cases and her invitation from the British Film Institute – and the subsequent withdrawal of that invitation – caught the public's imagination. In the second half of the 1960s, when she was making her long journeys to Africa and had no new projects to announce, she naturally received less attention.

This situation changed for good in the 1970s. For the first time there was talk of a 'Riefenstahl renaissance'. She assumed a public role as an artist again at the Munich Olympic Games of 1972, when she worked as a photographer for a British newspaper, and in 1973, when she published her first book of photographs about the Nuba. While Riefenstahl's image has not, perhaps, undergone any fundamental changes since then, it has acquired more subtle nuances. In particular, the conflicting interpretations of her work have become more clearly defined.

Relative Innocence

Probably in part because she was a woman, Leni Riefenstahl very quickly acquired a symbolic and uniquely enduring significance in Germany's attempts to come to terms with its Nazi past.

The underlying injustice is that, although many of Riefenstahl's colleagues had more to be ashamed of, they did not gradually become stigmatized as she did. Even directors of blatant propaganda films, such as Veit Harlan or Gustav Ucicky, were able to continue their careers in West Germany after the war. She appears even less deserving of her notoriety when compared to former NSDAP members who later went back into politics and held office. Measuring her conduct in these relative terms points up a fundamental issue in early post-war history. The reality in West Germany was that many artistic careers continued without interruption, just as many lesser offenders and Nazi sympathizers were integrated into society. When the guilt of respected members of society emerged subsequently, the equivocal aspects of their integration became a focus for the debate.

Clearly, however, Riefenstahl's case is also different from others simply because she was a woman. The way sexist prejudices were mobilized against her in the post-war reaction underlines the point. To that extent – but *only* to that extent – it is true that Leni Riefenstahl received unjust treatment. Yet the criticism was not based exclusively or even mainly on the fact that she was a woman, but rather on the fact that she had directed some blatant propaganda films. These films would have exposed even a male director to censure. Moreover, Riefenstahl's attempts to justify herself actually helped considerably to fuel the continuing criticism. She showed no inclination to take an honest look at her own record and she concealed or played down discreditable truths.

By comparing Riefenstahl with Veit Harlan – the other 'symbolic figure' of the film industry – we can obtain a clearer sense of the responsibility borne by these two propagandists. Harlan *invented* Jud Süss, wrote a role for him in his film and directed the actor. Ferdinand Marian may have been the man who became 'Jud Süss',[6] but it was the scriptwriter and director Harlan who brought him forth. This extremely questionable 'artistic high point' of his career was also a moral low point. Harlan used a popular art form, the melodrama, in order to disseminate his anti-Semitic message. He carefully honed the mechanics of the genre in order to adapt it to an undoubtedly ideological purpose. He *created* the world of the propaganda feature film.

Riefenstahl's contribution to Nazi propaganda was quite different. Her stylistic instinct spawned a new form, that of the 'heroic reportage'. Her work was, however, based upon a pre-existing, staged event and its political message. She did not have to *invent* a story, as Harlan did, but rather to distil one. She honed the events (such as the Party Rallies or Olympic Games) and stylized the way they were staged in order to popularize their undoubtedly ideological purpose. Riefenstahl translated the world of the Party Rally into that of the propaganda documentary. Her personal contribution to Nazi propaganda was thus confined to stylizing it for the cinema, whereas Harlan formulated the political message himself.

Harlan's relationship with his films was unambiguous. He was the scriptwriter and the director, he depicted his ideas. He treated 'Jud Süss' as a *character*, a figure of his own creation, not just as his actor. Riefenstahl's relationship with the 'actors' in her films was quite different. She had ideas about how the action might most effectively be depicted, but in *Triumph des Willens*, for example, she looked upon Hitler not as her character but rather, above all, as her actor. She treated him as the secret author of the film, but in order to make him seem impressive and powerful she had to rely on his own contribution. His 'acting' was an independent element beyond her control. She took what she considered to be the best parts of his performance and used this material to stylize 'her' Hitler. As observed above, she did not invent him. The difference may seem a minimal one: after all, both directors were producing Nazi propaganda. It is worth noting, however, that Riefenstahl did not use her skills to make inflammatory films dressed up as genre.

It may therefore seem unjust that, whilst Veit Harlan was able to continue making films after 1945, Leni Riefenstahl was not. In fact it is doubtful whether 'society' really did her wrong in any profound sense. Riefenstahl's impudent refusal to admit that there may have been anything at all questionable about her role during the Nazi era amounted to a provocation, ensuring that questions would always be raised. More importantly, the methods she had relied on for producing her films until 1945 were no longer available to her after the war. She had used 'special routes' to realize her projects, routes which had guaranteed her absolute artistic control. Personal contacts were important in this process. After 1945, these 'special routes' disappeared. There were no comparable financial backers outside the film industry, and of course the film industry itself was poorly developed. The smaller and medium-sized companies could never have financed a typical Riefenstahl film. Moreover, she was hardly a director known for her economy. The claim that *Olympia* had made between seven and eight million Reichsmarks was impressive but inaccurate.

There were unmistakable political reasons for the fact that, from this time onward, Riefenstahl kept being confronted with her past. Yet those political reasons were not what really prevented her from making any more films. Only once was she the victim of a genuine, albeit understandable, political intervention. In 1955, Jean Cocteau was the president of the jury at the Cannes Film Festival. He was so enthusiastic about *Tiefland* that he wrote to the West German Interior Ministry asking for the film to be nominated retro-spectively. His request was forwarded to the Foreign Ministry, which subsequently rejected it. Riefenstahl quoted the negative reply in her memoirs,[7] with the commentary: 'This showed I could expect nothing from the German government.' How could she have expected otherwise? This was just ten years after the war: there could have been no question of any government ministry officially supporting a film that had been produced in privileged circumstances during Nazi rule, and which featured interned 'gypsies'. The West German government had no option but to turn down the request if it was to avoid a diplomatic scandal. Complaining about the decision merely betrayed naïvety or political blindness.

Extras from the Camp

After three denazification court hearings in the French Zone, Riefenstahl was considered 'denazified'. Two of the hearings concluded that she was *nicht betroffen* (not affected). The third classified her as a *Mitläufer* (follower or fellow traveller). *Die Welt* reacted to the first verdict of 1 December 1948 by publishing documents from the archives of the former Reich Chamber of Culture (RKK). They included a telegram, which Riefenstahl claimed was not authentic,[8] and two letters from her to the director of the film department, Karl Auen, concerning the 'Schünemann affair'.[9] The newspaper published the documents in order to contest the court's verdict that Riefenstahl was *nicht betroffen*, as this meant 'that Leni Riefenstahl was not classified in any of the denazification groups, of which the two lowest are group V (*Entlastete* [exonerated]) and IV (*Mitläufer*).' In his letter to the editor, also published in *Die Welt*, Schünemann to some extent mobilized popular prejudices concerning Riefenstahl's closeness to the Führer and the villa which he had allegedly given to her. The newspaper itself, meanwhile, alluded indirectly to cracks in the image Riefenstahl had attempted to project of herself.[10]

The first direct attack on her version of her own story was launched by *Revue*. This was a popular magazine that frequently published stories about Nazi celebrities and was fond of providing what it considered to be titillating details. In an article of 1 May 1949, it brought up for the first time the circumstances surrounding the filming of *Tiefland*. The journal was unable to substantiate all its claims in court – for example, that Riefenstahl had personally selected the gypsies in the concentration camp – and its publisher, Helmut Kindler, was fined DM600. Nevertheless, the fact that the matter had been raised at all, even in such a trivial publication, was a significant development. The main points of the story were quoted in many national and local newspapers, achieving notoriety throughout the country.[11]

Kindler's trial at the district court in Munich also hit the headlines. The reports make it clear that the proceedings must sometimes have been turbulent.[12] Many of them dwell on the fact that Riefenstahl, whilst claiming legal aid, was elegantly dressed in court.[13] The case itself seems occasionally to have become some-thing of a public festival.

> The audience was very obviously split between two factions, the larger of which was composed of Riefenstahl supporters. From time to time, young girls would rub their hands in glee, and there was even the odd round of applause. The court did not even bother objecting to the frequent roars of laughter and interjections. This was regrettable, as it dragged the whole business down to a level below its dignity.[14]

Alfred Polgar also referred to the good 'atmosphere in the court':

> There were certain comic aspects to the idea of 'concentration camp inmates as film extras'. Testimony from witnesses with imperfect memories led to some amusing instances of mistaken identity which made everyone smile – even Leni Riefenstahl. At such moments her birdlike profile lost a little of its sharpness.[15]

Polgar saw the lawsuit not just as a way of addressing Riefenstahl's past, but also as a gauge for the current condition of post-war German society.[16] He thought the real shortcoming of the trial was 'that one matter remained an insignificant detail: the fact that, shortly after having the pleasure of serving Riefenstahl's cinematic art, the extras – including women and children – were shipped off to the gas ovens'. Polgar talked of the 'coldness' in 'Frau Riefenstahl's eyes and expression', and wrote: 'She told me in the courtroom that her pockets were full of foreign film contracts.' According to some reports, she also claimed that 'the allies had called upon her to clear herself of the . . . accusations'.[17] This may have been in connection with the impending third denazification court proceedings which had been instigated by the French forces of occupation.

The civil action produced a verdict on the issue of defamation, but it failed to resolve the decisive moral question. Riefenstahl had used the extras because she needed a certain physiognomy 'to enhance the Spanish flavour'.[18] Yet the extras came from a camp where they were interned – and later nearly all murdered – precisely because they were considered *different* and 'inferior' according to Nazi ideology. Leni Riefenstahl won the proceedings, which she had instigated in order to prevent damage to her reputation. It appears not to have occurred to her that her reputation did not actually depend on whether or not she had personally selected the extras at the Maxglan camp.

In the years to come *Revue* continued to play a special role in publishing accusations against the director. This was more than just a private feud between a tabloid and a celebrity. The amount of public interest in the legal wrangles about alleged insults and false allegations showed that, though these were mere details in the general scheme of things and far from unique, they were representative of the relationship between post-war society and the past. The reason the civil proceedings received so much attention was that Riefenstahl's attitude was prototypical of an inadequate response to one's own responsibility. She became a useful symbol. By taking Riefenstahl as a case in point, it was possible to discuss questions of great social relevance at, as it were, a personal level. She was neither the only, nor the most important person who might have served as an example of an inadequate attempt to 'come to terms with the past'. Her illustrious background and her chic appearance, however, meant that the press saw her as a perfect opportunity to confront an oft-suppressed issue: that of individual complicity.

The Massacre at Konskie

In April 1952, *Revue* again stoked up the debate concerning Leni Riefenstahl when, shortly after the re-release of *Das blaue Licht* in Germany and two days before the proceedings at the special denazification court in Berlin, it published further accusations. This time the magazine turned its attention to Riefenstahl's unremitting efforts after 1945

> to give the impression that she was completely unaware of the terrible atrocities committed by the National Socialist regime, crimes which still blacken Germany's image today and for which numerous innocent soldiers continue to be held unjustly responsible. In fact Leni Riefenstahl is one of the few German women who not only knew about these awful crimes, but also saw them with her own eyes.[19]

The allegations related to the events of 12 September 1939 in Konskie,[20] when twenty or more Polish civilians were shot by soldiers of the German army. The ensuing controversy did not concern the actual fact of the shootings. The contentious issues were the character of the crime (whether it was premeditated or a 'spontaneous act of violence'), the identity of those responsible (soldiers or SS) and the possibility that Riefenstahl knew about it.

Revue quoted a witness who claimed that thirty-one Jews died in the massacre and that Leni Riefenstahl had seen them die.[21] In her memoirs she refers to gunfire, but suggests she did not actually observe the incident. She claims that she only learned about it when she complained to General von Reichenau about the mistreatment of civilians. She has an alternative explanation for the photograph published in *Revue*, in which she stands, looking genuinely horrified, among some similarly affected soldiers. She alleges that Poles were being forced to dig a grave for German soldiers killed and mutilated by Polish civilians, and that she had protested about the way the gravediggers were being mistreated.

> The furious men then turned to me threateningly. One shouted 'Give her a punch in the face, get rid of the bitch!' Another one called out 'Shoot that bitch!' and aimed his rifle at me. I looked at the soldiers in horror. That was the moment when I was photographed.[22]

Revue's allegations inevitably came to dominate the proceedings at the Berlin denazification court. The proceedings were necessary, despite Riefenstahl's previous denazification trials, because a law had been passed in parliament tying the return of confiscated assets (principally, in this case, the villa in Dahlem) to a hearing in Berlin itself. After considering witness statements and statutory declarations, the court eventually decided not to condemn Riefenstahl's conduct at the time in question, declaring: '. . . it has been conclusively proven that the relevant photographs do not incriminate Frau Riefenstahl'.[23] The credibility of the *Revue* article was further undermined when it was proven that the photographs had been offered to Riefenstahl before being published in the magazine. She, however, had refused to buy them. *Stern* magazine later published the 'blackmail letter'.[24]

The *Revue* article was clearly a deliberate attack on the director's reputation. Yet it must be said that the version of events published in Riefenstahl's memoirs does leave some questions unanswered. According to Riefenstahl, a weapon had just been pointed at her when the photograph was taken – yet none of the soldiers around her appears anxious to move out of the way. It also seems unlikely that a grave for 'a high-ranking German officer and four soldiers' who had been 'murdered and terribly mutilated' by Polish civilians would have been dug in the middle of the market square in Konskie; Riefenstahl refers to 'a pit, the grave for the German soldiers'.[25]

This time the article in *Revue* never came to court: Riefenstahl and the publisher, Kindler, reached a settlement.[26] This may seem inconsistent with the policy she had pursued until then. Yet, even if *Revue*'s version of the execution she allegedly witnessed were true, it would not have indicted her in the way the magazine implied.

The versions of what happened in Konskie differ in various respects, but nobody denies that Riefenstahl did see Polish civilians being mishandled, did protest against the soldiers' conduct and did give up her war reporting. The fact that she 'resigned her commission' may, to some extent, be regarded as a point in her favour. In general, her behaviour in Konskie cannot be said to offer much scope for the critics – even if it seems the exception to the rule in the light of her congratulatory telegram to Hitler and, more particularly, her conduct during the making of *Tiefland*.

Leni Riefenstahl was not, however, being charged with a crime in any strictly legal sense: rather, she was seen as bearing a symbolic guilt. The accusations boiled down to her having witnessed a massacre. It is not possible to determine with any certainty whether she really did see the shootings themselves or 'only' the mistreatment of the men forced to dig the grave. In the denazification proceedings, there was no argument about her reaction to what she saw:

> According to her account, confirmed by witnesses, she was present by chance when a large number of Poles were forced to dig with their own hands a grave for four German soldiers, who had allegedly been horribly murdered. She protested to the army commander in charge, General von Reichenau, against the mistreatment and shooting of the gravediggers,

and the following day she gave up her activities as a frontline war correspondent.[27]

The Berlin court's decision was justified by the evidence available; nothing suggested that Riefenstahl was in any sense 'responsible' for anything that happened at Konskie, and her documented reaction spoke more for than against her.

The 'Manstein trial' offers a helpful insight into the context of the contemporary debate regarding Riefenstahl.[28] Field-Marshal Erich von Manstein was called to account at the end of 1949 (the verdict was issued on 19 December), principally for his conduct in the war against the Soviet Union. The war against Poland, in which Manstein had served as Chief of the General Staff under the Commander-in-Chief of the southern army group, Gerd von Rundstedt, also figured in the proceedings. Manstein denied any knowledge of executions and blamed the SS and SD (security police). His troops, he insisted, had not participated.

> When Sir Arthur asked the accused what he understood by the 'extermination of the Jewish-Bolshevik system' proclaimed in Reichenau's order, he answered that he had understood the extermination of a system, not of people. Sir Arthur showed the accused the passage in the order which reads: 'The German soldier must have understanding for the severe expiation against the Jewry.' He asked: 'Who was supposed to undertake the expiation and what did it involve?' When Manstein answered that the German soldier had nothing to do with it, Sir Arthur interrupted him: 'Who did have something to do with it?' Manstein again insisted that he had known nothing of the shooting of Jews by the security service.[29]

Manstein and other former army commanders were not the only ones still taking this position in 1949, and it continued to predominate for decades. It was a position that insisted on the honour of the German *Wehrmacht*, which allegedly neither committed nor participated in massacres – indeed the army was supposed not even to have been aware of the SS and SD atrocities. It was *Wehrmacht* soldiers, however, who were involved in the events at Konskie. The third staff officer under von Manstein,

Rudolf Langhaeuser, who was responsible for enemy intelligence and counter-intelligence, appeared at the trial as a witness for the defence and told the court about what had happened.

Questioned by the defence, Langhaeuser said that one day the film actress Leni Riefenstahl approached him, in a distressed condition. She had been assigned to the Tenth Army as a film reporter. She described the shootings of Jews at Konskiew and declared that she could not continue her work in such circumstances. Under cross-examination from prosecutor Elwyn-Jones the witness continued to stand by his statement.[30]

Later, von Manstein provided a similar account:

During the occupation of Końskie there had already been other shooting incidents, in which civilians had also taken part. A gathering at the market square led to a senseless outburst of shooting because of the nervousness of an anti-aircraft gun officer, who reached the square just as an unfounded panic erupted there. The shooting claimed several victims. The film troop witnessed this regrettable scene and our [female] visitor took her leave, thoroughly shaken. Moreover, General v. Reichenau immediately instigated a court martial, which sentenced the officer in question to demotion and a prison sentence of several years for manslaughter.[31]

The court martial mentioned by von Manstein did indeed take place. The files have been lost, but the delivery information to the army archive in Potsdam indicates that Lieutenant Bruno Kleinmichl was sentenced to two years in prison for manslaughter and illegal use of a weapon, although the punishment was deferred until after the war. On 16 January 1940, in response to the judgment, Kleinmichl was dismissed from the reserve officer corps, to which he had still belonged while serving in the air force.[32]

Insofar as Langhaeuser's testimony and von Manstein's reminiscences represent the whole truth, they generally support the version Riefenstahl gave in her memoirs – but contradict it in that they both suggest that Riefenstahl was a witness. Whilst casting a favourable light on Riefenstahl's behaviour in 1939, they also highlight the horrifying disregard for the truth which characterized contemporary discussion of the deaths in Konskie. In 1952 the German public was obviously less concerned with the iniquity of the murders as such than with the iniquity of having known about them. *Revue* had led the way when it played off Riefenstahl's alleged awareness of the shootings against the 'innocent soldiers'.

An article in *Welt der Arbeit* underlined once again that the criticism of Riefenstahl was founded on the suggestion that she had known about what happened. On 26 February 1954, the trade-union newspaper marked the premiere of *Tiefland* by repeating the accusations which had been made in *Revue*. It was forced to publish an alternative point of view on 12 November which it accompanied with the commentary:

> It is symptomatic of Riefenstahl's school of thought that she blames the ordinary German soldier for the atrocities which she trivialized . . . It is entirely improbable that this woman was unaware of the fact that Himmler's death squads were at work in Końsky. That she should here attempt to cover up the truth amounts to a monstrous defamation of the German soldier.

The desire – of *Welt der Arbeit* – to shift the burden of guilt is palpable in these lines. The suggestion that German army soldiers could have been to blame was simply unacceptable. Although even the witness quoted in *Revue* had accused an 'air force lieutenant' of giving the order to open fire, the honour of the ordinary German soldier is so important to the trade-union newspaper that it prefers to attack the witness than such a culprit. The fact that sections of the German *Wehrmacht* were also guilty of war crimes was clear long before the controversy surrounding the exhibition at the Hamburg Institute for Social Research. Controversies such as the one surrounding the massacre at Konskie helped consolidate the 'self-justifying legend'[33] that the army as a whole remained 'honourable' during World War II. The symbolic guilt weighed heavier than the crime itself. The real scandal was the disastrous failure on the part of the German press: at the time, no newspaper sought out the culprits.[34] It was not the person who instigated the evil deed who was held responsible for it, but rather the witness. The whole outcry amounted to a thoroughly unedifying spectacle and might well explain why Riefenstahl never subsequently deviated from her insistence that she had not seen the actual crime. Even if she was thought not to have told the whole truth, she surely deserved absolution for her conduct in Konskie. There cannot have been many war correspondents who protested against cruelty and shootings. Leni Riefenstahl's position was certainly a privileged one, but in this case she used it in a good cause. Her outraged reaction may not have achieved a great deal in 1939 – but it showed that there were things she was not prepared to accept.

Symbolic Guilt

There are few options open to a community which finds itself confronted with an unimaginable guilt. Germany's crimes, and in particular the technocratic organization of those crimes, were unique. Acknowledgement of a 'collective guilt', however, was not a realistic basis for a new social beginning. On the contrary, what this fresh start required was a symbolic sense of identity independent of the crime. East Germany declared itself the heir to the anti-fascist movement, a self-definition which superficially freed it from the issue of guilt (though not of guilty individuals and 'fellow travellers'). West Germany declared itself the succession to the German Reich, and undertook not to deny its guilt (although it was often criticized for taking a half-hearted approach). Yet this undertaking was partly founded on the unspoken consensus that the complicity of all those Germans who had turned a blind eye – who had preferred not to draw the obvious conclusions from what they knew or suspected – should not count as true guilt. In the early days of West Germany there was no attempt to address the everyday moral failure of the 'passive onlookers' or the general acceptance of systematic alienation and persecution. It seems unlikely that West German society could have survived such a self-examination. That was precisely why it needed individuals to function as categorical representatives and symbols. There was a need to define both 'good' and 'evil' in simple terms: clearly and unambiguously.

This was the principle underlying the attitude of *Revue* and *Welt der Arbeit* towards Leni Riefenstahl. Compared to other film artists, she possessed an almost singular symbolic significance, and there were various aspects of her career which made it very easy to portray her as 'incorrigible'. Although the two matters which came to public attention were distinct from one another – and each merited consideration in its own right – the general reaction in Germany was overwhelmingly similar in both cases. The community at large demonstrated a complete lack of interest in the victims and in identifying the real culprits. Quite apart from the implications for Leni Riefenstahl herself, today it seems absurd that so much dogged attention was paid to the question of what one person may or may not have seen, whilst the everyday victimization of gypsies, Jews and many others during the Nazi era was virtually overlooked. One day it may be possible to close the Riefenstahl 'case' and conclude that she was 'morally guilty' with regard to the extras from the Maxglan camp, and that she was 'not morally guilty' with regard to the Jews shot in Konskie. When she resorted to legal action to defend her 'honour' after the war, Riefenstahl demonstrated that she too was uninterested in either the victims or the culprits. She merely wanted not to be counted as one of the latter. Moreover, the descriptions of her court appearances reflect her horrifying self-righteousness – which itself contributed to the public perception of her.

The structure of the public dispute about an individual reputation (that of Leni Riefenstahl) in fact betrays a certain similarity between the symbolic figure and her accusers. There was a quite remarkable irony to the 'German public vs. Leni Riefenstahl' confrontation, for Riefenstahl's self-defence was precisely that she had 'known nothing about it all'. That was also the excuse of the huge majority in Germany as a whole. It was impossible to prove in court that Leni Riefenstahl was a liar, but the casual affirmation that 'Riefenstahl must be a liar' became the formula by which the silent majority excused itself.

In her review of Riefenstahl's memoirs, Margarete Mitscherlich wrote: 'She has managed to remain, right up to the present, in blissful ignorance of everything she wanted to know nothing about.'[35] This sentence (unintentionally) sums up what it was that Riefenstahl had in common with her fellow Germans. Riefenstahl's guilt offered an escape valve for the more general guilt which her compatriots were intent on suppressing. Her attempts to justify herself seemed unacceptable on principle – not because of the evidence available in each of the two cases, but rather because her excuses were identical to those of many of the 'small fry' – the passive onlookers in Nazi Germany.

CHAPTER TEN

Projects

Those of her films shown in public after the war served only to identify Riefenstahl even more firmly with the years before 1945. *Das blaue Licht* (in a new version), *Tiefland* (which had finally been completed) and *Olympia* (shorn of a few scenes) demonstrated the director's aesthetic competence, but it is not surprising that the critics picked up on their 'outmoded' aspects and expressed, at best, their respect. The films were outstanding in the context of popular German cinema, but when they were compared to international productions, it was difficult to overlook the fact that Riefenstahl's feature film aesthetics left little room for nuances and none at all for references to reality.

None of the three films reached the cinemas without encountering problems. The greatest complications surrounded *Tiefland*, the material for which had been confiscated by the French forces of occupation. It was stored in the *Cinémathèque*, where it seems to have been tampered with. It took years for Riefenstahl to succeed in getting it back. She used the leftover negatives from *Das blaue Licht* to create a new version of the film, which dispensed with the framework plot. Things were also more difficult than they seemed in the case of *Olympia*; she produced a slightly shortened version, cutting out shots of swastika flags and some of those featuring Hitler and other leading Nazis.

Repeating the Past

Das blaue Licht was the first of Riefenstahl's films to be shown after the war. It bore a particular burden not only at its premiere, but also at each of its two subsequent re-premieres. In 1932 the film had, in effect, to prove Riefenstahl's talent as a director. In 1938 it had to live up to its billing as a masterpiece of German cinematic art, long undervalued because of the machinations of the 'Jewish press'. In 1952, it had to vouch for the director's unpolitical temperament. Times had changed, and Riefenstahl was well aware of the competition her film faced:

> But today, just as I did then, I have to disappoint those who want to see the film as pure entertainment. It was not made for the moment, to be forgotten again by tomorrow. There is nothing sensational about it; it has no sex appeal or superficial effects. It is meant only for those still capable of actually watching. Perhaps the result will repeat itself: perhaps romanticism will again overcome realism, haste, restlessness and the modern, technical tempo.[1]

She thus attacked not only films made merely as popular entertainment, but also the much less numerous 'realist' (or neo-realist) films – with which *Das blaue Licht* did indeed have nothing whatsoever in common. Her attempt to differentiate her film in advance from two defining trends in contemporary cinema was a deft tactical move. It highlighted the qualities in the film which were as unique in the early 1950s as they had been in 1932.

Even before *Das blaue Licht* opened in Germany, the Italian version was shown in Italy. For Riefenstahl, the gala premiere in Rome was a rare moment of post-war glory, and the Zürich newspaper *Die Tat* judged it a great comeback: 'No less a figure than Vittorio de Sica complimented his fellow filmmaker warmly on her film.'[2] Despite such positive reactions, no distribution contract for the Italian version was forthcoming.

In Germany, *Das blaue Licht* was released by 'National-Film'. In her memoirs, Riefenstahl does not describe the premiere; contrary to the assumption of one cinema magazine, the film was not a success.[3] This was probably partly on account of the way that the article in *Revue* concerning the Konskie massacre had steered public perceptions of Riefenstahl in a particular direction. The same issue also invested the premiere of *Tiefland* with particular significance. Positive advance coverage meant that a great deal was expected of a film which had already achieved almost legendary status.[4] The premiere took place on 11 February 1954 in Stuttgart, and although the critics were less positive in their responses, Riefenstahl considered them thoroughly 'objective'.[5]

In fact there was almost unreserved praise for the direction and camera-work. In retrospect it seems almost surprising that Riefenstahl's achievement received such universal respect. There is no sense of rancour in the reviews themselves; the assessments were indeed objective. 'There is no doubt that its makers have succeeded in creating a film which, on account of its artistic and technical accomplishment, deserves praise and is likely to be a success.'[6] Approval outweighed scepticism in the film industry publications;[7] Riefenstahl was (once again) acknowledged as an *auteur*: 'Leni Riefenstahl deserves credit as an author, director and director of photography for achieving a perfect triad.'[8] There were only occasional references to cameraman Albert Benitz amid the general appreciation for Riefenstahl's photographic genius. The acting performances received mixed reviews: few critics thought Leni Riefenstahl's portrayal of Martha was successful, but otherwise most assessments were positive.[9] The daily press was generally more critical, but there were very few reviews which might be termed thoroughly 'malicious'.[10]

Nevertheless, the background to the making of the film means that it is hardly surprising that not everybody toed the almost programmatic line of the film magazines. The latter saw 'nothing that could conceivably be regarded as political',[11] but there were those who referred back to the fate of the extras from the Maxglan camp and took a generally cool view of the film. Some commentators considered that it would have been better not to release it, even though its content and style did not justify political reservations. Such objections, however, were few and far between, and they can hardly have been responsible for *Tiefland* doing so poorly. Most articles – for example the one in the *Neue Ruhr-Zeitung*[12] – did not even question Riefenstahl's 'artistic achieve-ments', and referred back to *Olympia*. Indeed, some elements of the German press even used the release of the film to sketch a positive picture of Riefenstahl's career.[13] This perhaps reflects the fact that a section of the West German media had made its peace with Riefenstahl as early as the 1950s.

That partial reconciliation is particularly evident from reactions to *Olympia*, when it too was re-released. According to one article, the 'disquiet caused by Leni Riefenstahl'[14] now meant the disquiet created by a masterpiece. It argued that there could be no doubt that this was a just description of a work which had just been voted one of the 'ten best films ever made': 'one left the "studio für filmkunst" deeply impressed by a great film document and – let us hope! – with that slight sense of disquiet' befitting the film. Other reviews resorted to the same, double-stranded argument. *Der Tag* called *Olympia* 'a great experience', a film which it had been possible 'to free from the political subtext which was indispensable at the time it was made' by just a few cuts.[15]

In fact, not many screenings actually took place, and they demonstrated for the first time the gulf between aesthetic and political arguments that was to become so typical of the controversy surrounding Riefenstahl from this point on. The two lines of argument were utterly independent: each was built on internally coherent foundations which took no account of the other. Disquiet created by a masterpiece may have characterized Germany's initial reencounter with the film, but it was a response which soon vanished from the debate.

The release of *Olympia* ended the first phase of Riefenstahl's post-war career. It had seen her begin all sorts of new projects – with Jean Cocteau, in Italy, in Spain. For various reasons, however, none of the projects came to fruition. In her memoirs, Riefenstahl blamed a sort of boycott for this. It is certainly true that aspects of her past were less than helpful when it came to getting new productions off the ground. In her attempts to make another film she came up against substantial and ultimately insurmountable obstacles – but not all the difficulties facing her were of a political nature. Indeed, political factors cannot even be said to have been decisive: the weak condition of the film industry, which consisted of small and medium-sized companies,[16] played an at least equally significant role.

Moreover, the fact that Riefenstahl's ideas appeared distinctly out of place in the new era naturally made it even harder to realize them successfully. The best example was *Die roten Teufel*, a project to which Riefenstahl dedicated many pages of her memoirs. At the time, this project received more press coverage than any others, and it seems to have been regarded as Riefenstahl's best chance of effecting a genuine comeback. In a typical response to adverse circumstances, she resorted to old, 'safe' material: ' "Die roten Teufel" was my pet project. The idea dated from the winter of 1930, when I had a role in the Fanck film "Stürme über dem Montblanc." '[17]

It appears to have been one of her earliest ideas for a film, which initially probably owed much to films such as Fanck's *Der weisse Rausch*. That certainly appears to be the implication of a *Film-Kurier* report published in 1930: 'It is a ski film, which is to be made as a sound-film and in colour. It will focus on the downhill skiers of Innsbruck, known as "Die roten Teufel" [The Red Devils].'[18] Riefenstahl's choice of material betrays her tendency to deal with any difficult situation by following a familiar route. Like her superficially strange decisions to follow up her first experience of directing with a modest role as an actress in *S.O.S. Eisberg* and to reactivate the *Tiefland* material after the failure of the *Penthesilea* project, her decision to make a ski film was founded on her need for a safety net. *Die roten Teufel* was to be about the contest between the Tyrolean skiers and the ski-Amazons. Today it seems positively grotesque that she should have viewed this combination of a ski film and a (comic) variation on the theme of *Penthesilea* – recycling two discarded ideas – as a serious comeback attempt.[19]

Yet that is precisely what this strange project amounted to. It was Riefenstahl's only real effort to make a new beginning within the film industry on the basis of a popular entertainment film and in a genre with which she was familiar. *Die roten Teufel* would have belonged firmly to the Fanck tradition, with spectacular mass starts of skiers dressed in various bright colours. Riefenstahl intended to use a helicopter for the first time to film particularly dramatic scenes, thus emulating Ernst Udet, whose artistic aeronautical stunts in the Alps had become the main attraction of *Die weisse Höle vom Piz Palü*. In accordance with the contemporary fashion, a 3-D version of *Die roten Teufel* was also to be made.[20] After the failure of several strategies for financing it, the film (along with Riefenstahl's hopes of a star-studded cast including Vittorio de Sica, Jean Marais and Brigitte Bardot) had to be abandoned – despite the fact that, by 1955, nearly all the groundwork had been accomplished. In her memoirs, the director blamed this setback on the fact that she had 'again . . . landed between the millstones of political interests'[21] – a reference to the Austrian government's decision to withdraw the funding it had agreed to provide for part of the production costs, following critical press reports.

This was the closest Leni Riefenstahl ever came to another large-scale production. All her subsequent plans for films which did at least enter the early stages of production – *Die schwarze Fracht* (Black Freight), the film about the Nuba and the underwater film – represented mere regressions. The director who had once worked with famous actors, with the best cameramen and film composers of her age, was reduced to planning on a scale as small as, or even smaller than, *Das blaue Licht*. The German film industry was now unable to support the professional, very capital-intensive productions she had worked on at the height of her career. Moreover, she had lost her tried and tested team; she no longer had a Schneeberger to conjure up magical images for her. It must have been a bitter pill to swallow for a director who had become used to working with a large team and ample resources since making *Triumph des Willens*. Her special status had been a thing of the past since 1945 – and Leni Riefenstahl interpreted the loss of that status as a boycott.

Africa

Die roten Teufel and Riefenstahl's other film projects all ended in failure. They turned out, in a sense, to be unproductive as well as unsuccessful attempts at making a fresh start. Her reaction to these failures, however, came in the long run to seem a prime example of productivity through escapism. Riefenstahl was always at her most brilliant when faced with a new challenge, when she was doing something for the first time. Whenever she could see no way forward, whenever she resorted to familiar recipes and still got nowhere, she always broke free – to the mountains, to working as a director, and now to Africa.

She was already over fifty years old when she visited the Dark Continent for the first time. Her experiences there were far from encouraging: another planned film (*Die schwarze Fracht*) came to nothing, and she suffered severe injuries in a car accident in Kenya. Leni Riefenstahl also found herself in dire financial straits at this time, as she emphasized in her memoirs: 'Since the end of the war I had been deserted by any glimmer of happiness; my life had turned into an unspeakable struggle for survival, the product of intrigues and political discrimination.'[22] In these reminiscences, her bitter complaints about insufficient support, the lack of film commissions and the protests against screenings of her films merge to form a kind of dull background, against which her experiences during those pivotal African journeys to the Nuba stand out all the more brightly.

As she looked back, 'Africa' doubtless seemed a word with symbolic resonance, standing not just for a liberating experience, but also for a counterweight to post-war German society, in which she had suffered 'systematic character assassination'.[23] That is why the whole of the last part of her memoirs – covering the time from the mid-1950s on and accounting for almost three quarters of the second volume – is entitled simply 'Africa'. It is clearly meant to contrast with the previous section, entitled 'The Post-War Years'. When she 'took stock of the fifteen years which had passed since the end of the war', Riefenstahl saw herself 'in a desperate struggle to defend myself, overwhelmed by slanderous mudslinging' – 'I had not lived since the end of the war, I had merely crept around in the filthy mire of human meanness.'[24]

'Africa' was the innocent alternative to that conspiratorial world. Riefenstahl saw it not as a continent dominated by war and civil war, but rather as a metaphor for naturalness and authenticity, defined by personal experiences. It was the place where her past did not matter. Once again, she assigns great significance to certain formative experiences: she was inspired to make her first journey by reading Hemingway's *The Green Hills of Africa*, whilst a photograph by George Rodgers of a black athlete being carried on the shoulders of his friend moved her to search for the 'Nuba of Kordofan'.[25]

The 'discovery' of the Nuba and her narrative were thus dominated by her dramatic requirements; her description of the tribe's living conditions cannot be said to constitute a realistic or convincing report. Portraying the Nuba as 'different' and 'natural' necessarily involved seeing them in splendid isolation. The Nuba had to seem almost unknown to the outside world, inhabitants of a remote region untouched by the passing of time and the influence of civilization. Nothing about the tribe could be 'similar'. The Nuba of the memoirs are as much a Riefenstahl invention as her Africa. 'It took a long time for me to find out where Kordofan lay, and even longer for me to discover the "Nuba Hills" on an English map.'[26]

The naturalness which Riefenstahl so missed on her later visits seems to have been partly fictional even by the time of her first visit. Complete isolation is hard to square with occasional visits 'to even the most remote corners of the Nuba Hills by trucks, from which Sudanese officials distributed free items of clothing to the natives.'[27] Later objections to Riefenstahl's description of the lifestyle of the Nuba tribes also appeared valid, even if the photographer did not see herself as engaged primarily in ethnographical research.[28] For her, the Nuba perfectly embodied an ideal: in this tribe Leni Riefenstahl saw 'biblical images, as if from the dawn of humanity'.[29] More specifically, she thought she had finally found her vision of 'naturalness', the quality she had identified in Rodger's photograph. The descriptions of her stays among the Nuba also give the impression that she enjoyed a sense of peace there which she could find nowhere else. The closeness, but also the possessiveness, of her relationship to the tribe was expressed in her references to '"my" Nuba'; the possessive pronoun was not always placed in inverted commas.[30]

During her expeditions to Africa, Riefenstahl was consistently on the lookout for the best possible photographs. She captured the Nuba lamenting their dead; when she arrived among the Anuak she discovered 'black people more beautiful' than those she had seen anywhere else in Africa; she photographed the unapproachable Masai – 'but they did not become as confiding as the Nuba'.[31] She seemed to have found paradise – but only for it to slip from her grasp. When she returned to the Nuba Hills in 1968 she noted 'that nearly all the warriors wore gaudy, multi-coloured trousers' – and was horrified.[32] She blamed the changes on the encroaching, money-based economy and the attempts of the Sudanese government to persuade the Nuba to wear clothes.[33]

In her hurry to capture 'naturalness' on film among the Masakin-Nuba despite this transformation, Leni Riefenstahl made another expedition. In dramatizing the 'journey of discovery' she claimed to have been inspired by the same kind of experience which, in her reminiscences, had preceded her debut as a director: a dream. This time it concerned 'two black figures with sharpened bracelets engaged in a fight'. The journey to these dream-figures, allegedly leading into the unknown, appeared to her to be a 'last chance to discover something special in this corner of the world'.[34] She found that special something in the Nuba of Kau, and immediately defined it entirely in terms of the distinction between them and the Nuba she had encountered before.

> [They] do not know one another, have a different language, and are the complete opposite of the Masakin Nuba in terms of their general character. The Masakin Nuba are peaceful and gentle; the Kau Nuba are wild and passionate. Photographing the Masakin Nuba was no problem at all, but it was almost impossible among the Kau Nuba.[35]

Critics argued that the differences between the two tribes were by no means so great as Riefenstahl had claimed. In fact the way she differentiated between them may simply reflect the dissimilar circumstances in which she photographed them. She had paid several, sometimes lengthy visits to the Masakin Nuba since 1962, but stayed with the Nuba of Kau only briefly, on three occasions. The first of these was in a purely private capacity, but her last two visits to the Kau were made with an eye to a future publication. They turned into veritable expeditions involving enormous amounts of luggage and material:[36] the whole character of her 'journeys' had changed. The camp, which had once been set up under a big tree, was now surrounded by a high, straw fence. Riefenstahl no longer lived among the Nuba: she viewed them as potential models and scanned the world before her eyes for spectacular images. Photography became something intrusive, a form of hunting. 'Despite all her protestations to the contrary, Leni Riefenstahl does buy the subject of her photograph – not with money, but with beads. She describes this with a disarming frankness quite alien to her own conduct.'[37]

In her memoirs she responded with faux naïve nonchalance to accusations that she had also made cash payments: 'Instead of money, we gave the Nuba oil, which was not cheap in Kau . . . Only in rare, exceptional cases when we had no more oil left did we also pay cash, but never more than one pound'[38] – rather than the eighty pounds she had allegedly been accused of paying. There is thus no doubt whatsoever – indeed, Riefenstahl herself provides the conclusive testimony – that she resorted to means which would have been taboo for any ethnographical investigation in order to obtain pictures.

Even on her first trip to Kau, she gave the impression of a dedicated photo-journalist with all the proper equipment:

> I had slung both my Leicaflex cameras around my neck and fitted them with motors and teleoptics. After getting a few long shots, I approached the fighters until I was right in the thick of the action. I was quickly chased away again. I then tried again from the other side. I knew that these were unrepeatable pictures, and I fought for every shot.[39]

The scenario is reminiscent of the alluring contests and the obstructive officials of *Olympia*. This time, however, Riefenstahl could only send herself and her companion, Horst Kettner, to the photographic front, and she lamented the lack of the resources she had previously enjoyed as a filmmaker:

> Several cameramen would have been necessary to capture the whole of the action at such a festival: for the faces of the onlookers and those of the fighters, the victors, the warbling women and dancing girls and above all for the fights themselves.[40]

There is no mistaking her longing to make a 'total' film of the Nuba bracelet or knife fights,[41] as she had of the Olympic Games, armed with 'special' support and a vast array of technical equipment.

In *Die Nuba von Kau* (published in English as *The People of Kau*) the photographer adopted a significantly more spectacular approach than in her first book of photographs. 'Leni Riefenstahl's initial amazement and curiosity about the Masakin Nuba are still evident in the pictures, but when she turns to the Kau Nuba, aesthetic calculation becomes her principle motivation.'[42] For the later book she worked from a great distance in every sense, using much more powerful telephoto lenses in order to obtain her photographs.[43] This perhaps also explains why many of the subjects are identified by name in the first book, but none at all in the second.

'Africa' also stood for disappointment. On Riefenstahl's third visit to Kau, in 1977, she failed to rediscover her ideal even among these remote tribes. 'They were distorted to the point of absurdity by impossible items of clothing and glasses. They were also aggressive, unlike the Masakin Nuba, and demanded all kinds of things from us, even our clothes.'[44] There were even visits from busloads of curious tourists: Riefenstahl was left to lament the destruction of another paradise.

In the course of her life, Leni Riefenstahl twice managed to create works which drew their beauty from the enthusiasm of those involved: *Das blaue Licht* and *Die Nuba von Kau*. Her first film as a director and her first series of photographs displayed her best sides. Both projects evolved without support from the film industry or publishers. In both enterprises she had to rely on herself, without the security of a financial backer. On the other hand, she was also more dependent than she was in any of her other projects – on Béla Balázs, Hans Schneeberger and the Sarntal farmers in the case of the film, and on the Nuba in the case of the photographs. She could dictate nothing at all: her whole achievement depended on collaboration. Each project was founded on trust. This, together with her natural curiosity and strength of will, enabled her to wrest optimum results from the most adverse circumstances.

After each of these successful beginnings she wanted more: a greater, more spectacular continuation of her debut. She evidently failed to see the extent of her own potential when she simply plunged into a new situation. She preferred the idea of controlling the situations, which is precisely why *Tiefland* turned into a much less satisfying film than *Das blaue Licht*. It is also why *Die Nuba von Kau* failed to live up to the standard set by her first book of photographs. Riefenstahl may have been in a vastly superior position when she came to make the 'sequels', but they both suffered from a loss of sensitivity. At her first attempt she had succeeded in developing her own form by determinedly – even obsessively – making the most of the limited resources available, but later she failed to exploit her embarrassment of riches. She tended to over-stylize; instead of coming across photographs, she simply sought them.

The first 'Nuba' book pays only cursory attention to the

everyday life of the tribe, yet it paints a much clearer picture than *Die Nuba von Kau*. Only in the second book is there a stylistic pathos which is unmistakably dedicated above all to 'heroic poses' and involves photographing the models against the sky again – isolated from their context. It is unfair to conclude without further ado, as contemporary observers did, that this produces a 'fascist aesthetic', but it does fit a certain pattern which the culture industry is fond of employing in order to invest individuals with significance and, if necessary (almost inevitably, so far as Riefenstahl is concerned), to heroize them.

The problem of the Nuba photographs is not that Riefenstahl's search for strength and beauty led her 'from the black uniforms of the SS to the black bodies of the Nuba'.[45] Nor does the suggestion that she saw the Nuba as 'the better Nazis, the purer Barbarians, the true Teutons'[46] offer a convincing explanation. In fact, something much more troubling can be observed in these photographs. An artist – whose talent is undisputed – is suddenly presented with more substantial resources, but she then allows herself to be distracted by effects which are easy (albeit expensive) to produce. An artist with an outstanding sense of form seeks her salvation in technical expertise, afraid of the risk represented by a lack of knowledge. She aspires to 'classical' solutions and achieves commercial art.

In its repetition of the 'Nuba' theme from the earlier book, *Die Nuba von Kau* recalls the way *Tiefland* drew on elements of *Das blaue Licht*. The photographs were also, to some extent, indebted to the aesthetics of the Party Rally films and *Olympia*. Suggestions of a direct ideological line of descent, however, are unjustified. Rather, the changed *attitude* of the photographer reflected in her two books is similar to the changed attitude of the director reflected in her two feature films, whilst the *aesthetical* transformation in the books of photographs harks back to Riefenstahl's experiences as a maker of documentary films. In *Die Nuba von Kau* she employed a pattern which would have seemed inappropriate to the first volume of photographs, but not to the films and books of photographs about the Party Rally or Olympic Games.

CHAPTER ELEVEN

Legal Questions and the Question of Tact

Riefenstahl's various activities, be they plans for films or legal battles, were widely reported, but her struggles to secure the rights to *Triumph des Willens* and *Olympia* went almost unnoticed by the general public. The question of who should properly own the producer's rights only began to exercise the minds of archivists and film historians from the 1970s onward. They unanimously concluded that the Party and the German Reich respectively should be regarded as the producers.[1] By then, however, a contractual settlement concerning the disputed copyrights had already been achieved.

Legal Claims

Leni Riefenstahl first asserted her rights to *Triumph des Willens* when she took action in 1954 against the production company responsible for the film *Bis fünf nach zwölf* (Until Five Past Twelve), a compilation which used excerpts from the Party Rally film. She demanded 'compensation, which she intended to pass on to charity'. The producer of the film, Wolfgang Hartwig rejected Riefenstahl's claims by arguing that 'the footage in question was the property of the German Reich, and had been seized by the Allies'.[2] According to Riefenstahl's memoirs, however, she was eventually paid for the material used, and donated the money to the 'Verband der Heimkehrer' (an association for repatriated prisoners of war).[3]

A few years later, legal rights became the subject of a broader public debate, when she threatened to take action against the company distributing *Mein Kampf* (a Swedish film directed by Erwin Leiser in 1960, originally entitled *Den blodiga tiden*) in Germany. The director of that film told a press conference in Stockholm about Riefenstahl's threat, which apparently involved a claim for DM100,000 plus 10 per cent of the film's takings and which she intended to pursue in the courts of France, Switzerland and West Germany.[4] Leiser's film was given its premiere on 12 July 1960 and proved very successful. In December 1960, Neue Film-Verleih GmbH (the distribution company) obeyed a temporary injunction by paying 'a substantial sum':

> The film company stressed that, in paying Leni Riefenstahl for the West German rights, it had gone against the wishes of the Swedish production company, Minerva. The Swedes continued to take the view that they had no need to buy anything from the beneficiaries of the Third Reich in order to make a film about that Third Reich. The legal arguments between Leni Riefenstahl and the Swedish production were [said Neue Film-Verleih] not yet over . . .[5]

In fact those arguments would drag on for several years.

Riefenstahl ceded her demands to the film producer Friedrich A. Mainz.[6] He wanted 'to freeze a part of Minerva's assets in Germany as a precautionary measure', and initially succeeded in doing so.[7] *Der Spiegel* expressed amazement when the regional court in Munich guaranteed possible claims against Minerva by freezing DM50,000 from the takings of the German version of the film. This initial ruling led to further litigation, which was not resolved until 1969, when the Federal Supreme Court decided in favour of the production company.[8]

Press comments about Riefenstahl's claims were remarkably uniform in tone. Moral arguments predominated over legal ones, as the headlines in West German newspapers make clear: 'The Reward for Immorality', 'Dirty Money', 'Leni Riefenstahl Profits from the Film *Mein Kampf*', 'A Question of Tact', 'A Right to a Fee?', 'Shameless'.[9] Their East German counterparts were even blunter: 'Nazi Morality', 'Shameless Demands', 'Old Fat Cat', 'The Resurrection of a Nazi Star'.[10]

The writers of such articles were particularly offended by the fact that the director of three Party Rally films should want to profit from a work designed to shed light on the crimes of National Socialism. They implied or stated openly that Riefenstahl had benefited from National Socialism and that this discredited her demands. The media either refused to take a view on the technicalities of the litigation or conceded that (in purely legal terms) Riefenstahl's demands were legitimate: in both cases they were skating on thin ice and risked inciting moral opposition to constitutional principles. The *Berliner Morgenpost* commentary referred to the 'cinematic poet laureate of the Nazi regime, the Führer's chronicler at the Reich Party Rallies' and went on: 'So Leni Riefenstahl has seen the film *Mein Kampf*. She did not just go quietly home and hide her shame. No, she remembered her hours of glory cranking the brown camera – and cashed in. Dirty money.'[11] *Der Tagesspiegel* pointed out: 'Today Frau Riefenstahl demands and receives a second fee for a propaganda movie which she was paid to make in honour of the "Third Reich". The trick is simply to stand up for your "rights" loudly and tactlessly.'[12]

The reactions in West Germany betrayed a certain sense of helplessness.[13] There seemed to be no possible legal objection to Riefenstahl's claims. The problem of how society would and should come to terms with the 'legacy' of National Socialism – with *Triumph des Willens* and 'Nazi art' in general – was never even raised. Though Riefenstahl was scolded for capitalizing on the past, there was no attempt whatsoever at a positive confrontation with that past through a critical engagement with the Party Rally film itself. That would have been the only way of focusing attention on the political position she represented in her film instead of the greed she was accused of displaying.

Riefenstahl also claimed the producer's rights to both parts of *Olympia*. At first she was successful, encountering no opposition. She had shown the film occasionally from 1957 onward,[14] initially at film club events. On 5 February 1958, after an appeal, the *Freiwillige Selbstkontrolle der Filmwirtschaft* (FSK – the 'voluntary self-censorship' authority) passed *Olympia* for audiences over six years of age, but it did not receive a rating from the *Filmbewertungsstelle* (the office which awarded films "positive" ratings tied to financial perks). This prompted Riefenstahl to submit expressions of support from Carl Diem (general secretary of the organizing committee for the 1936 Games), Otto Mayer (chancellor of the International Olympic Committee) and Karl Ritter von Halt (president of Germany's National Olympic Committee). She based her appeal – which was ultimately unsuccessful – on her claim that *Olympia* was 'neither supported nor screened by any organ of the National Socialist government, whilst it was being made or after its completion'. She thus failed to mention the financing of the film by the German Reich.[15] The approved version of the film, shorn of shots featuring Hitler and other top members of the Nazi regime, enjoyed successful runs in several West German cinemas over the next few years; the press reaction was also positive.[16]

The West German Foreign Ministry's reaction in November 1955 to an inquiry from the German embassy in Australia makes it clear that at this stage the government assumed that Riefenstahl owned the copyright for *Olympia* at least. The inquiry refers to screenings of a shortened version of the film and states that the Commonwealth National Library wished to continue showing the film as part of its programme. The department responsible named Riefenstahl as 'owner of the copyright' and advised strongly against supporting any further showings of the film.[17] There was a similar reaction when the German embassy in New Zealand asked, on behalf of the National Film Library, whether it would be possible to arrange a non-commercial distribution of 16mm prints of the English version.[18] Although the film library pulled out of the project for financial reasons, the Foreign Ministry's involvement in the matter continued, as a 35mm print of *Olympia* had been discovered in Wellington. The embassy presumed that the print had 'been seized during the confiscation of German property and then somehow been forgotten'. The Foreign Ministry, however, did not support the idea of making further prints from it, 'as Frau Riefenstahl has in the meantime regained full ownership of the proprietary rights to the film'.[19] In these instances, therefore, the Foreign Ministry pursued a policy which was aimed at securing existing copyrights or patent rights held by German citizens.

A Verdict

At 8.25 p.m. on Sunday, 29 September 1974, *Triumph des Willens* was shown against Riefenstahl's will[20] on the third programmes of the 'Nordkette' (an alliance of three northern German broadcasters – NDR, Radio Bremen and SFB). The *Hessischer Rundfunk* also broadcast the film, but at a different time. Viewers in northern Germany, Berlin and Hessen were given their first opportunity to see the controversial film on television – although at the time, the broadcast did not cause much of a stir.[21]

The necessary contract was signed on 13 June 1973 with the company 'Transit Film GmbH', and allowed for further broadcasts. It came about because the programme editor, Hans Brecht, had worked with Erwin Leiser and heard from him of the legal case against Minerva Film and the Federal Supreme Court verdict. This represented the end of the road for Friedrich A. Mainz's appeal against the decision of the senior district court (OLG) in Munich (29 December 1966).[22] From a legal point of view, it was now clear that the NSDAP should be regarded as the producer of *Triumph des Willens*, which meant that the West German state was responsible for the rights associated with the film. It seems probable that in 1974, at least partly in response to the television broadcast, Riefenstahl signed a contract relating to the use of *Triumph des Willens* with Transit Film GmbH, which now administered the rights associated with the former Reich film industry in trust for the state. Only by means of such an agreement could she guarantee that she would have a say and be able to prevent future showings of the film without her consent, based on the Federal Supreme Court decision.

In her memoirs, Riefenstahl attacks that decision as a 'miscarriage of justice',[23] and claims that Leiser used almost 600 metres of film from *Triumph des Willens*; in fact the appeal related to 337.31 metres.[24] She also refers to statutory declarations, alleging that the court disregarded some of them as they had not been notarized. These declarations indicated that neither the NSDAP nor the Reich had financed the production at all. In fact nobody disputed that the film had been financed by means of the Ufa distribution guarantee. Riefenstahl's only attempt to take account of the extant documents was her insistence that she had been termed the 'plenipotentiary of the NSDAP's directorate' only in one handwritten entry to a memorandum, and that the description was erroneous.[25] The statutory declarations to which she attached such importance[26] failed, in any case, to disprove that she had made the Party Rally film – financed in advance through Ufa – at the Führer's behest and for the Party.

Riefenstahl also quotes a letter from Arnold Raether, an adversary of hers at the time *Sieg des Glaubens* was made.[27] He stated 'that the NSDAP neither produced the film *Triumph des Willens* nor commissioned it', adding that Party films could not be 'made without my knowledge and my consent'.[28] He overlooks the fact that Hitler himself could commission a 'Party Rally film' – as he did from Riefenstahl in 1933, against Raether's will. Raether's support was thus less than entirely convincing, grateful though Riefenstahl herself was for it.[29] After the verdict, the only way she could pursue her claims was by trying to secure an agreement similar to the one concerning *Olympia*.

According to the Files . . .

At the start of the 1970s it became clear that Leni Riefenstahl claimed the rights to exploit the two most famous films she had made during the Nazi era. Her claims, however, were disputed, since the Bundesarchiv – West Germany's state archive – viewed the Federal Republic itself as owner of those rights, based on the extant documents. That difference of opinion was the reason for a remarkable agreement in 1964 between Transit Filmvertrieb GmbH and Leni Riefenstahl.[30] This represented an accord between two parties who both asserted their exclusive rights to the object in question. The agreement contains the following preliminary remark:[31]

Through the company 'Olympiade-Film GmbH' – later renamed 'Olympia-Film GmbH' – LR made the two films about the 1936 Olympic Games in Berlin, *Fest der Völker* and *Fest der Schönheit* in several different language-versions, as well as several short sports films. She alone created these films as director, artistic director and manager of the production company – the shares in which were held by her and her brother Heinz Riefenstahl. LR has so far been of the view that she was the sole proprietor of the copyrights and exploitation rights to the Olympia films. Conversely, Transit – which has the task of exploiting the former cinematic assets belonging to the Reich itself – has found documents which Transit believes constitute irrefutable evidence that the copyrights and exploitation rights to the Olympia films were really held by the German Reich, and that LR and her brother only held the shares to Olympia-Film in trust. In response, LR declares that she was hitherto unaware of these documents and that these documents could only have had a formal significance. She points out the possibility that such a trust may have been constructed for tax reasons or on account of other interests which can no longer be determined, and argues that the real proprietary rights relating to the Olympia films remained unaffected. In response, Transit refers back to the documents, which clearly indicate that the German Reich was the owner of the copyrights and exploitation rights.[32]

Irrespective of the obvious differences and in order 'to enable continued exploitation of the Olympia films without disruption', the agreement of 16 January 1964 contained provisions stipulating that Transit would cede 'the exploitation of the Olympia films of 1936, including all the associated short films and the archive material' to Leni Riefenstahl, thereby granting her the right 'to describe herself as the owner of the exploitation rights when signing contracts relating to exploitation' of the films. The profits were to be divided, with Riefenstahl receiving 70 per cent and Transit 30 per cent. Claims each Party had made against the other in the period before 1 January 1964 were to be set aside. The agreement was to remain in force for a period of three decades: '30 years after the date this contract comes into force, the rights relating to usage return to Transit.' It was agreed that the details of the contract would remain confidential between the parties.

After the dissolution of Transit-Filmvertrieb GmbH, the company which succeeded it continued to respect this contract. The Aktiengesellschaft für Filmverwaltung i.L. (Joint-stock Company for Film Administration (In Liquidation)) sent several reminders to

Riefenstahl concerning outstanding payments which referred to the agreement. The company took a similar stance in its dealings with the Bundesarchiv, although here it encountered a different interpretation of the story:

> After the state-owned Olympia-Film GmbH was dissolved on the instigation of the Reich in 1941, the Olympia films passed into the direct ownership of the Reich. They should therefore now constitute a part of the package which, in the contract of 28/30.6.1966, passed to the West German state and which is currently administered by Transit-Film-GmbH, Munich.[33]

This response caused the plot to thicken still further. The new company, the Aktiengesellschaft für Filmverwaltung i.L., operated as a trustee on behalf of the West German state – just as Transit-Filmvertrieb GmbH had done (until its dissolution). This new trustee now found itself notified by the Bundesarchiv that the contract concerning *Olympia* did not, despite the apparently diplomatic balance achieved in its preliminary remarks, represent a final clarification of the situation with regard to the rights to the *Olympia* films and their exploitation.

The 'Transit Film GmbH' named in the letter of 17 January 1968 is *not* identical with the dissolved 'Transit-Filmvertrieb GmbH' (despite the fact that the same abbreviation, 'Transit', which used to designate the former continues to designate the latter). Rather, it was a new company, the upshot of failed attempts to found a new film production company from the Ufi Film stock. The task of the new Transit Film GmbH was (and still is) to exploit the rights relating to the former Reich's state-owned assets.[34] In 1968 the new company became active, evidently at the instigation of the West German Interior Ministry, and turned its attention to the dispute regarding the succession to the old Transit-Filmvertrieb GmbH. Its aim was to achieve a resolution to the issue of the rights to *Triumph des Willens* and *Olympia* favourable to its own interests. First it wrote to Ufa Film GmbH:

> . . . In a letter of 8.1.1968, the Interior Minister cites §§ 1 and 6 of the weekly newsreel contract and bids us take appropriate steps in order to secure the [West German] Federation's exploitation rights to the films 'Triumph des Willens' and

'Olympiade 1936'. May we therefore request that you send us the files in your possession relating to the film 'Triumph des Willens' for our inspection.[35]

An answer was sent immediately, emphasizing that Ufa Film GmbH had never 'claimed the copyright and exploitation rights to the film "Triumph des Willens"':

> The Bundesarchiv instigated detailed legal investigations and concluded that this film was almost certainly an NSDAP production. As far as we are aware, the exploitation rights are exercised by the Bundesarchiv . . . With regard to the film 'Olympiade 1936', Transit and we have so far taken the common view that this film does not come under the provisions of the weekly newsreel contract of 28/30 June 1966 and is not covered by the decision of the liquidation committee of 1 April 1966, as it does not involve footage from PK [army 'Propaganda Company'] reporters or old German weekly newsreels, but rather full-length films. We request clarification of the facts which have now led you to a different interpretation of the legal position.[36]

This question did indeed require clarification, as it was clear that Transit Film GmbH's initiative was primarily concerned not with *Triumph des Willens*, but rather with *Olympia* (which was referred to by the wrong name throughout almost all the correspondence).

Next, Transit Film GmbH turned to the administration company for films, the *Aktiengesellschaft für Filmverwaltung*. This time the subject of its letter was ' "Olympiade 1936" ' (no reference at all was made to *Triumph des Willens*):

> The Interior Ministry has instructed us, within the scope of our management in trust of the Federal film assets, to take appropriate steps in order to secure the Federation's exploitation rights to films including the two films made about the 1936 Olympic Games ('Fest der Völker' and 'Fest der Schönheit'). We were able to gather from the documents which Frau Riefenstahl made available to us that Transit-Filmvertrieb GmbH signed an agreement with Frau Riefenstahl on 16.1.1964. This stipulates that Frau Riefenstahl holds the exploitation rights to the film until January 1994, whilst

Transit-Filmvertrieb GmbH is entitled to 30 per cent of the proceeds from exploitation. We were also able to discover that your company now handles business dealings with Frau Riefenstahl. Before we institute further investigations pertinent to our task, we request that you inform us of the reasons for not applying the regulation in § 8 of the contract Treuko/ BRD of 28/30.6.66 in the agreement with Frau Riefenstahl.[37]

The reaction was one of prevarication, but Transit did not give up and 'respectfully requested' that the Aktiengesellschaft respond to its position.[38] Finally in the reply of 15 April 1969 the other side (this time signing itself Ufa Film GmbH) capitulated:

The content of your letter of 14.4.1969 is accurate in every respect. Some time ago already we forwarded a draft contract to the Federal Interior Ministry, which would provide for the withdrawal of the two films from the list of those administered by the liquidator of Ufa Film GmbH.

The whole, somewhat absurd saga of the infighting between various agencies operating in trust for the Federal Republic, each armed with a different interpretation regarding the rights to *Olympia*, finally seemed to be over. The contract sent to the minister specified:

There has so far been uncertainty among the signatories to the contract about whether the two Olympia films 'Fest der Völker' and 'Fest der Schönheit' . . . were transferred to the Federal Republic of Germany. In its meeting of 5.2.1969, the Ufi liquidation committee considered this matter and determined that documentary films are subject to the decision of 1.4.1960, and that documentary films also include full-length films without a dramatic plot. The two Olympia films mentioned above are full-length films of this sort.[39]

To start with, it had seemed that *Triumph des Willens* was the main bone of contention; within a year, the focus had switched to *Olympia*, and both films were now defined as the property of the Federation – albeit only by the state's own agencies, which had not always shown all their cards during the dispute. In formal terms, the consensus was only made possible by invoking the decision of the Ufi liquidation committee, which in fact related exclusively to (wartime) weekly newsreels.[40] The differences which had been resolved were not between Leni Riefenstahl and her potential adversaries in a lawsuit, but rather between those potential adversaries themselves. It would now have been reasonable to expect the Federal Republic to pursue its rights against Frau Riefenstahl. Whether it actually did or not remains unclear, due to the thirty-year rule for files of the Federal authorities. It is known, however, that – despite the position adopted by the Federal Interior Ministry in 1968 – a contract was signed in 1974[41] between Transit Film GmbH and Leni Riefenstahl regarding the use of *Triumph des Willens*. It is also clear that, although the 1964 contract stipulated that all rights to *Olympia* should pass to Transit Film GmbH on 1 January 1994, this did not happen. Transit's supervisory board does not appear to have negotiated any extension to the agreement in question.[42] The question remains of whether and when the Federal Interior Ministry changed its position and what information might have caused it to do so. No information on these matters is forthcoming from those involved.

Today, Transit Film GmbH only authorizes showings of *Triumph des Willens* after consulting Leni Riefenstahl. This has regrettable but more or less inevitable consequences. The first example came in 1979, when the director refused to approve an application by the Berlin Free Democratic Party (FDP) to show the film at an event against the rise of neo-Nazism.[43] Similar difficulties impede the use of the film in university courses or political education work. Riefenstahl's restrictive attitude also prevented the showing of excerpts from the film at the large exhibition dedicated to twentieth-century art in Germany ('Das XX. Jahrhundert. 100 Jahre Kunst in Deutschland'). It is quite evident that the Federal government has given up the attempt to claim exclusive rights to the two films, and in fact it is questionable whether administering those rights on its own would have been in its political interests – particularly in the case of *Triumph des Willens*.

Even if the government had managed to win an unavoidable legal battle against Riefenstahl, what political advantage would have come of it? Showings of the films or excerpts from them could have come back to haunt the government which authorized them. Any criticism – sparked above all by screenings of *Triumph des*

Willens, but also of *Olympia* – would be directed at the government instead of Transit or Riefenstahl herself, as it would have had to take unequivocal charge of the copyright and thereby responsibility for the use of the material. It is easy to see that such a prospect might seem less than alluring. Even the application from German rock band 'Rammstein' to use excerpts from *Olympia* would probably have proven problematic. Whatever company or institution was chosen to administer the rights for the Federal Republic, its management would surely have had to consult the supervisory board in such instances, and it in turn would have had to consult the relevant ministry.[44] The Federal Supreme Court verdict may have clarified the legal situation, but the television broadcast of *Triumph des Willens* showed that sticking to the letter of the law would have entailed a host of difficult decisions. If a court case had been won, somebody would have had to determine, on behalf of the Federation or in its name, which documentaries should be allowed to use excerpts from the Party Rally film and at what price, and in which circumstances Riefenstahl's films might be shown. Who would that have been?

It is a matter for conjecture whether such considerations really did play a part. What is certain is that, in this case at least, the generally less than transparent treatment of National Socialism's cinematic legacy worked out to Leni Riefenstahl's advantage.

CHAPTER TWELVE

A Renaissance – But No Rehabilitation

Leni Riefenstahl's second volume of photographs had already appeared by the time she returned from Sudan in 1977, after an expedition destined to be her last for some time. She had needed only 'a few extra scenes and the new photographs for *GEO* [magazine]'.[1] Publication of the Nuba books a few years previously had restored her high public profile – although some of the attention she received was of a new and critical kind. In the 1970s and early 1980s serious consideration was finally given to the aesthetic and political significance of Riefenstahl's *work*. It had always been Riefenstahl herself, through her obstinate-seeming insistence on her own innocence, who had caused most offence. Now, at last, her work and its function began to be examined independently of her personality. The idea of 'everyday fascism' now seemed vital in order to understand not just the lives of the majority, but also the careers of particularly prominent individuals. Riefenstahl had always protested her political naïvety, and for the first time people seemed ready to consider the possibility that such an interpretation really might be helpful in understanding certain aspects of the propagandist.

In the Public Eye

The slogan of 'fascinating fascism', coined by Susan Sontag, signalled a new interest in Riefenstahl, although Sontag's essay contained several errors and was based on a contention that came to seem increasingly problematic.[2] Once again, Riefenstahl was regarded as a symbolic figure, but this time her symbolism was not seen in an exclusively negative light. In the 1970s, at least, she enjoyed a hitherto unimaginable degree of success. Along with her two books, several special issues of cinema magazines appeared, as well as numerous tributes in the German press to mark her seventieth and seventy-fifth birthdays. She was honoured at film festivals and received invitations from television stations – which also, for the first time, broadcast some of her films.

The decisive year was 1972. Riefenstahl celebrated her seventieth birthday, and all the main newspapers published lengthy articles about her career and her films. It was the year of the Munich Summer Olympics, and once again she was present at the Games, observing the various competitions. This time she represented the *Sunday Times*, and was without the huge team she had led back in 1936; her position was based instead on her own reputation as a photographer. Even before the great sporting occasion began, *Olympia* was shown at a Munich cinema, as if in anticipation of her appearance. It was a considerable popular success. It had also been intended to show the film in Berlin, but vigorous protests had been organized in the former capital of the German Reich. In the end, following objections from the umbrella organization of associations representing the victims of Nazi persecution, the screenings at the Zoo-Palast cinema were cancelled. The different reactions in the two cities probably had much to do with the announcement that the director was to make an appearance at the cinema in Berlin:

> One has to ask, moreover, whether it was wise to organize a press conference with Leni Riefenstahl a few days before the film was shown, announcing her attendance at the first matinee event. There has been publicity for the film in the show-case in front of the Zoopalast for some time which has not apparently aroused any opposition.[3]

Riefenstahl the person thus remained a thorn in the eye of at least some sections of the public, but responses to the film itself were very different. Only a few critics viewed it as propaganda; they were greatly outnumbered by positive voices. Two years after the controversy in Berlin, when the third programme of the northern

German broadcaster NDR showed *Fest der Schönheit* (the second part of *Olympia*), there was no comparable outcry.[4] The 'best sports film of its kind' convinced a new generation of audiences that it was one of the 'great achievements of cinematic history'.[5] The film might seem strange and outmoded, but it continued to overwhelm its audiences:

> This film is a monumental event, in every sense of the word. Far from being a propaganda film for the Third Reich, it revels in the beauty of the human body and attempts to use it to reawaken a sensuality which fell victim long ago to the process of alienation.[6]

The new admiration for *Olympia* and Riefenstahl's commission to photograph the Olympics led commentators to talk for the first time of seventy-year-old Riefenstahl's comeback – her 'renaissance'. Wolf Donner published a carefully considered article in *Die Zeit*, justifiably criticizing the 'far from creditable' attitude of the post-war German press towards Riefenstahl. At the same time, he noted that Riefenstahl herself was 'so untroubled by political considerations that it takes one's breath away even today'. In his discussion of *Olympia*, he paid homage to the 'abstract montages', 'the treatment of the "sound backdrop", revolutionary for its time' and the 'retouched image of sport'. That image, he observed, was 'stylized and aestheticized'.[7] He was probably the first prominent German commentator to pay tribute to the form of the film without lapsing into uncritical eulogy. Only after his article, did people in Germany really begin to look at Riefenstahl's work in a way which attempted to do justice to its stylistic brilliance whilst also taking its political function into account.

This was the start of a process which has yet to be concluded. Only if Riefenstahl's films are also seen as aesthetic constructions, only if the style underlying those constructions is recognized, is it valid to speak of 'fascinating fascism'. Before the 1970s, if only because of the lack of opportunities to see the films themselves, examinations of her work rarely went beyond the comforting but false assertion that both Riefenstahl as a person and the films she made were infected by the same disease: National Socialism. Only when the example of *Olympia* brought the formal quality of her work to people's attention and when Riefenstahl ceased to be dismissed without further ado as a fascist did other, more troubling questions emerge. These concerned the relationship between art and ideology, between artists and morality. Could there really be such a thing as Nazi art which was not downright bad and unspeakably kitschy? Could there be such a thing as a work of art which was also Nazi propaganda? And how should an artist who achieved such a thing be regarded?

The publication of Riefenstahl's Nuba books threw up another issue: how much continuity was there in her work? This was a question Siegfried Kracauer had already asked with regard to the period before 1933, since when it had generally been answered by, at least implicitly, linking the Party Rally films to the mountain films (*Bergfilme*). Now the same question had to be asked about the period after 1945, for *Tiefland* was produced before the fall of National Socialism. It was quite clear that, far from being new, the 'Riefenstahl aesthetic' exhibited in the Nuba books was basically the familiar one; they were provocative precisely because of their brilliant stylization.

By realizing that Riefenstahl's films were of aesthetic merit the public had, in effect, forced itself to confront a problem that had remained comfortably hidden so long as the director was regarded as a symbol of evil. 'Where is the "missing link" between Riefenstahl and the Nazis?'[8] asked one commentator. One way of answering the question was to separate subjective political convictions from the message of the films,[9] a strategy which by no means excluded the possibility that an unpolitical artist had been used for political ends. According to such a view, Riefenstahl's guilt meant, above all, the inherent irresponsibility of an apolitical individual.[10] Such an approach made it possible to concede Riefenstahl's mastery as an artist whilst also making the perfectly fair observation that her mastery involved repeating only a few basic models. This restored Riefenstahl's reputation as an artist, but still left her under a somewhat smaller cloud of guilt. If the popular image of Riefenstahl in the years immediately following the war was of a 'culprit' or at least a 'conniver', the new image was of an 'unwitting director' – a director, however, whose narrow-minded, apolitical outlook meant that she was partly to blame.

The monster image, heavily laden with symbolism, which had been so enthusiastically constructed in the post-war years, thus gave way to a more banal kind of figure. There was nothing threatening about Riefenstahl's new image, but her films now seemed all the more threatening in their own right. They had hitherto been overshadowed by the 'guilt' of their director; now they acquired a new independence as aesthetic products worthy of serious attention. The idea of 'fascinating fascism' implied a form of seduction which arose solely from the aesthetics of the films. Riefenstahl's longed-for 'renaissance' made her socially acceptable again, but it was accompanied by a new need to engage with her films. The number of detailed critiques of *Olympia* in 1972 is a clear indication of that need.[11] For Riefenstahl, this did not represent the total vindication she had always expected, but rather a change in the kind of questions she was asked. Previously, she had in effect been made to deputize for the whole Nazi regime and take responsibility for what happened under it. Now the public wanted to hear her apologize and express regret in a manner appropriate to what was seen as the 'share of the guilt' she had acquired by her 'unpolitical attitude'. Such demands, however, were utterly at odds with her whole temperament, and they were also incompatible with the legend she had been disseminating for so long.

The transformation in the general view of Riefenstahl was a subtle one. Her earlier accusers tended to assume Riefenstahl's guilt without much ado *because* she had made the films. Now, by contrast, interest was focused on the questions of *why* she had made the films, *why* she had failed to see the truth about the dictatorship. She found herself confronted with such questions – and probably taken by surprise – when she appeared on the chat show *Je später der Abend* . . . . The programme was produced by WDR, hosted by Hansjürgen Rosenbauer and broadcast live by ARD (the main public broadcaster in West Germany) on 30 October 1976. It was Rosenbauer's final show in the series and turned out to be altogether out of the ordinary. It was grist to the mill of the conservative press, which was delighted to see the end of the controversial presenter. The ambitious choice of some particularly distinguished guests to mark the occasion betrayed a degree of recklessness: those invited were a political singer-songwriter (Knut Kiesewetter), a committed seventy-year-old trade unionist (Elfriede Kretschmar) and a seventy-four-year-old film director and photographer (Leni Riefenstahl).

At the start of the 1970s, the new distinction between the apolitical artist Riefenstahl and her ideological films – between understandable, albeit lamentable, complicity on the one hand and contemporary documents on the other – seemed to make a new kind of discussion possible. This was doubtless what the programme makers had in mind when they issued the invitations, but even the guests they had chosen were unable to skirt round one particular question. It was a question Riefenstahl had never before encountered so directly in Germany: 'Why did you do it?' The image of the unpolitical artist was not altogether without drawbacks: if it was accepted, her work would henceforth be subject to purely aesthetic scrutiny, but otherwise she was destined to remain problematic. In this case, the question acquired a sharper edge: instead of 'why', it became 'How could you have?' The ensuing conversation was dominated by the same question, and Riefenstahl failed to give any answers. She probably had none to offer. Her outrage was evidently undiminished by the time she came to write about the chat show in her memoirs. Not for the last time, she treated a public appearance as a celebration of her as a person and of her work, rather than as an opportunity for explanations and justification. Only at a late stage during the programme did she realize the – entirely foreseeable – predicament in which the questions had left her: 'I cannot explain why I did it – that's impossible.' That, however, was what her questioners wanted to know. It was, moreover, an inevitable question in the wake of the new attitude towards Riefenstahl. Since nearly everybody now agreed that Riefenstahl had behaved unpolitically and had been neither a Nazi nor a racist, there had necessarily to be an alternative explanation for her collaboration in such patently propagandist films.

Leni Riefenstahl failed to see the chance this public discussion offered her. She probably could not even comprehend it. She pursued the same strategy she had already adopted in countless interviews, insisting on the identity between her as a person and her films. For her everything seemed very simple: she was an unpolitical director, ergo she made unpolitical films. Her fellow guests did not object to the embellishments she made to her story – she claimed, for example, to have spent over three years in prison and in camps after the war. It was simply that they did not understand the logic of Riefenstahl's equation, and they therefore also failed to understand why there could be no debate. Rosenbauer's last chat show deserves to be remembered as a public object lesson in mutual misunderstanding. *Bild* newspaper later provided a poetic description: 'As the spotlights dimmed there was an embarrassed silence in the studio. Suddenly Rosenbauer found himself alone. Even the stage-hands avoided him. The cold buffet organized to mark his departure was called off.'[12]

It is worth noting that most of the telephone calls to WDR and most of the readers' letters to the magazines were supportive of Riefenstahl.[13] This may have been a result of her final remarks in the programme, when she spoke of the shock she felt on hearing of the reports from the concentration camps after the war. Her world fell apart, she said, 'to the extent that I – and other people too, I believe – will never be able to recover'. Yet the scars which, according to her, would never heal would also never coax from her an admission that she was guilty of turning a blind eye, of not wanting to know.

The chat show, which brought together two elderly ladies who had led utterly dissimilar lives and two relatively young left-leaning intellectuals, seemed to have set itself the goal of forcing this confession from Leni Riefenstahl in front of a six-figure audience. Yet the fundamental flaw of the show was that its very composition militated against any such confession. That composition made candid conversation most unlikely, particularly since Riefenstahl, who told the story of her life as though it were pure melodrama, seemed in one respect to have modelled herself on Scarlet O'Hara – another character who preferred to leave thinking for another day.

In her almost total refusal to heed the calls for her to make a believable admission of her mistakes or to concede her guilt, Riefenstahl also demonstrated the poor tactical awareness of an egocentric. Riefenstahl felt that she was being unfairly treated above all because she had been invited, as she claimed, on a very different basis:

> The WDR editor in charge, Herr Wulffen, told me he did not want a political discussion, it was to be a discussion about my

work: about the sensational photographs in my new book about the Nubas and about my expeditions. I told Herr Wulffen quite clearly that I did not want to talk about politics, as I have been involved in enough of that in the course of three decades . . . And as far as my art is concerned, in that regard Frau Kretschmar . . . was no partner at all for me. My art and my destiny mean nothing to her, so she was unable to summon any understanding.[14]

Elfriede Kretschmar could not understand why the director had gone on to work on the Party Rally films after making *Das blaue Licht* (which had apparently impressed Kretschmar greatly) and she asked Riefenstahl what had led her to do so. Riefenstahl did not understand that she was supposed to answer the question; she could not comprehend that the chat show was not a forum for paying homage to an individual but rather an opportunity to represent oneself in conversation with others. Instead of taking that opportunity, she defended herself – and this led, as ever, to a general offensive.

Towards Cult Status

Ironically enough, although the chat show had been decidedly short on chat, it had said more or less all there was to be said. The headline chosen by *Das Neue Blatt*[15] for its selection of readers' letters concerning the programme, 'We're Standing By Leni Riefenstahl!', signalled a change in the public debate. Ever since the early 1950s, the press had been favouring the director with occasional apologias and profiles of her as a star, but it was only in the 1970s that her symbolism truly acquired its second dimension. Before then she had represented guilt, but now she also became a symbol of unfair persecution. The obligatory articles to mark her birthdays took a softer line, and Riefenstahl began to appear more frequently in interviews, presenting the public with her by then well-established legend.[16]

The proliferation of interviews – featuring mostly the same answers to mostly the same questions – suggests that the public was hungry for such material. Although these conversations tended to reveal little or nothing new, the interest in Leni Riefenstahl did not seem to wane. One after another all the major German newspapers seemed to feature some kind of 'Riefenstahl interview', in much the way that museums all seemed to be acquiring a Warhol screen-print. There were only shades of difference between these interviews, as (despite knowing the answer in advance) every interviewer naturally felt constrained to ask about the filmmaker's views on the moral responsibility of the artist. Questions about the notorious enmity between her and Goebbels were also very popular. The result was that Riefenstahl regularly talked at length about a production which had enjoyed relatively little support from the Nazi Party – *Olympia* – and enlarged on the fact that it was in no way a piece of propaganda. In other words, the conversations became little more than rituals as the interviewers gave up any attempt to get beneath the surface. They should perhaps be forgiven – for what was there left for them to ask that she had not been asked before? Riefenstahl was fond of comparing herself to Marlene Dietrich,[17] who famously complained that she had been 'photographed to death'. In recent years, it could be said that Leni Riefenstahl has been interviewed back to life. This naturally tenacious woman needed the rush of adrenalin provided by the questions: it kick-started her fighting spirit. Self-justification became an expression of vitality. More aggressive questions would probably have invigorated her in much the same way, but in the face of the increasingly obliging way she was generally treated, she made her peace with post-war society and largely refrained from pursuing her own grudges. She even brought herself to make a sort of admission of guilt.[18]

For all her newfound equanimity, there were things which could still upset her, as certain moments in Ray Müller's film portrait, *Die Macht der Bilder* (the English version is entitled *The Wonderful, Horrible Life of Leni Riefenstahl*) make clear. Asked (at the site of the Party Rallies in Nuremberg) about *Sieg des Glaubens*, Riefenstahl initially offered a variation on one of her standard answers and then began to lose her composure. She would have been happy to talk about *Triumph des Willens*, but not about her improvised debut. In her comments she so played down the significance of *Sieg des Glaubens* that she seemed to be trying to bury it completely. The little woman energetically shook her director in a physical indication of how unwelcome the topic was to her. This was the Leni Riefenstahl of *Olympia* all over again: infuriated by every obstacle. Her outrage was equally evident when Müller confronted her with the Goebbels diary entries for 1933 relating to meetings with Riefenstahl and discussions about a 'Hitler film'. None of this was true! Never – at this point she could no longer constrain herself to remain seated on the sofa – never had she visited Goebbels privately. The longstanding, carefully maintained legend of continual obstruction from her sworn enemy did not crumble even in the face of Müller's direct assault. Either Riefenstahl's memorably incensed reaction was evidence of how firmly entrenched her version of events had become – to the point that it was quite invulnerable even to verifiable objections – or it was one of her greatest achievements as an actress. Seldom has she been so challenged.

Although research into cinematic history produced a detailed picture of the circumstances in which Riefenstahl's films were produced, this had no effect on the structure of the public debate concerning her. The number of friendly voices rose, the attacks decreased, indifference predominated. One after another, as if by force of habit, interviewers approached the elderly lady and put their questions to her – but even if they harboured any hopes of finding out something new, they never did. Riefenstahl's public image thus became established as one of controversy personified. At some point the vehemence of the criticism directed at this utterly steadfast individual seemed to exhaust itself, until even the journalists themselves began to notice with some astonishment just how tame their colleagues had become when faced by the spirited old lady. Reports of Riefenstahl's press conference in February 1999 contain many surprised references to how restrained the questions were. Far from constituting a real question-and-answer session, the occasion turned into what one newspaper punningly dubbed the 'birth of Leni Riefenstar'.[19]

Yet it was not as if there had been no arguments about Riefenstahl in the quarter of a century since the first Nuba book. In fact it is fair to say that the understandable political criticism of the early post-war years was often based on mistaken assumptions, while subsequent, more detailed proof regarding the director's relationship with the Nazi regime played a lesser part in the public debate. The vehemence of the critics was already subsiding by the time her new books of photographs appeared, and the publication of underwater photographs left advocates of the 'fascist aesthetics' angle at something of a loss: can a photograph of a coral really be 'fascist'?

The past did, however, catch up with Leni Riefenstahl once more. Her civil case against Nina Gladitz received more attention than any of the other litigation in which she had been involved. Gladitz's film *Zeit des Schweigens und der Dunkelheit* (A Time of Silence and Darkness) revived the issue of the circumstances concerning the making of *Tiefland*, and by the time of the trial, at least, Gladitz had stronger arguments to offer than Helmut Kindler had done in 1949. Part of Riefenstahl's version of events collapsed: the Maxglan camp was not a 'welfare centre of a unique kind, led by criminal investigation police and welfare management', as Anton Böhmer, former chief of the Salzburg criminal investigation police (*Kriminalpolizei*), had claimed. Riefenstahl had enthusiastically cited this witness's statement following the verdict against Kindler, but she had failed to mention that Böhmer was a *Sturmbannführer* (equivalent to a major) in the SS and had in that capacity signed the list of 'gypsies' used in the making of *Tiefland*.[20] The police were indeed in charge of the camp, which meant that in formal terms it was not a concentration camp (for which the SS would have been responsible). Nevertheless:

> The routine in the camp involved forced labour, inadequate food, makeshift accommodation and the most extreme restriction of personal liberty. The rigid order in the camp and the threat of possible transfer at any time to concentration and extermination camps were important disciplinary tools.[21]

The first session of this civil action received very much more press coverage than the appeal. Riefenstahl's comment on the final verdict was:

> It is the same as the initial finding. The defendant Gladitz is prohibited from showing her film unless the Auschwitz allegations relating to me are cut from it. She is permitted, however, to go on claiming that the gypsies were 'forced to work' and not paid and that I selected them myself in

Maxglan. Despite the fact that the latter claim, in particular, could not be proved in the trial, the judges still decided in favour of the defendant Gladitz. This was because they did not view her allegations as defamation which could diminish my reputation. An incomprehensible verdict.[22]

Die Zeit took a different view: 'This judgment, for which detailed grounds were given, is an acceptable one.' It was, however, not entirely satisfied by the strictly juristic evaluation of witness statements unfavourable to Riefenstahl:

[The judges] should for once have looked beyond Leni Riefenstahl's courtroom tears and her wailing about the injury to her honour. She, as the beneficiary of the fact that the gypsies were already in the Maxglan concentration centre. . . – she could surely have been expected (in the successor state, founded on the rule of law) to put up with testimony which was imprecise in minor matters regarding what was, for [them], a thoroughly disagreeable film.[23]

It is to the court's credit that it did no such thing; it stuck conscientiously to its remit – which did not involve reassessing the past. The judges' duty was to consider only whether certain allegations in Gladitz's film were slanderous to Riefenstahl – they were not meant to clarify any wider issues in their judgment.

The real problem was, in any case, a more fundamental one. What mattered was not whether Riefenstahl had personally selected the gypsies in the camp, but rather her attitude in retrospect towards the ultimately undeniable fact that her extras did indeed come from a camp. It is perfectly conceivable that making the film was less arduous than the other kinds of forced labour they endured – but it was forced labour nevertheless. Subjectively, perhaps, Riefenstahl really was unconscious of bearing any guilt, as she did nothing blameworthy herself – except in once again making the most of the opportunities thrown up by the Nazi regime. Indeed, it could even be argued that everything she did until 1945 was, in a certain sense, understandable. After the war, the core of the problem *with* Leni Riefenstahl had relatively little to do with the clarification of her function and role within the Nazi system. Rather, the powerful symbolism she acquired in the post-war debate was due to the fact that her approach to her own life story revealed a layer of impenetrable armour.

Riefenstahl seemed to forbid herself even to think about the way she had benefited from the regime, representing herself as an artist whose successes had been achieved in spite, rather than because, of the Nazi dictatorship. This in itself was scandalous enough in the light of the financial backing her films had enjoyed from the Party or state, and the situation was exacerbated by her reaction to criticism concerning the Konskie massacre and the camp internees from Maxglan. The really astonishing thing about the debate concerning Leni Riefenstahl, however, is that her armour-plating has caused so little offence in the course of the last decade. The last time her protective layer came to the fore as a constituent in the Riefenstahl legend was when her memoirs appeared, and this was the last time it caused people to regard the incorrigible director with horror.

> Even today she bears an invisible emotional coat of armour. Whenever the master race's most talented propagandist is confronted with the possibility that she actually contributed to the mass hysteria of 'holy Germany', and that she therefore bore a share of the responsibility for the mass misery caused by that Reich, she reacts with fury and outrage – never by grieving or looking back in a way that might lead towards self-understanding and a desire to atone.[24]

The memoirs demonstrated once again that Riefenstahl was never going to address the link between a privileged position and a share of the responsibility, and they gave rise to a suspicion that the problem was not necessarily a purely moral one. It was perfectly true 'that even today the old lady has yet to see through this curtain which she has woven for herself and which she mistakes for her life'.[25] It now seemed possible to view her rigid refusal to allow herself to reflect on art and responsibility as a kind of amorality which was far from unusual in certain artists, and to explain her tenacity as the blind loyalty of an artist to her own vocation. The shift towards a more apologetic view of Riefenstahl as a great but naïve figure took hold abroad earlier than it did in Germany. Advocates of such a view were unfazed by all the things about Riefenstahl which might seem difficult to reconcile with such naïvety: her extraordinary business acumen, her ambitious cultivation of important contacts, her calculated, almost mechanized formal language and her evident determination to turn her works into popular successes.

From as early as the 1950s, there was anger and fear in Germany about the 'Riefenstahl renaissance' whenever one of her projects seemed to be close to completion. The renaissance began to be accepted as a possibility, and ceased to be viewed as a threat, in the 1970s. Only in the 1990s, however, did it become a reality, when a series of exhibitions and retrospectives, along with fictional adaptations of her life story and attempts to film them, combined to make it impossible to overlook Riefenstahl's ongoing influence. She modelled for Helmut Newton, not merely inspiring his photographs but also influencing the aesthetics of advertising. Rammstein used *Olympia* in a pop video, and the Italian magazine *L'Espresso* launched a successful marketing campaign with a 'Riefenstahl issue', featuring a video of *Triumph des Willens* as a special offer.[26]

First there was a rash of retrospective surveys of her work. An exhibition opened in December 1991 in Japan, which defended its complete neglect of the works' context with the motto of 'reassessment'. It isolated the artist from world and artistic history and presented her as a consistent stylist. The exhibition, which made waves even in Germany,[27] did not attempt to 'inform or illustrate or criticize'; in fact it was 'a festival, a celebration of the object of the occasion itself'.[28] This was followed by purely photographic exhibitions in Italy (Milan, July 1996[29] and Rome, May 1997), Hamburg (August 1997) and finally Berlin (May 2000), while the exhibition at the Filmmuseum Potsdam (from December 1998) featured as wide a range of exhibits as the one in Tokyo. None of the exhibitions would have been possible without Riefenstahl's consent and support, and they all shared her own narrow focus on her work. Even in Potsdam, critical asides were more evident in the accompanying publication[30] than in the show itself.

It was probably Riefenstahl's need for a homage which also led her to initiate the documentary film about her life. In fact, Ray Müller's *Die Macht der Bilder* is much more than a mere tribute to Riefenstahl's genius, although it does betray the precarious balancing act which Riefenstahl's collaboration made necessary. The film was only made possible by Müller's ultimately supportive attitude towards his 'star', and he did not attempt to hide his sympathies. Such a balance was vital in any case, as any film which relies to such an extent on the role of its main character needs to give that character some leeway; it cannot afford to distract its audience by permanently intruding. Müller described his own position and the dilemma of the film in an interview:

> She always expected us to make a homage to her – and I always said: if we make a homage, it will never be broadcast. She probably failed to understand that right to the end. I wanted to be as fair, but also as critical as possible. The resulting struggle between the maker and the star colours the whole film.[31]

Thus, in its constitutional respect for its 'star' and its acceptance of the star's version of her story, Müller's film could indeed be said to represent 'belated reconciliation'.[32] In some ways, *Die Macht der Bilder* made it possible for Riefenstahl to play the role of her self.

Yet she did not finally enter the new era – that of posthumous fame within her lifetime – until she became a dramatis persona in other productions. Once again there was a conspicuous lack of anger in the way the fictional, invented 'Riefenstahl' was characterized. After demolishing other legends in previous adaptations, Johann Kresnik disappointed his critics by doing no such thing in his dance theatre production, *Riefenstahl*. His approach seemed 'unexpectedly kind':[33] the long and nervously awaited 'homage'[34] finally appeared from a most unexpected quarter. It was thus by no means inappropriate to invite Riefenstahl to the premiere: 'This was no affront. What was acted out under the title "Riefenstahl" was, after all, not so much a brown witches' sabbath as the visit of the old lady.'[35]

The fictional 'Leni' had an even easier time of it in Thea Dorn's radio play *Marleni*,[36] which was at least based on a witty idea: the old lady, Leni, scrambles up the outside wall to reach Marlene's Paris flat and persuade her to act in her production of *Penthesilea*. The suggestive comparison in the radio play between Marlene Dietrich and Leni Riefenstahl[37] was by no means unflattering to 'Leni'. Dramatic considerations alone required a reasonable balance between the characters in a two-person play. Dorn's perspective orientated itself above all towards two poles: the actress and the director, the woman directed by men and the woman who directed men. Her 'Leni' inevitably emerged with the better part.

Through Kresnik's choreography and Dorn's radio play, Riefenstahl entered pop culture. Although Warhol had already taken an interest in her films, her life itself now became art. The planned films are a further example of the same process. Jodie Foster has plans to use her own company to make a film in which she will play the part of 'Riefenstahl'. German producer Thomas Schüly, well known for his work on difficult and controversial projects such as *Der Totmacher* (directed by Romuald Karmakar), acquired the rights to Leni Riefenstahl's memoirs and is also preparing to make a film.

In retrospect this appears a necessary development: a step forward from the time when 'Riefenstahl' was only ever cited as an example of a failure to engage with the past. It was made possible by the separation of the person from her work: the 'Riefenstahl' who inspired new works of art no longer aroused automatic condemnation. There was increasing wonderment at her vitality, and the incorrigibility which went hand in hand with that vitality began for the first time to seem attractive. The more banal, commonplace facets of Riefenstahl's character came to light, creating a counterbalance to her well-publicized tendency to suppress unpleasant truths. This made her appear more 'normal' – less of a symbolic figure and more of a person. The exceptional phenomenon which had been the female genius of Nazi cinema acquired a new, slimmed-down identity as the female artist in a man's world. In that sense, 'Riefenstahl' shared the fate of many ordinary people, and the public displayed a significantly greater readiness to accept her. In the 1990s she was able to dispense with all the standard lines which had been expected of her even by the time she made her chat show appearance. Now it was the Riefenstahl characters who spoke those lines.

In the same way that Riefenstahl the person lost concrete historic significance to these characters and reformed herself as the classic 'special case' among women artists, a transformation occurred in the way her work was assessed. In losing its relationship to the circumstances in which it was made, it seemed to gain quality. On the occasion of the 'Leni Riefenstahl' exhibition, the Berlin gallery 'Camera Work' sold a selection of fifty photographs at prices of DM2000 and more; all were signed by the director. Most of the pictures were familiar motifs – frame enlargements from *Olympia*. They first appeared in 1937 in the book *Schönheit im olympischen Kampf* (Beauty in the Olympic Struggle), where they were arranged to correspond to the film, and thus according to the cameramen: 'Most of the pictures are enlargements from the Olympia film. The shots of the temples, sculptures and nudes are by Willy Zielke.'[38] The audience at the private viewing in May 2000 did not care about such niceties: their admiration of Riefenstahl as a photographer embraced even photographs she had certainly not 'taken' in the technical sense. They had no quibbles about buying a 'Riefenstahl' which would have been considered a 'Willy Zielke' back in 1937. The new 'persona' was now well and truly established.

CHAPTER THIRTEEN

In Conclusion: A Change of Persona

Inevitably, consideration of Leni Riefenstahl has nearly always concentrated on two outstanding issues: the moral and political evaluation of her work for National Socialism on the one hand, and the aesthetic quality of her works – particularly her propaganda films – on the other. The director herself would have liked precisely those four films and her contribution to Nazi filmmaking to be left out of the equation for a change. She tended anyway to behave as though none of the party rally films except *Triumph des Willens* really existed and to present her career as a Nazi filmmaker as a matter of just seven months' work for Hitler. Her message was destined to fall on deaf ears for many years. It was the propaganda films which dominated every portrait of her, and they will always continue to do so. After all, if Riefenstahl can be said to have achieved something unique, then it was in those films, starting with *Sieg des Glaubens* and ending with *Olympia*. If any aspect of her work is destined to retain its influence in times to come, then it is those stylistic statements. Her whole stature and influence was founded on the films she made under – and largely in homage to – the Nazi regime. The quotations taken from her work – famous takes, perspectives and tracking shots – all come from those films. Sometimes these quotes are treated ironically, but more often they are invoked as authoritative references. Riefenstahl's greatness lies in having been the most innovative filmmaker of the Nazi era.

Today the influence of her work is felt in sports reporting, advertising and in historical films. Neither her feature films nor her photographs will ever rival the significance of those four films. Riefenstahl has taken this personally as an injustice, but it is the consequence of a collective historical memory which will always view the Nazi era as a time during which unique crimes were perpetrated, rather than dismissing it (as Riefenstahl has done) as a short period within the course of a long life. Riefenstahl cannot be personally blamed for any of those crimes – certainly not in a legal sense. The fact that she, as an individual, was 'not guilty' – that she could thus claim to have done no wrong – seemed to her an adequate excuse. Her critics insisted that it was an inadequate basis for a clear conscience. The fact that she was so obviously always at peace with herself was nothing short of provocative. Whatever she may have witnessed or suspected was irrelevant to the way she regarded herself. Like so many Germans, Riefenstahl refused to take account of any arguments other than strictly legal ones when examining her own conscience. She was a symbolic figure for National Socialism, and she inevitably also became one for post-war society. She seems never to have properly understood either role. She accepted honours and privileges as just rewards for her art, but dismissed criticism as personal persecution. Her tenacity was always associated with an astonishingly egocentric attitude – a fact which perhaps makes her reactions understandable. Yet, although her experiences after 1945 were destined to remain bitter ones for a long time, her situation could not be described as tragic. The way she reacted to criticism, controversy and sometimes to slander in the early years after the war merely underlines that point.

There were attempts to completely separate her moral and political responsibility from her aesthetic achievements, but only by early critics who feared a 'Riefenstahl renaissance' (and who refused to recognize that her films possessed any formal qualities) and later by a few apologists for Riefenstahl as an artist (who ignored the way her films give aesthetic design to ideological content). There have been two distinct phases in the reception of her work, each of which produced two very different Riefenstahl 'personae' – two stable constructions of her image. One of them arose immediately after the war and was predominant in Germany until the 1960s; the other began to develop in the 1970s and has been the predominant one since the 1990s. Both 'images' are forms enabling Riefenstahl's symbolic persona to be understood within a certain social consensus; both amount to incomplete appropriations of a 'life and work' viewed as essentially representative.

These constructions played a role – albeit a marginal one – in post-war West German society's process of self-justification, but not in East Germany, which 'saw itself as the final goal of antifascist resistance in the form of a state' and in which, therefore, only a partial 'engagement with individual, even entirely personal, involvement' was possible.[1] For West Germany, however, the structure of Riefenstahl's self-justification – which amounted to the insistence that she had known as little as everybody else and had done nothing wrong – represented an unreasonable provocation. People suspected that the famous director knew more than the average German: so how dare she employ the same excuse? The majority of her compatriots rejected her because they were not truly at ease with their own moral defence: for while the majority might have *suspected* something, it seemed obvious that Riefenstahl must have *known* something.

The truth was that, in general, she had been by no means as unwitting as the great majority of Germans now believed themselves to have been. That fact triggered a sort of projected protection mechanism, which condemned Riefenstahl to hope in vain for a comprehensive absolution. Regardless of how credible her defence might be in detail, it simply could not be acceptable in general. That was why the court cases were so significant, and it was also why the debate sparked by the allegations against Riefenstahl took no account of the real victims – something which today seems astonishing and even horrifying. She was a convenient scapegoat. This explains but does not excuse the public reaction against her – for her failure to examine herself critically was mirrored within the society so eager to inculpate Riefenstahl and thereby symbolically exculpate itself. Nevertheless, it would be wrong to label the director as a victim. It is true that other artists and (above all) many lawyers, doctors, administrators and industrialists might have been inculpated for similar or even more convincing reasons, but to conclude that the accusations against Riefenstahl were therefore all due to conspiracies is to overlook her own contribution to the intractable nature of the debate. Even immediately after the war, when she was interrogated by the US army, she built some patently false claims into her defence; small wonder, then, that her sanitized legend should be contradicted vehemently and continually.

The second Riefenstahl image to be constructed in West Germany defined her as an 'unpolitical artist', as French and British commentators had begun to do somewhat earlier. This approach separated the works from the person – partly in order to understand the aesthetic and ideological significance of the work, but also in order to understand the person. Irrespective of whether the question was formulated in relatively neutral ('Why did you do it?') or more aggressive terms ('How could you have!'), it assumed that Riefenstahl bore the moral guilt of an accomplice rather than a culprit. For the first time, there was recognition of the popular support for Hitler's dictatorship, and the questions directed at Riefenstahl implied, in a sense, that she was no different from many others. They were asked in order to elicit insights into the popular support for the dictator – now that this phenomenon was beginning to be acknowledged – from an artist who had played her part in cementing that support. Yet, amazingly enough, the director refused to answer the questions, or at least not in the way expected of her. Instead, she continued to take the same line as before, maintaining that not only she as a person, but also her work, should be regarded as unpolitical. It is difficult to judge whether her attitude arose from a lack of intellectual capacity or whether it was calculated.

Despite her stubborn insistence on the idea that even the Party Rally films possessed only artistic and documentary – in other words, historical – significance, today her propaganda films, including *Olympia*, are regarded as National Socialism's most refined formal expression of its own ideology. In the public perception, these works and the director stand side by side almost independently of one another – a consequence of the separation of the works and the (naïve) artist. It could be said that the more people know about Riefenstahl's propaganda films, the less important her authorship becomes. Such simplifications, however, underestimate Riefenstahl's significance as the *auteur* of Nazi filmmaking. It may seem both grotesque and futile to wish to discover 'something new' from Riefenstahl concerning the propaganda for which she was responsible: but her creativity, vision and tenacity meant that she was the one person able to make cinematic spectacles out of the Party Rallies and the Olympic Games. It might be argued that anyone could make a memorable film out of 400,000 metres of film – but who else would have been capable of turning the Olympic Games into *Olympia*? Who else could have portrayed the Party Rallies as 'love stories' between Hitler and his people – and also as submission rituals, in which that same people enthusiastically went down on its knees before the Führer?

These days there are few attempts to reconnect the naïve artist and the sophisticated productions she staged. If the films really are 'fascism – felt and filmed',[2] the work and the person certainly belong together. This would solve the dilemma between accepting Riefenstahl as an unpolitical artist on the one hand and examining her carefully constructed ('art-ificial') propaganda films on the other, and it would finally eliminate the element of chance from the Riefenstahl story. It would also guarantee the coherence of the œuvre: all the works would belong together in interdependence. *Das blaue Licht*, for example, would have to be related not just to *Tiefland*, but also to *Triumph des Willens*, which in turn would be seen in the light of not just *Olympia* and the Nuba photographs, but also the underwater pictures. The 'fascism' of her work would not just mean the synergy between an aesthetic founded on classical ideals and a huge event based on mass choreography; rather, it would amount to a fascist outlook on the world. Even the 'heroic reportage' would be no more than a special case within a pre-existent 'fascist sensibility': it would no longer represent a one-off combination of event and temperament, of a pre-filmic, staged event and a neoclassical orientation.

It is, however, much more likely that Riefenstahl's work is neither consistently fascist nor consistently magnificent. Comparisons between Riefenstahl and Eisenstein are popular, but they are fundamentally inappropriate, and not just because of the entirely different ways the masses are portrayed in their films.[3] The comparison is also infelicitous because Eisenstein had a different approach to both propaganda *and* art. In political terms, the crucial difference is that the filmmakers of the Russian Revolution never claimed that their work was not propaganda: on the contrary, they emphasized that it was. Their explicit propagandistic intent is also what tied them to a particular system, triggering the decline in their reputations which has today left them quasi-tragic figures, as the example of avant-garde idol Dziga Vertov shows. In aesthetic terms, however, the decisive factor is that Eisenstein and the others acknowledged their propagandist intent in the way they employed the cinematic techniques at their disposal. On the whole, therefore, they did not regard those techniques as illusionist or 'classical', but rather as disruptive and disturbing: as ways of jolting their audience. Their early films did not aim to engender approval for what they were presenting, or to achieve illusionist acceptance of the way they presented it. In a formal sense, they aimed to provoke.

Leni Riefenstahl's reputation has not suffered any such 'tragic' decline, and nor does her work display the slightest hint of formal provocation. The Party Rally and *Olympia* films are the best, most intelligently made propaganda National Socialism ever produced. Yet Riefenstahl regards such an assessment as slanderous. She insists that the propagandist effect of her work was at most coincidental – it was never her aim, never the result of a purposeful artistic effort. Nevertheless, these films offer the only available measure of the director's greatness. They alone are 'great', simply because they are 'famous'. Their formal qualities, however, account for only a small part of their fame, which has more to do with the events the films depict, the circumstances in which they were made and their functions. Riefenstahl is not the 'cinematic genius' her apologists like to pretend she is. She is the master of transforming mass-participation events into successful films which achieve 'aesthetic effects' without themselves 'being of aesthetic origin'. In other words, the films are great because they are notorious, and Riefenstahl will continue to be regarded as a great director for as long as she too retains her aura of notoriety. For it is true that *Triumph des Willens* and *Olympia* are outstanding films; they are particularly effective and confident and sometimes their construction is not merely perfect but also poetic. The way they are crafted is more convincing than any other art produced under the Nazi regime and as propaganda on its behalf. This implies that Leni Riefenstahl is only 'great' for having been the 'Nazi filmmaker' she has always denied she ever was. It was that role which gained her a reputation she would otherwise have been denied. Without the spice of notoriety, Riefenstahl would have been no more than

Riefenstahl in the flagstaff elevator at the Party Rally

A directors' meeting: Hitler and Riefenstahl studying the schedule for the Party Rally

Covering every spectacular aspect of the event: manufacturing the spirit of the Nuremberg days

Enjoying the enthusiastic response of the masses

Gala premiere of
Triumph des Willens at
Ufa-Palast am Zoo

Riefenstahl receiving flowers
and congratulations after
the premiere of *Triumph
des Willens*

In just the right place: cameraman Walter Frenz on an extended ladder filming personnel carriers for *Tag der Freiheit*

Taking a low-angled shot of marching soldiers for *Tag der Freiheit*. Riefenstahl looks on

The new Wehrmacht reviewed by Hitler, von Blomberg and others. (*Tag der Freiheit*)

Riefenstahl framing a shot for *Olympia*

Working on the prologue to *Olympia* in Greece, 1936

Planning the filming of
Olympia: Riefenstahl and her
crew members

Devising a schedule

One of the most beautiful sequences in *Olympia*: the airborne men of the high-diving sequence

Catching the right moment: shooting *Olympia*

Preparing a staged scene for the decathlon sequence: gold medal winner Glenn Morris and Riefenstahl

Glenn Morris posing as the discus thrower by Myron (*Olympia*)

Premiere of *Olympia* on Hitler's forty-ninth birthday (20 April 1938) at the Ufa-Palast am Zoo

'Dedicated to my Führer with eternal devotion and profound gratitude in memory of the Olympic Games in Berlin. Christmas 1936. Leni Riefenstahl'

Riefenstahl in the editing room

Riefenstahl's villa in Berlin

Hitler and Goebbels visiting Riefenstahl's home (1937)

Riefenstahl in the role of Martha in *Tiefland*

Pedro (Franz Eichberger) and Martha (Riefenstahl) in *Tiefland*

Leni Riefenstahl in Kitzbühel, May 1945

interesting as a director, for her aesthetic ideal was 'harmonious', whilst her approach to stylization was characterized by her lack of interest in ambiguity and contradictions and by her disregard for everyday phenomena and in particular for anything unattractive. Her films do indeed seem 'stylized' and reminiscent, to a point, of advertising art. Her stylistic intent is evident in every picture; the films are free of any ambivalence. She described the editing of her documentaries as a continual process of trial and error, an attempt to make the transitions between the cuts seem 'automatic'. That process is akin to the ideal which informs the montage technique of narrative films. The aim is not to wrong-foot the audience, but to beguile it and win it over. Riefenstahl never wanted to jolt or provoke her audience: throughout her career she pursued a different goal. The romantic 'legend', the 'Nuremberg experience' and the 'beauty of the Olympic competition' were all designed to do one thing: to seduce her audience.

Notes

1 Introduction: The Problem with Leni Riefenstahl

1 *Frankfurter Allgemeine Zeitung* magazine, 25 March 1994.
2 The two films were *Josef Thorak – Werkstatt und Werk* (Josef Thorak – Workshop and Work, 1943) and *Arno Breker* (1944).
3 W. Benjamin (1985), *Gesammelte Schriften*, Vol. 6. Frankfurt am Main: Suhrkamp, p. 321.
4 *Ibid.*, p. 136.
5 *Die Macht der Bilder. Leni Riefenstahl* (English title: *The Wonderful, Horrible Life of Leni Riefenstahl* – directed by Ray Müller, Germany, 1993); *Riefenstahl* (a work of dance theatre choreographed by Johann Kresnik, first performed at the Schauspielhaus, Cologne, on 3 November 1996, text by Andreas Marker); *Stripped* (video by 'Rammstein', 1997).
6 Cf. J. Monaco (1985), *American Film Now: The People, the Power, the Money, the Movies*. New York: Oxford University Press (revised edition: 2000). Monaco identifies a parody of the Party Rally films in the shots of military formations in *Star Wars* (directed by George Lucas, USA, 1977). In his discussion of *The Lion King* (directed by Roger Allers and Rob Minkoff, USA, 1996), Daniel Kothenschulte alludes to 'perspectives copied from Riefenstahl' (*Berliner Zeitung*, 28 November 1996).
7 Thea Dorn's radio play *Marleni. Preussische Diven blond wie Stahl* (Marleni. Prussian Divas, Blonde as Steel) was broadcast for the first time in November 1988.
8 *Variety* quotes Foster as follows: 'There is no other woman in the twentieth century who has been so admired and vilified simultaneously' (6 December 1999).
9 There were no similar protests against the exhibition at the Filmmuseum in Potsdam – presumably because the organizers could not be accused of commercialism, but probably also because the change in the public perception of Riefenstahl had already moved a stage further.
10 For a recent example of an apologetic image of Riefenstahl, cf. A. Schwarzer (1999), 'Leni Riefenstahl. Propagandistin oder Künstlerin?', *Emma*, No. 1, 39–47. Kay Sokolowsky (1999) responded with his polemic 'Die neue Rechte', *Konkret*, No. 3, 12–17.

2 Beginnings

1 L. Riefenstahl (1996), *Memoiren 1902–1945*. Frankfurt am Main, Berlin: Ullstein, p. 36 (henceforth cited as *Memoiren I*). Riefenstahl's memoirs were published in the United Kingdom in a single volume as *The Sieve of Time: The Memoirs of Leni Riefenstahl* (1992, London: Quartet Books) and in the United States as *Leni Riefenstahl: A Memoir* (1993, New York: St Martin's Press). The original of this letter was an exhibit at the Potsdam Filmmuseum exhibition in 1998–9.

2 *Memoiren I*, p. 30.

3 *Ibid.*, p. 33. This must have taken place before spring 1919, when – not least because of the performance – she was sent to a boarding-school in the Harz mountains. She was therefore no more than sixteen years old at the time.

4 Cf. P. Schille (1977), 'Lenis blühende Träume', *Stern*, No. 35, 18 August, 34–43. Schille cites the 'five careers' – dancer, actress, director, photographer, diver – and anticipates a sixth: the writer of memoirs. Cf. also, C. Lenssen (1996), 'Die fünf Karrieren der Leni Riefenstahl', *epd Film*, No. 1, 27–31.

5 *Memoiren I*, p. 61.

6 The brief review is signed 'HB', *Münchener Zeitung*, 26 October 1923, 2.

7 -t., 'Tanz-Abend', in 'Telegramm-Zeitung', *Münchener Neueste Nachrichten*, 25 October 1923.

8 *Memoiren I*, p. 61.

9 In the young dancer's PR brochure, which dedicates seven pages to positive press comments, the quotation from the *Münchener Neuesten Nachrichten* is dated correctly: 12 December 1923. It is, however, edited in the same way as the version reproduced in the memoirs. Cf. *Die Tänzerin Leni Riefenstahl. Auszüge aus Pressekritiken* (n.p., n.d., unpaginated); the sections it quotes are presented here in italics.

10 Riefenstahl hints at an attempted comeback, but in 1925: 'I asked Herr Klamt, my pianist . . . to come to Freiburg, where I recommended my training. The first exercises after the knee operation and after a year's break were very hard. No sooner was I over the worst than I was called away to the film' *Memoiren I*, p. 87. Even in the late summer of 1924, however, she was evidently planning a return to the stage. In a letter from a Dr Otto Pflaum to Oberregierungsrat Heydel (a senior administration official) on 8 August 1924, the former asks whether it would be possible for Riefenstahl to make a guest performance at the Residenztheater, and if so, what costs would arise. 'The dancer would be keen to organize a guest performance at the Residenztheater at the end of September if possible.' 'Excerpts from press reviews about the dancer Leni Riefenstahl' were enclosed with the letter – probably the PR brochure with the same title. The inquiry was turned down, as was the one from the Leonhard concert promotion agency (the date stamp indicates this was received on 12 September 1924). The agency put together 'a tour for the excellent dancer, Leni Riefenstahl' and sought additional engagements to follow dates between October and January which had already been arranged (Bayerisches Hauptstaatsarchiv, Staatstheater file, 12123).

11 *Berliner Tageblatt*, 21 December 1923. The text is reprinted in F. Hildebrandt (1925), *Tageblätter*, Vol. 1 1923/24. Berlin: Landsberg-Verlag, pp. 139–40. As far as I am aware, the first commentator to draw attention to this text was Claudia Lenssen (1999), 'Leben und Werk' in Filmmuseum Potsdam (ed.), *Leni Riefenstahl*. Berlin: Henschel, pp. 23–4. She does not, however, quote any other contemporary critics. Other descriptions of the early career completely fail to examine the source material. The passage in Hildebrandt's review not quoted here contains particularly negative opinions.

12 The distortion of critical comment is not limited to the examples cited above. The thoroughly negative reviews (such as those in: *Vossische Zeitung*, 1 November 1923; *Vorwärts*, 31 October 1923; *Kölner Tageblatt*, 17 March 1924) were, of course, omitted entirely. There are carefully trimmed versions of other quotations. The *Neue Zürcher Zeitung* wrote: 'Leni Riefenstahl is certainly not an outstanding, grippingly individual dancer, but her performances do bear the stamp of high culture and decent taste; the latter is appealingly evident not least in the costumes, which are free of arty extravagances' (21 February 1924). For obvious reasons, the advertising brochure does not quote the start of the sentence.

13 J. Schikowski (1923b), 'Mit der Wünschelrute', *Vorwärts*, 16 November.
14 In her memoirs Riefenstahl quotes the review by Franz Servaes (1923), 'Eine neue Tänzerin', *Der Tag*, 29 October.
15 *Kölner Tageblatt*, 17 March 1924.
16 *National-Zeitung*, 17 December 1923.
17 *Deutsche Allgemeine Zeitung*, 29 October 1923.
18 *Münchener Neueste Nachrichten*, 25 October 1923.
19 *Züricher Post*, 22 February 1924; quoted from *Die Tänzerin Leni Riefenstahl*.
20 *Kämpfer*, Zürich, 24 February 1924.
21 *Ibid.*
22 J. Schikowski (1923a), 'Animalisches und seelisches Temperament', *Vorwärts*, 31 October.
23 *Deutsche Zeitung Bohemia*, 29 November 1923. The article is signed with the abbreviation 'à.st'.
24 *Ibid.*
25 This took place in a Berlin underground railway station, Nollendorfplatz. Her first full description of the moment (to which she has frequently alluded) and of her similar reaction to the film itself, was in L. Riefenstahl (1933), *Kampf in Schnee und Eis* (A Struggle in Snow and Ice). Leipzig: Hesse and Becker, pp. 10–11.
26 A. Fanck (1973), *Er führte Regie mit Gletschern, Stürmen und Lawinen*. Munich: Nymphenburger.
27 According to her memoirs, after leaving school at the age of 16 she was approached several times by directors who wanted to screen-test her or engage her for their films. 'But I always resisted such temptations, because such plans seemed too good to be true. One director would not give up; he and his wife followed me every day. Eventually I gave in. Behind my father's back, with the help of my mother, I spent a few days filming. In a small studio room in Belle-Alliance-Strasse, I played the role of a young charcoal burner's girl. I cannot recall the name of the director in question, I just remember that he prophesised that I would have a great future', *Memoiren I*, p. 29.
28 'After a break of one and a half years, I am back on stage again. I start at the Schauspielhaus in Düsseldorf. The first dances are uncertain. When I return for the second half of the programme, however, I have completely lost my heaviness. I am a success once again. Nevertheless, I feel depressed. I have to admit to myself that I have failed to make progress. I have not moved on from before. People expected more from me . . . At the Deutsches Theater in Berlin . . . I taste real success again. I have overcome all my inhibitions . . . It almost seems as if I am going to return to dancing . . . And then, suddenly, the film is there again' Riefenstahl (1933), p. 26.
29 *Memoiren I*, p. 65. Here, as elsewhere in her memoirs, Riefenstahl fails to give dates. However, she places the offer during the time of her dancing tours, which means between October 1923 and, at the latest, mid-1924. Filming took place between August and October of 1924, which fits her version. Cf. W. Jacobsen (1989), *Erich Pommer. Ein Produzent macht Filmgeschichte*. Berlin: Argon, p. 176.
30 H. Bock (ed.) (1984 ff.), *CineGraph. Lexikon zum deutschsprachigen Film*. Munich: edition text und kritik (entry for Leni Riefenstahl, p. F1). Also, K. Kreimeier (1992), *Die Ufa-Story*. Munich, Vienna: Hanser, p. 296; H.M. Bock and M. Töteberg (eds) (1992), *Das Ufa-Buch*. Frankfurt am Main: Zweitausendeins, pp. 132 and 152 ff. On page 153 of the latter volume there is a publicity photograph in which one of the scantily clad actresses is identified as Leni Riefenstahl. Claudia Lenssen is more sceptical, arguing that Riefenstahl's involvement cannot be proved (Lenssen (1999), p. 116). Leni Riefenstahl has told the author that she had nothing to do with the film, even denying that she ever saw it. C. Ferber (ed.), *Der Querschnitt*. Berlin: Ullstein, p.

31 also reproduces the photograph and the accompanying caption. In the original edition, however, only the photograph appeared: the actresses were not identified.

31 American grotesques were certainly inspirational models for Fanck's two comic films, *Der weisse Rausch* (The White Rapture) and *Der grosse Sprung* (The Great Leap), and the final scene in *Der grosse Sprung* quotes from the ending of Keaton's *Three Ages* (1923).

32 It has been compared to a death-mask, E. Rentschler (1996), *The Ministry of Illusion. Nazi Cinema and its Afterlife.* Cambridge, Mass., London: Harvard University Press, p. 36.

33 Hertha von Walther, who played the female lead in Fanck's *Berg des Schicksals* as a modern, sporty, ambitious woman, is reduced to helplessness by the end of the film. The only options left open to her are crass clichés. Riefenstahl always managed to avoid such belittlement. Horak describes her (in the context of *Der grosse Sprung*) as 'the archetypal phallic woman, before whom every man can only kneel' (J. C. Horak (1997b), 'Dr Arnold Fanck: Träume vom Wolkenmeer und einer guten Stube', in J. C. Horak (ed.) (1997a), *Berge, Licht und Traum. Dr Arnold Fanck und der deutsche Bergfilm.* Munich: Bruckmann, p. 36. T. Brandlmeier, 'Sinnzeichen und Gedankenbilder', in *Berge, Licht und Traum,* p. 81, describes Riefenstahl's specific double-role: 'In American westerns the role she plays is divided between the school-ma'm and the Mexican woman, the passive and the active, the saint and the whore, the woman you love and the woman you desire. She plays two female abstractions rolled into one.'

34 Along with the scenes from *Tiefland,* the shots from *Der heilige Berg* are the only surviving evidence of Riefenstahl's qualities as a dancer. Unfortunately, they do not offer a basis for conclusive judgements. Slow-motion shots have a distorting effect, whilst cuts fragment the continuous movement. John Schikowski thought the way the dances were adapted to the requirements of a two-dimensional medium was remarkable. Riefenstahl 'adapted her *Traumblüte,* for example – a dance we are familiar with from the stage – for the cinematic perspective. Her movement is now almost always from left to right or vice versa. She avoids any engagement with the depth of the space. This means that, although the superficial form is very different, the original rhythm is preserved. And as the composition folds wonderfully together towards the climaxes of its final position, a perfect work of art develops. It is at least as effective as the original dance on stage', 'Der Filmtanz', in *Vorwärts* (undated cutting, Filmmuseum Potsdam, Riefenstahl file). It is true that this dance makes the most harmonious impression. It is also less interrupted by cuts (which Schikowski also lamented).

35 The caption reads: 'But the friend storms off to get his overwhelming feelings under control. He rushes away – high into his mountains.'

36 The captions are '(Diotima:) "Have you come from up there? (Trenker removes the pipe from his mouth.) It must be beautiful up there." – (The friend:) "Beautiful, hard and dangerous!" – (Diotima:) "And what does one look for up there?" – (The friend:) "Oneself." – (Diotima:) "And nothing else?" – (The friend:) "And what are you looking for up here . . . in nature?" '

37 In various articles for *Film-Kurier,* Riefenstahl described the difficult conditions in which filming took place, betraying a subliminal scepticism about the need for such hardships. Cf. the issues of 21 December 1927, 4 November 1929, 27 May 1930 and 17 July 1930. Her book *Kampf in Schnee und Eis* (1933), dedicated mainly to the filming of *S.O.S. Eisberg,* first appeared as a preprint in the magazine *Tempo,* and excerpts were also printed in other newspapers. It appears that *Der weisse Rausch* was an exception to the rule among the films she made with Fanck: in her memoirs, at least, she mentions no ordeals during the filming.

38 Riefenstahl (1933), p. 39. The equivalent passage in the memoirs is *Memoiren I,* p. 98.

39 The two German fragments are held by the Bundesarchiv Filmarchiv, Berlin. The Italian version was restored by Film-Archiv Austria, Vienna.
40 Although Riefenstahl claims that the filming took place in Schönbrunn Castle, the surviving scenes offer no evidence whatsoever for this. Cf. *Memoiren I*, p. 104.
41 According to her memoirs she was surprised and delighted 'finally to be offered an interesting role in a film which Fanck was not producing', but was so ill with diphtheria that her role had to be shortened to the extent that she was only needed for six days of filming. *Memoiren I*, p. 104–5.
42 Even Fanck himself seems to have profited from the collaboration: in *Stürme über dem Montblanc* and *S.O.S. Eisberg* the expositions are exceptionally concentrated and lead in much more directly to the dramatic situation than in any of his previous films.
43 *Memoiren I*, p. 98 and Riefenstahl (1933), p. 39.

3 The Film *Auteur* Emerges

1 Reviews of such films typically praised the photography whilst regretting the quality of the plot. The more subtle analysis by Béla Balázs – 'Der Fall Dr Fanck', in B. Balázs (ed.) (1984), *Schriften zum Film*, Vol. 2. Berlin: Henschel, pp. 287–91 – was a rare exception. On Balázs cf. also H. Loewy (1999), 'Medium und Initiation. Béla Balázs: Märchen, Ästhetik, Kino'. Frankfurt am Main: MS (diss.).
2 In 1933 she remembered realizing even at a very early stage – while she was viewing the screen tests for her role in *Der heilige Berg* – 'that I had to find out all about the technology – that cinema is nothing without technology. I am itching to discover these secrets already, to start experimenting today or tomorrow, to busy myself with all the incredible possibilities and surprises of film technology right away, in *Der heilige Berg*. But it is still too early. I only know that first I have to look and learn for a long while. And indeed, several years pass before I succeed in imposing my will on a film. Not until *Das blaue Licht*, the film that was to become entirely my own, did I manage to work with the same dedication as in *Der heilige Berg*', L. Riefenstahl (1933), *Kampf in Schnee and Eis*. Leipzig: Hesse and Becker, p. 15.
3 'Underlying these rejections was the notion that even though Leni Riefenstahl was a fine athlete, she was really a minor acting talent, besides which she had had no previous experience in directing,' P. Wallace (1974), 'The most Important Factor was the "Spirit": Leni Riefenstahl During the Filming of "The Blue Light"', *Image*, Vol. 17, No. 1, 18.
4 Quoted by Wallace, *ibid.*, 21.
5 There are various indications that Balázs directed the scenes involving Riefenstahl as an actress and that Carl Mayer contributed to the script.
6 When the film was relaunched, the *Film-Kurier* (No. 224, 24 September 1938) described *Das blaue Licht* as a 'film created by a collective of one woman and six men'. This article, of course, did not mention Balázs or Harry Sokal. Both had already emigrated.
7 Leni Riefenstahl (1933), pp. 24 and 30. Cf. also *Film-Kurier*, No. 171, 24 June 1926, which quotes Riefenstahl (discussing *Der heilige Berg*) as follows: 'I have every reason to call it my own. It is not just that I play the main part in it. I was also involved in the direction, working together a great deal with my director, Dr Fanck.'
8 Riefenstahl (1933), p. 39.
9 'Curiously, it is not just the form of the acting which so fascinates me, but something else as well. I have studied the camera and the lens; I am familiar with the film stock and the filter. I have edited films and have a sense of how new effects can be achieved. Despite myself, I am increasingly drawn to these things. I resist, for I am an actress, after all, and do not wish to fragment myself. Nevertheless, I cannot change

the fact that I see everything through the eyes of a filmmaker. I would like to create pictures myself. I see mountains, trees and human faces quite differently in particular moods and movements,' *ibid.*, p. 67.

10 *Memoiren I*, p. 137.

11 *Ibid.*, p. 138.

12 *Ibid.*, p. 139. From the 1987 perspective, it seems that it was only difficult financial circumstances which forced her to become more than an actress – to take sole responsibility for a film and construct it herself. 'Because of the limited financial resources, I had decided to take over the direction myself,' *ibid.*, p. 142.

13 Riefenstahl (1933), pp. 70–1 and *Memoiren I*, pp. 142–3.

14 Cf. F. Grafe (1985), 'Leni Riefenstahl. Falsche Bauern, falsche Soldaten und was für ein Volk', in F. Grafe, *Beschriebener Film: Die Republik*, No. 72–5, 41, and E. Rentschler, (1996), *The Ministry of Illusion. Nazi Cinema and its After-life*. Cambridge, Mass., London: Harvard University Press, pp. 27 ff.

15 The plot of *Das blaue Licht* is a simple one. Ever since a landslide, a blue light has emanated from Monte Cristallo at full moon. It is the reflection of the moonlight from crystals in a cave near the summit of the mountain. The painter, Vigo, who wishes to spend a few days in the village, discovers that four youths have already died this year attempting to climb the mountain at full moon. Only Junta knows of a safe route, a fact that earns her a reputation as a witch in the village. When another young man falls to his death, the villagers start stoning the outsider, Junta, who only escapes thanks to Vigo's intervention. She flees to her hut, where she lives together with a shepherd boy. Vigo visits her there and falls in love with her. At the next full moon Junta leaves the hut as if sleepwalking; by following her up the mountain, Vigo finds the route to the grotto. At the same time a villager, Tonio, attempts the ascent, but he falls. Vigo returns to the village and makes a sketch for the farmers, upon which they rush en masse to the grotto and plunder its crystals. Junta comes across fragments of the crystals on her way to the village; horrified, she climbs Monte Cristallo and finds the grotto completely ransacked. She stumbles as she makes her descent, and Vigo finds her corpse as he makes his way elatedly back to her after the celebrations in the village.

16 Leni Riefenstahl enjoyed reading fairy-tales, not just in her youth. Cf. *Memoiren I*, p. 17.

17 *Memoiren I*, pp. 137–8, p. 151. In 1932 the magazine *Tempo* published a portrait of the star as Junta, knocking six years off her age.

18 'In *Das blaue Licht*, as if in a premonition, I told the story of my subsequent fate: Junta, the strange mountain girl, who lives in a dream world and is persecuted and rejected, perishes because her ideals – in the film these are the glittering rock crystals – are destroyed. Until the early summer of 1932, I too had lived in a dream world, ignoring the harsh reality of the age and hardly aware of events such as World War I with its dramatic consequences,' *Memoiren I*, p. 151.

19 In the framework story a couple arrives at the remote village and repeatedly comes across references to the Junta legend. Their landlord sends for an old book, in which they discover Junta's story. In formal terms that story is a flashback: only in the 1951 version did it come to occupy the whole film. Cf. Rentschler (1996), p. 46.

20 In this the film differs from one of the sources which inspired it. In Gustav Renker's *Bergkristall* (Rock Crystal), Gütersloh: Bertelsmann (n.d., but first published in 1930), blue light from a mountain grotto (which 'appears at midnight when the moon is full', p. 45) also plays an important part. The main character is a painter (!) who suspects that the effect may be due to reflection from the rock crystal. When an expedition sets out to solve the mystery, its members agree not to plunder the grotto. The reflection eventually turns out to come from a mountain lake within a cave.

21 Contemporary critics occasionally mocked Riefenstahl's fondness for symbolic scenes such as this one.

22 The 1932 version of the film highlights this more clearly. Before Vigo finds Junta's hut, the camera gradually pans to focus on Riefenstahl's legs – effectively presenting them as the main attraction in the landscape. In addition, the scene in which Vigo sketches his partner begins earlier in the 1932 version. It opens with Vigo chopping wood. He glances at Junta, outstretched on the grass, and is so fascinated by what he sees that he decides to draw her.

23 Hermann Sinsheimer wrote a very negative review, entitled 'Zwei Legenden' (Two Legends), in the *Berliner Tageblatt*, 26 March 1933. He spoke of an 'inwardly sick film'. The positive reactions, however, were much more numerous. The *Film-Kurier*, No. 73, 26 March 1932, offered a paean of praise: 'A film to be ranked alongside the unforgettable greats. On Maundy Thursday, at its first showing, its transporting effect was unmistakable. By the time the lights came on, the audience had tasted life in another world. Everyday life was slow to reassert itself. A brave woman, trusting in her work and in her obsession, had made the faded cinematic sky fall in. Above us shone the moon and the dubious nights of the mysterious mountain landscape. Leni Riefenstahl has achieved what she was striving for: a unique film-poem.'

24 *Memoiren I*, p. 150.

25 The Tobis press-pack for the film's re-release in 1938 read as follows: 'Seldom has a film received such a mixed reception at its premiere (at the end of March 1932) as this one. Although it was a considerable and ongoing popular success, the press reaction was overwhelmingly negative – apart from a few Aryan exceptions among the reviewers. The treatment the film received from the Jewish press, however, can only be described as calculatedly malicious. This tactic ensured that the film was largely wasted, and that only a relatively small section of the German public ever even saw it.'

26 Riefenstahl (1933), p. 6.

27 S. Kracauer (1947), *From Caligari to Hitler. A Psychological History of the German Film*. Princeton, N.J.: Princeton University Press, pp. 258–60.

28 The film was never made because of the government's general reservations about themes involving espionage. Ufa, the production company earmarked for the film, was sceptical in any case: 'The board has decided only to sign a contract with Leni Riefenstahl after her artistic qualities have been subjected to careful scrutiny, which should be undertaken in absolutely objective terms' (*Protokoll* of the board meeting of 5 September 1933, BA R 109 I/1029a), p. 101.

4 A New Kind of film: *Sieg des Glaubens*

1 This and the following quotations are from 'Urlaub zur Premiere' (Time Off for the Premiere) in *Illustrierter Beobachter*, No. 37, 16 September 1933.

2 'At the premiere . . ., Leni Riefenstahl raises her hand in the Hitler salute on stage after the film. Paul Kohner will never forgive her that gesture. Paul Kohner suffers a nervous breakdown and retires to Marienbad to take a cure'. Horak (1997b), 'Dr Arnold Fanck: Träume vom Wolkenmeer und einer guten Stube', in J. C. Horak (ed.) (1997a), *Berg, Licht und Traum. Dr Arnold Fanck und der Deutsche Berg Film*. Munich: Bruckmann, p. 49. Kohner's widow confirmed Riefenstahl's gesture when she was interviewed for the television documentary *Der Agent von Sunset Boulevard*.

3 On 18 May 1932, the *Film-Kurier* referred to the impending departure of the expedition 'at the end of the month', and it reported Riefenstahl's return to Berlin on 28 September.

4 F. Moeller (1999), 'Die einzige von all den Stars, die uns versteht', in Filmmuseum Potsdam (ed.), *Leni Riefenstahl*. Berlin: Henschel, p. 145.

5 'Yesterday: wonderful trip to Heiligendamm. Picnic a failure. Wonderful lake! With the boss. Also Leni Riefenstahl. Marvellous trip home' from the Goebbels diaries: E. Fröhlich (ed.,) (1987), *Die Tagebücher von Joseph Goebbels*. Part 1, Vol. 2. Munich, London, New York, Oxford, Paris: K. G. Saur, p. 424; entry for 26 May 1933. Regarding Riefenstahl's visit to Goebbels, see entry for 16 August 1933, p. 458.

6 *Ibid.*, p. 421, entry for 17 May 1933.

7 *Ibid.*, p. 433.

8 Both Martin Loiperdinger (1993), '*Sieg des Glaubens*. Ein gelungenes Experiment nationalsozialistischer Filmpropaganda', in U. Herrmann and U. Nassen (eds), *Formative Ästhetik im Nationalsozialismus*. Weinheim and Basel: *Zeitschrift für Pädagogik*, Supplement 31, p. 36, and Moeller (1999), p. 146, mention Riefenstahl's meeting with Goebbels, but they draw different conclusions from the reference to a 'Hitler film'. Loiperdinger draws a continuous line from the discussion of a 'Hitler film' project in May to the filming of *Sieg des Glaubens* in September 1933 and concludes: 'in any case, work on the project began as early as spring 1933'. Moeller sees the diary entries rather as a reference to a project that was never subsequently realized, being abandoned for unexplained reasons. As a result, Loiperdinger views the Goebbels diary entries as a strong indication that Riefenstahl had a far longer period to prepare for her first Party Rally film than she herself claimed, while Moeller does not share the assumption that preparations for *Sieg des Glaubens* began as early as June 1933. 'At least, notes about the planning of a political film project from May 1933 onward suggest that another Party Rally film was under discussion before *Sieg des Glaubens* – a "Hitler film", as Goebbels calls it – which then only turned into the spectacle of the Nuremberg Rally at a late stage. This certainly dispels one myth: the one that Leni Riefenstahl nearly always discussed her film projects exclusively with Hitler, causing Goebbels to oppose them out of jealousy.'

9 *Memoiren I*, pp. 204 ff.

10 There was a complete 16mm copy of the film in the 'Staatliches Filmarchiv' of the former East Germany. It remains a mystery why this was not publicized even after the debate surrounding the incomplete version and in particular after Germany's unification. I am indebted to Kerstin Stutterheim for informing me of the copy and for making her draft transcript available to me. *Sieg des Glaubens* is one of the themes in her book: K. D. Stutterheim (2000), *Okkulte Weltvorstellungen im Hintergrund dokumentarischer Filme des "Dritten Reiches"*. Berlin: Weissensee.

11 *Memoiren I*, pp. 212–13.

12 Loiperdinger (1993), p. 36.

13 'On the instructions of the national leadership of the Reich propaganda administration Division IV (Film), a film is to be made of the NSDAP Party Rally in Nuremberg. At the Führer's special request, Fräulein Leni Riefenstahl will be the film's artistic director. The general supervisor will be the leader of Division IV (Film), Pg. [Party Member] Arnold Raether, and Pg. Eberhard Fangauf will be in charge of technical organization. After detailed discussions with Pg. Raether, Miss Riefenstahl will travel to Nuremberg next week to undertake preparations for the film', *Film-Kurier*, No. 199, 25 August 1933. There was a similar report in *Kinematograph*, No. 164, 1933.

14 Similarly, in the following year it was announced only just before the opening of the Party Rally that she had overall charge of *Triumph des Willens*, although preparations had begun much earlier.

15 *Licht-Bild-Bühne*, No. 200, 1933.

16 Cf. Loiperdinger (1993), p. 38. On 23 November 1933, the *Nationalsozialistische Parteikorrespondenz* reported that Riefenstahl only found out about her new

appointment four days before the Party Rally began. Loiperdinger sees this as a kind of precautionary excuse, in case there was criticism of the film's quality. 'And, as if there was a desire to head off objections to Riefenstahl's Party Rally film in advance, it was emphasized before the premiere that: "Her job was not made any easier for her. The Führer's commission arrived just four days before the beginning of the Party Rally, meaning that it was not even possible . . . to make preparations for important, decisive, indispensable shots." '

17 'The artist was commissioned some time ago to turn her hand to the new Party Rally film too, making it possible to begin already with preparations for the film', *Film-Kurier*, No. 195, 21 August 1934. The *Lagerzeitung des Deutschen Arbeitsdiensts* (No. 8, 1935, p. 2) similarly notes: 'But while *Sieg des Glaubens* necessarily ended up as an "extended weekly newsreel", having been made without preparation time and without the necessary personnel, *Triumph des Willens* will be constructed in exemplary fashion, "with all the extras" so far as direction, film technology and the niceties of post-production are concerned'.

18 An article in *Filmwoche* can be interpreted along similar lines: 'Leni Riefenstahl, the creator of *Das blaue Licht*, was entrusted with this task by the Führer. She was in the town where the Party Rally took place from the start of the preparations. Thanks to her foresight and the skill of her cameramen, it was possible to capture the whole context of the event, thereby achieving a wider, more profound perspective than that of the sober, prosaic weekly newsreel, –s: 'Der Sieg des Glaubens', *Die Filmwoche*, No. 50, 1933. The question is: what does the 'start of the preparations' actually mean?

19 Peter Warneke suspects that the Film division's hostility was sparked by rumours suggesting Leni Riefenstahl might be of Jewish descent: cf. P. Warneke (1998), 'Recherche für die Ausstellung "Leni Riefenstahl"'. N.p. (Potsdam): MS, p. 39. To me it appears that the Party men's antagonism had a great deal to do with the fact that a woman had been given the job.

20 Cf. *Licht-Bild-Bühne*, 30 August 1933 and *Kinematograph*, No. 171, 5 September 1933.

21 *Film-Kurier*, 31 August 1933 (original emphasis).

22 The *Völkischer Beobachter* constitutes an exception. In that newspaper's interview with Riefenstahl, which was carried by the *Licht-Bild-Bühne* on 1 September 1933, it credits her with 'overall responsibility for the filming'. Cf. Loiperdinger (1993), p. 38, n. 5.

23 Cf. *Licht-Bild-Bühne*, No. 208/209, 1933. When Hess and Raether visited the possible locations for filming, the *Film-Kurier* (No. 205, 1 September 1933) only referred to Riefenstahl as one of six others who were 'also present'.

24 *Film-Kurier*, 4 September 1933.

25 A. Speer (1969), *Erinnerungen*. Frankfurt am Main, Berlin, Vienna: Ullstein, p. 74. Riefenstahl also mentions being denounced to Hess, cf. *Memoiren I*, p. 207.

26 BA BDC-RKK Leni Riefenstahl. The report is signed 'v. Allwörden' and is addressed to Party Member Auen (Director of the Film Department). On 8 September, Raether wrote to Hinkel: 'Your letter regarding Riefenstahl was forwarded to me on my holiday. I had brought the matters, of which I too was aware, to Herr Hess's attention in Nuremberg. He decided to investigate the case. From Berlin I learn that it has not been possible to discover anything detrimental to her regarding her descent . . . One thing is certain: until 1 year ago, even Fräulein Riefenstahl still knew nothing about National Socialism. And her landscape films – or rather, the landscape films created by the expert members of her crews – were only made for commercial reasons.' Lenssen (1999) observes that in her reminiscences Riefenstahl does 'not question a matter such as the exclusion of non-Aryan artists'; rather, Riefenstahl reserves her indignation 'for the "machinations" against her person by top Party functionaries in the propaganda ministry.' ('Leben und Werk', in Filmmuseum Potsdam (ed.), *Leni Riefenstahl*. Berlin: Henschel).

27 'Here a trained National Socialist has to be behind the camera, someone who knows what it is all about, whose heart is in it and for whom the camerawork – and the enormous effort required to cope with the endless list of duties in Nuremberg – is a way of thanking the Führer and the movement itself', *Film-Kurier*, 8 September 1933.

28 Cf. S. Dolezel and M. Loiperdinger (1995), 'Hitler in Parteitagsfilm und Wochenschau', in M. Loiperdinger, R. Herz and U. Polhmann, *Führerbilder. Hitler, Mussolini, Roosevelt, Stalin in Fotografie und Film*. Munich, Zürich: Piper, pp. 77 ff. In his look back, Arnold Raether (1943) 'Die Entwicklung des nationalsozialistischen Filmschaffens', *Der deutsche Film*, Vol. 7, No. 7, 6) mentions that in the 1932 election campaign 'shorts of the speeches by the Führer, Hermann Göring and Dr Goebbels were filmed on new, as yet unpatented sound-film equipment which was, however, "accessible" to us'.

29 Fröhlich (1987), p. 432, entry for 12 June 1933.

30 *Film-Kurier*, 11 October 1933.

31 *Ibid.* On 24 October the same magazine wrote: 'Leni Riefenstahl has been entrusted with the most powerful material conceivable, which the National Socialist movement wishes to set before the whole people as a document for all time.' The sheer amount of work performed by the director, which would also earn her praise in her subsequent films, was first drawn to the public's attention with reference to *Sieg des Glaubens*.

32 Leni Riefenstahl in an interview with the *Film-Kurier*, No. 277, 25 November 1933.

33 'Adolf Hitler, surrounded by his loyal staff, descends the giant flight of steps like a king: not a king with a crown, but a king of work and duty. His hand soars massively into the picture: this is no longer a stereotypical salute, but rather a symbol of the blessing bestowed upon the Hitler Youth' ibid. This passage also appears, almost word for word, in the film's programme notes.

34 *Film-Kurier*, No. 239, 11 October 1933.

35 *Film-Kurier*, No. 281, 30 November 1933.

36 P. Hagen (1933), ' "Der Sieg des Glaubens". Die Welturaufführung des Films vom Reichsparteitag', *Angriff*, 2 December.

37 The *Film-Kurier* (No. 283, 2 December 1933) employs the metaphor of a 'cinematic oratorio'; there was talk of the '*Eroica* of the Reich Party Rally' and a 'pictorial symphony' even before the premiere (*Film-Kurier*, No. 250, 24 October 1933).

38 Occasionally parallels were also drawn with other representative, large-scale forms: 'The film never comes across as a reportage. It seems more like a historic, monumental painting, to be regarded with due solemnity', *Reichsfilmblatt*, No. 49, 1933.

39 Cf. Loiperdinger (1993), pp. 47–8, on the relationship between *Triumph des Willens* and *Sieg des Glaubens*: 'A year later it seemed as if the 1933 film was always waiting in the wings; it was used as a comparison over and over again.'

40 *Film-Kurier*, No. 239, 11 October 1933.

41 Cf. M. Loiperdinger and D. Culbert (1988), 'Leni Riefenstahl, the SA and the Nazi Party Rally Films, Nuremberg 1933–1934. "Sieg des Glaubens" and "Triumph des Willens" ', *Historical Journal of Film, Radio and Television*, Vol. 8, No. 1, 3–38.

42 Loiperdinger (1993), p. 48.

43 *Ibid.*, p. 46.

44 Loiperdinger and Culbert (1988) provide an overview and divide the film into 'scenes'. These correspond to the 'sequences' in the present volume, but the numeration is different, as Loiperdinger and Culbert were working on the basis of the incomplete version and could not take the first sequence into account. Here, 'sequence 2' therefore corresponds to their 'scene I'.

45 Loiperdinger and Culbert (1988) stress the politically calculated message of *Sieg des*

Glaubens and regard Marpicati's appearance as a reference to the 'triumph of Fascism' in Italy.

46 Preparations in Nuremberg (1), Hitler's arrival at the airport and journey to the hotel (2), reception at the town hall (3), opening of the Party congress in the festival hall (4), review of the *Amtswalter* (Party Leaders) at the Zeppelin meadow (5), review of the Hitler Youth in the stadium (6), parade of various Party sections on the market square (7), tribute to the fallen, review of the SA, SS and *Stahlhelm* (the 'Steel Helmet' units), consecration of the flag (8).

47 Examples of these well-constructed stylistic elements include Hitler's journey in an open car into the city, his appearance at the hotel window in response to the crowd's appeals, the idealized eye contact between Hitler and individual representatives of the units on parade (achieved by intercutting between shots and reaction shots). Loiperdinger (1993), p. 47, also refers to 'the review of the *Amtswalter*, the Hitler Youth rally and the march past at the main market square' as scenes which occur in both films in nearly identical form. 'All the innovations in cinematic aesthetics with regard to photography and cutting which define the style of *Triumph des Willens* are already clearly evident in *Sieg des Glaubens*.'

48 Examples include the 'feature film scenes' (as Loiperdinger (1993), p. 47, calls them) – the scenes in which cutting from a shot to a reaction shot achieves a relationship between Hitler and his individual followers.

49 For example when people in the background on the speaker's platform move through the picture, when the tips of the standards behind Hitler noticeably sway, or when Röhm fiddles with the belt of his uniform during Hitler's speech.

50 For more on this see Loiperdinger and Culbert (1988). The prominent part played by Röhm in *Sieg des Glaubens* and the emphasis it placed on his special relationship with Hitler made it impossible to use the film after Röhm's murder. It also features representatives of the Italian fascists, members of the government (such as Goebbels, Göring and von Papen) and the diplomatic corps, regional NS leaders and even the then largely unfamiliar figure of Albert Speer (twice with his wife).

51 The city awakens, decks itself (with flags), prepares for the event (the stands are erected and the streets cleaned) and finally receives its visitors (SA troops in the city and on the march).

52 Riefenstahl did not, of course, invent this enthusiasm: there is plenty of evidence of the 'spontaneity' in Nuremberg. Cf. C. Lenssen (2000), 'Unterworfene Gefühle. Nationalsozialistische Mobilisierung und emotionale Manipulation der Massen in der Parteitagsfilmen Leni Riefenstahl', in C. Benthien, A. Fleig and I. Kasten (eds), *Emotionalität. Zur Geschichte der Gefühle*. Cologne, Weimar, Vienna: Böhlau, pp. 198–211. I am grateful to the author for making her manuscript available to me before it went to print.

5 The *Auteur* of Nazi Filmmaking

1 'Leni Riefenstahls Abschied von Nürnberg', *Fränkische Tageszeitung*, 13 September 1934. The following quotations are from the same source. 'PO' denotes the NSDAP's 'Political Organization'.

2 Riefenstahl claims that, following completion of the work in Nuremberg and immediately after suffering a nervous breakdown, she told Streicher that she found his anti-Semitic attitude distasteful. (*Memoiren I*, p. 207). The oft-quoted, but rather dubious note on Hotel Kaiserhof letter paper ('I grant Gauleiter Julius Streicher of Nuremberg – editor of the *Stürmer* – power of attorney with regard to the claim made by the Jew, Belá Balács, against me. Leni Riefenstahl' 11 December 1933, BA BDC/ RKK Leni Riefenstahl) might suggest a different kind of relationship, as might

Streicher's letter of 17 July 1937 to Riefenstahl, in which he delights in his recollections of her new house *(ibid.)*

3 'Julius Streicher besucht die Tobis', *8-Uhr-Blatt* (Nuremberg), 26 February 1938. The following quotation is from the same source.

4 There are occasional claims that the film was not a popular success, but they are clearly inaccurate. By 31 May 1935 – within two months – the film had earned 815,000 Reichsmarks (BA R 109 I/1030b, p. 83). Ufa considered it one of the three best films in the production year 1934/35 *(ibid.,* p. 112).

5 M. Loiperdinger (1987a), *Rituale der Mobilmachung*. Opladen: Leske und Budrich, p. 83.

6 To this end, Riefenstahl opted not to follow the chronological order of the Rally. 'It is not important that everything should appear on screen in the correct chronological order. The structural concept involves taking account of the actual experience of Nuremberg and instinctively identifying the coherent way forward, thereby structuring the film in such a way that each successive act and impression takes the listeners and viewers higher and higher,' L. Riefenstahl (1935a), *Hinter den Kulissen des Reichsparteitags-Films*. Munich: Eher, p. 28. After the war, Riefenstahl stated that Ernst Jäger had written this text. There is a corresponding receipt in the files (BDC-RKK, Riefenstahl file). This hardly means, however, that Riefenstahl was not responsible for the text: she described it as hers when it was received into the *Reichschrifttumskammer* (Reich Chamber of Literature).

7 The opening address by Hess and then the speeches by Frick, Lutze and finally Hitler include hints to this effect. The audience could hardly have missed their significance. Kanzog therefore even imputes a 'ritual significance' to the film and sees it as a political catechism for (re-)instilling Nazi dogma: K. Kanzog (1995), 'Der Dokumentarfilm als politischer Katechismus', in M. Hattendorf (ed.), *Perspektiven des Dokumentarfilms*. Munich: Schaudig and Ledig (= *diskurs Film*, Vol. 7), pp. 57–84.

8 Cf. S. Neale (1979), ' "Triumph of the Will". Notes on Documentary and Spectacle', *Screen*, Vol. 20, No. 1, 63–86.

9 Cf. the *Protokoll* of the Ufa board meeting of 28 August 1934: 'The board approves the signing of a distribution contract with Leni Riefenstahl as the special authorized representative of the NSDAP's Reichsleitung [the Party directorate] . . . Fräulein Riefenstahl has artistic and technical responsibility for the film, having been appointed by the Führer in the name of the NSDAP's Reichsleitung according to a letter of 19.4. 34. According to a letter of the same day, Miss Riefenstahl has 300,000. – RM at her disposal. The Führer has given his approval for the film to be distributed by Ufa,' BA R 109 I/1929b, p. 28.

10 Riefenstahl (1935a), p. 16.

11 The description in her memoirs of the planning for *Triumph des Willens* is inconsistent on this point. Riefenstahl claims to have selected Ruttmann to direct the film *(Memoiren I,* p. 217), and only to have discovered in mid-August that Hitler wanted her to be the director. She then inspected Ruttmann's footage and rejected it as useless *(ibid.,* p. 221). 'Nearly two weeks were' still available, and she claims that within that time she 'finally did manage to get eighteen cameramen together' *(ibid.,* p. 223). These claims do not tally with the source material.

12 This is well documented in the Riefenstahl file in BA BDC-RKK. Riefenstahl wrote to Karl Auen, head of the film department: 'When my secretary contacted Herr Schünemann by telephone, Herr Schünemann said he was busy, but asked which film he was being considered for. To this my secretary replied that it *(sic)* was being considered for the Reich Party Rally film. The response to this was another question: this doubtless meant the film which Leni Riefenstahl was making? When an affirmative answer was given, Herr Schünemann said: "I would not do that on

principle, it is below my dignity." Since I regard this comment as a belittlement of my work, with which the Führer has entrusted me, I consider it my duty to inform you of it. I leave it up to you to state your point of view on the matter' (17 August 1934). Schünemann, having been questioned by Auen, claimed that his objection was to working under any woman on principle (later he said that this was merely an evasion), and did manage to pacify Auen. Riefenstahl, however, was not mollified, and she responded that she 'would just like to make it clear that I understood his remark in precisely the sense he described to you – but that does not alter the fact that Herr Schünemann's comment amounts to a boycott against the Führer. The Führer has given me overall artistic responsibility and I therefore feel duty-bound to hire cameramen and other crewmembers who are answerable to me in artistic matters. If the Führer does not feel it beneath his dignity to give me overall artistic responsibility for this project, it is curious, to put it mildly, if Herr Schünemann feels it beneath his dignity to recognize that fact. It would be impossible for me to fulfil the Führer's commission if other crewmembers also adopted Herr Schünemann's attitude. That is why I felt it necessary to inform you about the matter' (29 August 1934). This was certainly the most distasteful manifestation of Riefenstahl's absolute self-assurance, founded on Hitler's appointment of her, and it is characteristic of the way she approached her own story that she should fail to mention the incident altogether in her memoirs, although it had long since become public knowledge.

13 In one of her ingenious attempts to construct myths about herself, Riefenstahl claimed in an interview with Michel Delahaye (September 1965), 'Entretien avec Leni Riefenstahl', *Cahiers du cinéma*, No. 170, p. 62) that she had never had any artistic collaborator or co-director. Ruttmann, she said, did not shoot a single metre of film in *Triumph des Willens* or *Olympia*. Quite simply, he was not present while those films were being shot. If only the material actually used in the films is taken into account, Riefenstahl's claims are true to the extent that only the text for the opening of the film originated from Ruttmann. They are not true of the production of the film in general. In her memoirs, Riefenstahl no longer insists that Ruttmann was 'not even present'. Brandt blames 'Leni Riefenstahl's egocentric attitude and vanity' for this confusion: H.-J. Brandt (1986), 'Walter Ruttmann: Vom Expressionismus zum Faschismus. 3. Teil', *Filmfaust*, No. 51, 42. It appears that, in fact, Ruttmann was given responsibility for the prologue (which was to constitute a third of the film) and Riefenstahl for the shots of the Party Rally. Nor is the claim that Riefenstahl had rejected Ruttmann's footage even before the start of the Party Rally (*Memoiren I*, p. 221) accurate. As late as October 1934, she worked together with him on scenes for the prologue. Cf. *Licht-Bild-Bühne*, 23 October 1934.

14 *Film-Kurier*, No. 198, 24 August 1934. The report was evidently based on an official press release: the article in the *Völkischer Beobachter* (24 August 1934) was phrased almost identically. A few days later, reports suggested that the Party Rally would form 'the culmination of a prologue . . . which would revisit all the movement's historic venues and the stages in its development', *Film-Kurier*, No. 206, 3 September 1934.

15 *Licht-Bild-Bühne*, No. 208, 7 September 1934.

16 'Die deutsche Bewegung und seine (*sic*) lebendigen Zeugen. Walter Ruttmann über seine Mitarbeit am Reichsparteitagsfilm', *Film-Kurier*, No. 217, 15 September 1934. Ruttmann's involvement is also mentioned in similar terms in the *Film-Kurier* on 27 September 1934 (No. 227).

17 'Elend, über das der Wille triumphierte', *Film-Kurier*, No. 235, 6 October 1934.

18 *Film-Kurier*, No. 243, 25 October 1934.

19 *Licht-Bild-Bühne*, No. 247, 23 October 1934.

20 Cf. *Memoiren I*, pp. 203 and 221. Riefenstahl also hints at differences of opinion

concerning the structure of the film: cf. *ibid.* p. 217. In her memoirs she described Ruttmann as a communist, in order to emphasize that all kinds of people, not just she, collaborated with those in power. That point is a valid one, but Ruttmann's alleged communist sympathies were unknown to the Communist Party itself.

21 On the basis of the extant newspaper and magazine articles, both J. Goergen (n.d. (1989)) 'Walter Ruttmann – Ein Porträt', in J. Goergen (ed.), *Walter Ruttmann. Eine Dokumentation*. Berlin: Freunde der Deutschen Kinemathek and Brandt (1986) estimate that Ruttmann was expected to contribute about a third of the film. H. Barkhausen (1973), 'War auch Walter Ruttmann politisch blind?', *Neue Zürcher Zeitung*, 18 August was the first to highlight Ruttmann's role.

22 Goergen (1989), p. 41. This outstandingly researched essay contains many revelations about Ruttmann's career and his relationship to *Triumph des Willens* (as does the rest of the volume).

23 Brandt (1986), p. 45, also mentions the lecture Riefenstahl gave at the Lessing University to mark the film's premiere, in which she declared that her initial doubts regarding a film entirely dedicated to the Party Rally had subsequently been resolved. She does not appear to have mentioned Ruttmann.

24 'The three ideal scenes [street, hall and field] correspond to three actors, which can be summarized under the titles of the people, the Führer and the Party, or alternatively as the citizens, the Führer and the soldiers', Loiperdinger (1987a), p. 65.

25 Both in principle – as the portrayal is always 'faithful' and therefore also constructs a document of the situation in front of the camera – and in a stylistic sense – as certain forms and kinds of narrative, or sometimes just certain scenes, privilege an attitude which can be construed as 'documentary' towards the presentation of a fictional story. Cf. R. Rother (1990), 'Die Form der Abbildung und die Struktur der Erzählung', *filmwärts*, No. 17, 34–9.

26 Cf. K. R. M. Short and S. Dolezel (1988), *Hitler's Fall. The Newsreel Witness*. London, New York, Sidney: Croom Helm.

27 Susan Sontag (1980) attempts to do this in 'Fascinating Fascism', in *Under the Sign of Saturn*. New York: Farrar, Straus, Giroux, pp. 71–105. She describes *Triumph des Willens* and *Olympia* as perhaps 'the two greatest documentaries ever made' (p. 95), but also declares that anyone who 'defends' them as documentaries is 'being ingenuous' (p. 83). She evidently assumes that a propaganda film cannot also be a documentary film.

28 Loiperdinger (1987a), p. 163, offers an overview of the various points of view surrounding the documentary and propagandist 'alternatives'. He himself treats the film as an 'affirmative document of the Reich Party Rally 1934. The selection and organization of the footage is determined by the cinematic condensate, the "model of an ideal Party congress". Reproducing the Party Rally as an authentic cinema experience signifies heightening an already idealized staging of the actual Party Rally to turn it into the ideal Party Rally.'

29 Kracauer (1947), pp. 257–8. He also sees a parallel between the choreography in Fritz Lang's *Nibelungen* and the Party Rally film. For criticism of this thesis, from which various authors took their lead, cf. Loiperdinger (1987a), pp. 36–7.

30 Neale (1979), p. 66, describes '*spectacle* as the principle of the film's operations'.

31 Cf. *ibid.*, p. 70, on the opening of the film: 'It insists over and over again not only upon the activity of looking as the basis of the relations between the actants the sequence signifies, but also upon looking as the key term in the articulation of its own internal consistency: in a very similar manner to that of classical "fictional" cinema.'

32 E. Leiser (1989) '*Deutschland erwache*'. *Propaganda im Film des Dritten Reiches*. Reinbek: Rowohlt, p. 29.

33 Riefenstahl (1935a), p. 12.

34 Later she gave a clear description of the procedure: 'The director has no influence over the progress of the events, he only has a general idea of the programme. His first task, therefore, is to capture the event completely with a large number of cameras, to document every detail, every moment from near and far. The camera lenses really need to penetrate the whole event,' L. Riefenstahl (1940/41), 'Über Wesen und Gestaltung des dokumentarischen Films', in *Der Deutsche Film. Zeitschrift für Filmkunst und Filmwirtschaft. Sonderausgabe.* Berlin: Max Hesses, p. 147. She used large teams to enable her to realize her uncompromising approach to the 'event'. That approach related entirely to the event as a 'show', and was thus defined by the official ideology. For *Triumph des Willens* she had a crew of 120 at her disposal, including 16 cameramen and 16 assistant cameramen with 30 appliances (Riefenstahl, 1935a, p. 13). Her filming of *Olympia* was an even bigger operation. Cf. the detailed description in C. C. Graham (1986), *Leni Riefenstahl and Olympia*. Metuchen, N. J., and London: Scarecrow Press, and T. Downing (1992), *Olympia*. London: BFI.

35 In order to simplify the challenge, Riefenstahl seems to have concentrated on certain events, particularly those which appeared in the official programme for the Party Rally.

36 For a Protokoll of the film, cf. M. Loiperdinger (1980), *'Triumph des Willens'. Einstellungsprotokoll.* Frankfurt am Main: Institut für Historisch-Sozialwissenschaftliche Analysen (= Arbeitspapier No. 12).

37 The enormous mobility of the camera struck even contemporary critics as the *new* characteristic of the film.

38 Neale (1979) describes Hitler as the 'privileged object of the gaze' (p. 69); 'he himself is the ultimately significant spectacle – for the crowd *in* the film and for the spectators *of* the film' (p. 70). This is certainly true, but within the shot–reaction-shot logic the privileged object is also tied into the *exchange* of gazes. What is of immediate importance to the spectators of the film is that they can follow this from an 'ideal position'. They 'identify' with the action, not with a character, even if one character – Hitler – dominates the eye contacts. They thus identify with the obvious enthusiasm for the Führer.

39 Loiperdinger (1980), p. 88, refers to the portrayal of Hitler as the 'political saviour' and the 'messiah of the nation'. Kanzog (1995), p. 71, describes the opening sequence as the 'arrival of the messiah'. This deification of Hitler is inherent in the ritual but is not apparent from the participants in close-ups; it is achieved by the montage. With regard to the light effects, cf. Neale (1979), pp. 71–2.

40 'We want to see our leader' is the chant at the end of the first sequence, as the crowd pleads with Hitler to make his appearance.

41 This is why Loiperdinger (1987a), p. 71, notes that in the first half of the film, after travelling to the hotel, Hitler 'really only appears on screen in order to disappear from the scene again'.

42 Kanzog (1995), p. 73, argues that this section of the film has the function of 'representing the community'.

43 Cf. H. Regel (1970), 'Triumph des Willens', *Filmkritik*, Vol. 14, No. 5, 249–51: '*Triumph des Willens*, however, does not recognize individuals, it recognizes only the statues of the Führer and the satraps, along with the "sections" which people in the film always represent whenever they appear to act as individuals.'

44 In total there were five separate tributes to the dead at the Party Rally. The first marked the opening of the Party congress, and there were 'short choir performances' at the reviews of the Hitler Youth, the Reich Labour Service and the Politische Leiter (political leaders), as well as the tribute to the dead at the review of the SA and SS which is included in the film. Cf. S. Behrenbeck (1996), *Der Kult um die toten Helden. Nationalsozialistische Mythen, Riten und Symbole.* Vierow: SH-Verlag, pp. 326–7.

45 For a description of the ceremony cf. *ibid.* (pp. 362 ff.).

46 Loiperdinger (1987a), p. 104, therefore describes this scene as 'cinéma vérité'.

47 With regard to the different placing of the scene in the copies held by the Institut für den Wissenschaftlichen Film and the Bundesarchiv, cf. *ibid.* p. 60. With regard to the *Wehrmacht* sequence, which is also at odds with the film's overall context, cf. Kanzog (1995), pp. 68 ff.

48 Loiperdinger (1987a), p. 109.

49 Riefenstahl has claimed that, except for her 'colleagues, nobody had seen the film before the premiere'. According to her, it was only finished a few hours before the premiere and had not been presented to the censor. Apparently she did not even have time to visit the hairdresser before the premiere and only arrived at the Ufa Palast when 'Hitler and all the guests of honour, including the diplomats, were already seated in their boxes' (*Memoiren I*, p. 231). On the other hand, two days before the premiere the *Filmprüfstelle* (censor's office) approved the film (cf. Kanzog (1995), p. 69). Moreover, Riefenstahl herself found the time to give a lecture about the film *before* it was premiered. This took place at a press conference organized by the propaganda ministry (cf. *Film-Kurier*, 26 March 1935 and *Münchener Neueste Nachrichten* and *Germania* of the same day). Whilst editing, Riefenstahl received visits from Goebbels, Hess and Hitler (cf. Loiperdinger (1987a), pp. 45–6). The *Völkischer Beobachter* (8 December 1934) reported Hitler's visit to the editing room as follows: 'The Führer was then shown excerpts from the film, which was in the process of taking shape. The presentation made a great and obvious impression on the Führer, and he expressed his exceptionally warm appreciation to the artiste and her colleagues as he left their workplace.'

50 Loiperdinger (1987a), p. 47, illustrates this with an article from the *Frankfurter Zeitung* of 29 March 1935.

51 *Dresdener Anzeiger*, 30 March 1935.

52 *Deutsche Filmzeitung*, No. 14, 1935 (pp. 3–4).

53 The Gold Medallion was not a singular award; it was also awarded, for example, to *Jugend der Welt* (Youth of the World, directed by Carl Junghans, Germany 1936).

54 The censor card for the 35 mm version has not been found, but the one for the 16 mm cine film version names the NSDAP as producer.

55 Cf. the published decrees issued by the NSDAP's Reichsleitung in September 1934: 'If images from the Reich Party Rally were to be shown in individual film recordings, it would contradict the idea underlying the production of a unitary film.' The ban applied to all sections of the Party, all offices and even 'each individual national comrade'. It is hard to believe that the NSDAP would have acted so vigorously on behalf of a privately produced film.

56 Cf. the letter from Walter Taut to the *Reichsfachschaft Film* (Reich Film Department), 5 November 1934, with regard to an insurance matter: 'In this case, however, I do not feel that I am authorized to represent the interest of the NSDAP, for whom we are making this film at the Führer's behest, and have therefore referred the matter to the lawyer allocated to us by the Party' (BA BDC-RKK, Taut file). The two other letters are from Walter Groskopf to the Reich Ministry for the People's Enlightenment and Propaganda, 25 July 1935 and to the Reichsfachschaft Film, 26 September 1935 (BA BDC-RKK, Lantschner file).

57 She did not forget, however, to send a postcard to the *Film-Kurier*, No. 140, 19 June 1935.

58 Cf. D. Culbert and M. Loiperdinger (1992), 'Leni Riefenstahl's "Tag der Freiheit": the 1935 Nazi Party Rally Film', *Historical Journal of Film, Radio and Television*, Vol. 12, No. 1, 3–40.

59 Cf. *ibid.*

60 *Film-Kurier*, No. 121, 11 September 1935. On 13 September the same publication specified some of the footage which was shot in addition to that used in the film: 'The Führer's arrival was again a particular target for the cameramen. The laying of the foundation-stone in the conference hall, the Reich Labour Service – in short, the "Riefenstahl film crew" is again on hand at every phase of Nuremberg 1935.'

6 The Best Sports Film of All Time

1 Cf. D. Wildmann (1998), *Begehrte Körper. Konstruktion und Inszenierung des 'arischen' Männerkörpers im 'Dritten Reich'*. Würzburg: Königshausen und Neumann.

2 'At that time the task was a quite unimaginable one; I was entrusted with it because my films *Sieg des Glaubens*, *Triumph des Willens* and *Tag der Freiheit* had been big successes and because I am familiar with sport and sports film techniques after working on so many mountain and ski films', Leni Riefenstahl, in Tobis Filmkunst-GmbH, Olympia-Pressedienst (Olympic press service, 1936), *Olympia. Fest der Völker. Erster Film von den Olympischen Spielen*. Berlin, p. 27.

3 The *Völkischer Beobachter* (2 August 1936) referred to 300 workers, and the *Film-Kurier* suggested a similar figure (No. 178, 1 August 1936). *The Deutsche Illustrierte* (30 June 1936) published a photograph of Riefenstahl in Kiel, where the navy was helping her shoot the film, and showed her in a 'directorial discussion' with Lieutenant-Commander Hauck.

4 Bella Fromm's description of the director is well known: 'Leni Riefenstahl is the official photographer. She wears a pair of long, grey flannel trousers and a kind of jockey's cap and is unpleasantly conspicuous wherever one looks. She attempts to give the impression of untiring activity, thereby underlining her importance. Meanwhile her colleagues calmly and expertly get on with the job in hand. Leni need do no more than give the results her blessing', B. Fromm (1993), *Als Hitler mir die Hand küsste*. Reinbek: Rowohlt, pp. 249–50. Graham (1986), pp. 100–1, quotes similar comments from the *New York Times* correspondent Frederick Birchall and from the reminiscences of Hans Ertl.

5 *Film-Kurier*, 4 August 1936.

6 'What makes these pictures unique is that cameramen have never been allowed to work so close to the athletes at any other Olympics. It was a hard battle to obtain authorization for this from the IOC. Despite permission being granted, there were vehement disputes with the judges on a daily basis. One had to go to war to get the shots', L. Riefenstahl (1937), *Schönheit im olympischen Kampf*. Berlin: Deutscher Verlag, p. 5. The *Film-Kurier* also reported difficulties during filming (No. 180, 4 August 1936).

7 Letter from Riefenstahl to Kohner, 16 September 1936, Kohner collection, Stiftung Deutsche Kinemathek: 'Never before has it been possible to use such techniques and artistic resources to make such a magnificent sports film . . . Within the next few weeks we will discover whether Ufa or Tobis obtains the film. The ultimate authority when it comes to deciding who gets the film is Herr Reichsminister Dr Göbbels [*sic*] . . . If an American company as large as Metro-Goldwyn-Mayer makes [even] a very modest offer for foreign distribution rights, it might quite conceivably obtain the film for distribution abroad.'

8 Cf. 'Die Aktiven der Kamera', *Völkischer Beobachter*, 18 August 1936.

9 Riefenstahl (*Memoiren I*), pp. 278–9, blames the reduced press interest on Goebbels, claiming that he had ordered a press boycott out of resentment against her. There is, however, no proof of this. Cf. Graham (1986), pp. 145 ff.

10 Cf. *Memoiren I*, pp. 236 ff. In 1958 Riefenstahl summarized her defence in a manuscript entitled *Über die Herstellung der Olympia-Filme (Falsche Behauptungen und*

ihre Widerlegung). This later appeared in English: L. Riefenstahl (1973b), 'The production of the Olympia Films. Incorrect statements, their refutations', *Film Culture*, No. 56–7, 170–4.

11 H. Barkhausen (1974a), 'Footnote to the History of Riefenstahl's "Olympia"', *Film Quarterly*, Vol. 28, No. 1, 8–12; H. Barkhausen (1974b), '"Auf Veranlassung des Reiches". Leni Riefenstahl und die Olympia-Filme 1936', *Neue Zürcher Zeitung*, No. 367, 10 August; Graham (1986).

12 Quoted after Leiser (1989), pp. 127–8.

13 R. G. Reuth (ed.) (1992), *Joseph Goebbels. Tagebücher 1924–1945*. Munich: Piper (p. 874, entry for 17 August 1935). As early as 23 August, the Ufa board considered Riefenstahl's suggestion 'of distributing the film to be made by her on the occasion of the Olympiad in Berlin 1936', but rejected it (BA R 109 I/1031a, p. 215).

14 *Film-Kurier*, 21 September 1935. Ernst Jaeger was probably responsible for this indiscretion. On 18 November, while Riefenstahl was preparing to dub the *Wehrmacht* film, it was reported that 'after this she will have to prepare for the next great task, about which official information will probably soon be available'. It materialized on 10 December: 'Reichsminister Dr Goebbels commissions Leni Riefenstahl' to design the Olympia film; preparations were already being made. Later, Hitler was sometimes credited with commissioning the film: the *Kölnische Illustrierte* (17 February 1938) published a photograph of Riefenstahl and Hitler in her garden with a caption to that effect.

15 Reuth (1992), p. 896 (entry for 5 October 1935): 'Went over Leni Riefenstahl's plans for her Olympiad film with her. A woman who knows what she wants! . . . Concluded the business concerning the film at home with Leni Riefenstahl.' On 13 October, Hitler and Goebbels discussed the matter, and Hitler seems to have given his basic approval for the contract with Riefenstahl (p. 899). On 7 November (p. 906), Goebbels wrote: 'Miss Riefenstahl gets her contract for the Olympia film. A property worth 1.5 million. She is very happy.'

16 H. Dörlöchter, 'Erläuterungen zur Abschlussbilanz und der Gewinn- und Verlust-rechnung der Olympia-Film GmbH', in BA R 55/1327, pp. 81 and 82.

17 Letter from the Reich Ministry for People's Enlightenment and Propaganda to the District Court of Berlin, 30 January 1936. Quoted after Leiser (1989), p. 128.

18 The text of the contract between the ministry and Leni Riefenstahl is reproduced in Leiser (1989), pp. 127–8. There is no doubt about the disagreements with Goebbels, and it appears that he really did make a sudden attempt to replace Riefenstahl as director. The financial audit, which identified an expenditure policy not necessarily in line with the regulations for the use of public money, probably seemed to offer a good line of attack, especially since it was foreseeable that the budget would be exceeded.

19 Riefenstahl (*Memoiren I*, pp. 239–40, claims that the film was pre-financed with a Tobis loan guarantee of RM1.5 million. She does not supply a date for this, but implies that it was as early as 1935. On 3 July 1936, however, the Ufa board discussed whether an alternative offer – also to Tobis – to take over *Olympia* for a guarantee of RM800,000 was reasonable. It concluded that RM500,000 at most would be acceptable (BA R 109 I/1031b, p. 177). This corresponds to details given by Riefenstahl herself in a letter to Kohner. There is much to suggest that the contract with Tobis was actually agreed on 4 December 1936 (BA R 55/503, pp. 200 ff.). Warneke (1998) argues that the date should have read 4 December 1935.

20 Quoted after Moeller (1999), p. 155.

21 BA R 55/1328, p. 6, note of 16 March 1939.

22 The final balance was made on 29 July 1942 (BA R 55/1327, pp. 80–91). With regard to Riefenstahl's fee, cf. BA R55/1328, p. 6 (note of 16 March 1939), Riefenstahl's letter

of 6 March 1939 (BA R 55/1327, p. 258) and the letter from the ministry to Olympia-Film GmbH of 29 March 1939 (BA R 55/1328, p. 9). With regard to the contract cf. BA R 55/1327, p. 137.

23 H. Hoffmann (1993), *Mythos Olympia. Autonomie und Unterwerfung von Sport und Kultur*. Berlin: Aufbau, p. 155. A host of more or less significant errors seriously restricts the value of this work.

24 Cf. J. Spiker (1975), *Film und Kapital. Der Weg der deutschen Filmwirtschaft zum nationalsozialistischen Einheitskonzern*. Berlin: Volker Spiess, p. 143. Spiker estimates the average production cost of German feature films at RM425,000 in 1936, and at RM537,000 in the following year. Even the original estimate for *Olympia*, which was subsequently exceeded, was thus based on a budget three times greater.

25 Downing (1992), p. 90.

26 T. Koebner (1995), 'Olympia', in T. Koebner (ed.), *Filmklassiker*, Vol. 1. Stuttgart: Reclam, p. 372. This evaluation does not take into account the central role given to Hitler in the prologue, but its assessment of the way the individual sporting competitions are presented is not inaccurate.

27 A point made by Graham (1986), pp. 255–6: 'Another major goal of the National Socialists was to depict the friendliness and good will of Germany. The film reflects this propaganda aim in several ways. The author is aware that this comment . . . puts Leni Riefenstahl in something of a double bind. If she had made a racist, chauvinistic film, then she would clearly have been making a National Socialist film. But by making a film that does not reflect racism or nationalism, she is still making a National Socialist film. To be fair, it must be remembered that artists and writers who produce sociological propaganda may be entirely unaware that they are doing so.'

28 With regard to the instructions given to the press, cf. *ibid.*, pp. 254 ff.; D. Welch (1983), *Propaganda and the German Cinema 1933–1945*. Oxford: Clarendon Press, pp. 112 ff.; T. Alkemeyer (1996), *Körper, Kult und Politik. Von der 'Muskelreligion' Pierre de Coubertins zur Inszenierung von Macht in den Olympischen Spielen von 1936*. Frankfurt, New York: Campus, pp. 449 ff.

29 Downing (1992), p. 91, summarizes the sense in which *Olympia* may be regarded as a political film: '*Olympia* is an intensely political film. It was set up for political motives, it described an immensely political event. It was made and promoted with government money using several agencies of the Nazi state.'

30 The commentary in the English version is less martial in tone than the German original. Hitler's first appearance is not until the parade of the athletes, instead of in a conspicuous close-up at the end of the prologue. Cf. Downing (1992), p. 55 and Graham (1986), p. 92.

31 Sontag (1980), p. 92.

32 Hoffmann (1993), p. 115.

33 Wildmann (1998), p. 110.

34 Wildmann *ibid.*, p. 13, bases his analysis on a distinction between the 'Arian body' celebrated in the film and the 'Jewish body' which is excluded from it. In that sense he regards the prominent role of Jesse Owens, for example, as largely immaterial, since the 'black body' was not the antithesis of the 'Arian body' within Nazi ideology (p. 103).

35 *Völkischer Beobachter*, 22 April 1938: 'We repeatedly see the Führer, genuinely and profoundly involved, as he follows the contests and spurred our athletes on to their surprising and splendid performances – not just by his personal presence, but because he has given both them and the spellbound spectators the pride and dignity of a great and self-confident fatherland.'

36 M. Loiperdinger (1988), 'Halb Dokument, halb Fälschung. Zur Inszenierung der Eröffnungsfeier in Leni Riefenstahls Olympia-Film ''Fest der Völker'' ', *Medium*, Vol. 18, No. 3, 43.

37 Loiperdinger (*ibid.*) describes the shot of Hitler as the 'dramaturgical hinge' of the film.

38 *Ibid.*, p. 46.

39 Cf. H.-J. Brandt (1987), *NS-Filmtheorie und dokumentarische Praxis.* Tübingen: Niemeyer, pp. 123 ff. Brandt also mentions (p. 154) that the film won both the Italian 'Luce' trophy for the best documentary film (1 September 1936) and the Grand Prix at the World Exhibition in Paris of 1937. The latter, in particular, casts further doubt on Riefenstahl's arguments (she also won both prizes).

40 In his sequence, Junghans cuts in shots of flying eagles. Unfortunately, the visual metaphor tends to disrupt rather than intensify the effect he is aiming at (as Brandt (1987), p. 148, agrees). It may have represented his attempt to compensate for shortcomings in the individual shots.

41 This solution only works if the distance in time from the event is not excessive. Brandt (1987), p. 147, doubts if this was achieved in every case.

7 The Function of the Genius

1 'Leni Riefenstahl zum 10. April', *Film-Kurier*, 10 April 1938: 'The greater Germany is now reality; increasingly confident and moved, we have watched it grow from year to year. The creator of *Grossdeutschland* [Greater Germany] is also its most artistic human being . . . During these years the Führer's voice has often urged us to "Make a start!"; often the artists followed the call to join ranks with the millions of Germans and declare their loyalty to the Führer and their support for one of his undertakings on behalf of Germany's liberty, honour and grandeur.' Riefenstahl cannot, in most cases, be said to have been the last to join ranks.

2 Cf. F. Moeller (1998), *Der Filmminister.* Berlin: Henschel, p. 117.

3 *Völkischer Beobachter*, 5 May 1934.

4 *Film-Kurier*, 2 May 1934.

5 Cf. J. Fraser (1982), 'An Ambassador for Nazi Germany', *Films and Filming*, Vol. 2, No. 5, 12–14.

6 When Germany's troops marched into the former Czechoslovakia, *Triumph des Willens* arrived with them. The *Film-Kurier* (No. 66, 18 March 1939) described this in the following terms: 'Following the recent political events in the former Czecho-Slovakia, cinema-goers are keen finally to see the German films which had previously been banned from that territory.'

7 Cf. C. C. Graham (1993), ' "Olympia" in America, 1938: Leni Riefenstahl, Hollywood, and the Kristallnacht', *Historical Journal of Film, Radio and Television*, Vol. 13, No. 4, 436. Graham describes the organization as 'non-sectarian' and points out that in this it was different from the Hollywood Anti-Nazi League, which was led by well-known leftists and was soon under attack as a communist organization, despite the fact that its membership certainly also included many non-communists (*ibid.*, 440).

8 *Memoiren I*, pp. 323–4.

9 *Der Spiegel*, 18 August 1997.

10 *Völkischer Beobachter*, 7 November 1938: 'Leni Riefenstahl arrived on board the *Europa* in New York for an extended tour through the United States. There too she is a well-known artist, and she was greeted by a large detachment of press representatives and photographers, who showered her with questions about her work in films.'

11 Graham (1993), p. 435.

12 Riefenstahl's explanation was printed in the *Film-Kurier* (No. 8, 10 January 1939). The same journal (No. 2, 3 January 1939) also featured a translation of the positive article which was published by the *Hollywood Citizen News* following a private screening. The *Völkischer Beobachter* commented: 'The anti-German powers which control

cinema and the movie parks are more powerful than these uninhibited reviewers of the film.' Contemporary readers will have had no difficulty in identifying these 'powers' and 'people'. The *Berliner Illustrierte* (19 January 1939) was more explicit. It provided a photograph of Riefenstahl in jeans and a check shirt, holding a horse by the bridle, with the following caption: 'Leni Riefenstahl on a visit to a Californian farm. Jewish influence in Hollywood is preventing any public screening of the Olympia film, although Leni Riefenstahl received enthusiastic applause when it was shown to film critics.'

13 Reuth (1992), p. 1307. Moeller (1998), pp. 445–6, points out that 'the cheap anti-Semitic propaganda clichés . . . belonged to the standard repertoire of the Goebbels image of America' and that his diary entry should not automatically be used to draw conclusions about Riefenstahl. She herself, however, undoubtedly promoted prejudice in her public statements. The *Film-Kurier* (No. 27, 1 February 1939) quotes her as follows: ' "I cannot tell you which other directors or actors I saw [other than Disney], as it would cost them their jobs. I had to promise them faithfully not to 'betray' them." Leni Riefenstahl's answer does not require much elucidation: anyone not already aware of the fact will have realized from it that the Jews dominate the American film industry in a reign of utter terror, and that public opinion is also very strongly influenced against Germany by the Jewish atrocity propaganda – but fortunately not to the same extent.'

14 'Schule Riefenstahl. Der absolute Film', *Film-Kurier*, 25 January 1936.

15 *Ibid.*

16 *Ibid.*

17 Cf. G. Albrecht (ed.) (1979), Film im Dritten Reich. Karlsruhe: Schauburg, for details of the 'Kaiserhof speech' of 28 March 1933, in which Goebbels referred to Eisenstein's *Battleship Potemkin* as one of the standards for future films. Cf. also R. Schnell (2000), *Medienästhetik. Zur Geschichte und Theorie audiovisueller Wahrnehmungsformen.* Stuttgart, Weimar: Metzler, pp. 131 ff. and O. Bulgakowa (1999), 'Riefenstein – Demontage eines Klischees', in Filmmuseum Potsdam (ed.), *Leni Riefenstahl*, Berlin: Henschel, pp. 132 ff.

18 The journal cited films by Ritter and Harlan, for example, and of course *Der ewige Jude* and *Feuertaufe*, as positive examples; there can be no doubt that the kind of 'German cinema' advocated here is both anti-Semitic and chauvinistic. The journal was, after all, a *Reichsfilmkammer* publication.

19 H. Gressieker (1936), 'Leni Riefenstahl', *Der deutsche Film*, Vol. 1, No. 2, August, 40–41.

20 'Gibt es einen deutschen Kamerastil?', *Der deutsche Film* Vol. 3, No. 7, 1939, 176–7.

21 F. Maraun (1938), 'Der wichtigste Film des Monats. Triumph des Dokumentarfilms', *Der deutsche Film*, Vol. 2, No. 11, May, 317). In a subsequent issue of the same publication, Maraun restates his claim, sometimes in the same words: 'The documentary film can therefore only achieve artistic status if it makes visible an idea pervading the reality which is the film's object. National Socialism, with its power of spiritual guidance which pervades every detail of the whole life of the nation, has created the ideal conditions for such films . . . This explains why documentary films have given the most convincing, brilliant cinematic expressions of German socialism so far. The National Socialist movement created its own style of state representation in the Reich Party Rally films of Nuremberg. The Reich Party Rally films *Sieg des Glaubens*, *Triumph des Willens* and *Tag der Freiheit* captured those eventful days on film with impressively liberal creativity, with an imagination steeped in the energy of the action', 'Deutscher Sozialismus im Film', *Der deutsche Film*, Vol. 4, No. 11, 1940, 206.

22 H.-H. Gensert (1938), 'Die neue Kunstanschauung und ihr Ausdruck', *Der deutsche*

Film, Vol. 2, No. 12, June, 323–6. The contributors to *Der deutsche Film* thought that contemporary Nazi cinema offered very few examples of the 'grand form' other than Riefenstahl. In the first few issues of the journal, *Jugend der Welt* is the only film honoured in remotely similar terms; after 1938, Party opinion elevates *Westwall* (Siegfried Line) to a place beside Riefenstahl's films, as it does *Feuertaufe* (Baptism of Fire), *Sieg im Westen* (Victory in the West) and *Der ewige Jude* (The Eternal Jew) during the war. These films are thus not merely the earliest model examples of 'heroic reportage', but also – for a long time – the only ones available. This explains why many articles prescribing the kind of work which would conform to those theories (which they were to some extent able to discern in other forms such as the cultural film or *Bergfilm*) are accompanied by illustrations from Riefenstahl's films even if there is no reference to her in the text.

23 L. Fürst (1937), ' "Woran liegt es?" Von der Problematik des Filmschaffens', *Der deutsche Film*, Vol. 2, No. 5, November, 125 ff.

24 A. Melichar (1937), 'Entstofflichung des Films', *Der deutsche Film*, Vol. 2, No. 1, July, 13.

25 F. Maraun (1939), 'Warum sieht man das nie im Spielfilm?', *Der deutsche Film*, Vol. 3, No. 8, February, 212.

26 The daily press and the trade journals also sometimes found space for such ideas. Even *Filmwelt*, otherwise dedicated largely to film industry gossip, produced a theoretical article in honour of *Olympia*. 'If one traces the course of Western culture from the present day back to early antiquity, one perceives a constant pattern of wave-like movement, a continual interchange between wild, stormy, baroque periods and tranquil, balanced, classical ones. Our task today is to overcome the consequences of a chaotic time of spiritual and material inflation and reaffirm the healthy basis of human culture. This essential truth also gives the general development of our art its new character . . . A work to which this particularly applies is Leni Riefenstahl's Olympia film', K.: 'Neue Klassik', *Filmwelt*, No. 16, 15 April 1938.

27 'Imposante Wochenschauberichte', *Licht-Bild-Bühne*, 6 September 1933.

28 Leni Riefenstahl, 'Wie der Film vom Reichsparteitag entsteht', *Der Deutsche*, No. 14, 17 January 1935, 5. Quoted after P. Nowotny (1981), *Leni Riefenstahls 'Triumph des Willens'. Zur Kritik dokumentarischer Filmarbeit im NS-Faschismus*. Dortmund: Arbeitshefte zur Medientheorie und Medienpraxis, Vol. 3, p. 99.

29 'All reports which involve us in an authentic relationship with great events become documents, whether they achieve this by means of the spoken word, painting or photography,' Riefenstahl (1940/41), 'Über Wesen und Gestaltung des dokumentar-ischen Films', in *Der deutsche Film. Zeitschrift für Filmkunst und Filmwirtschaft. Sonderausgabe*. Berlin: Max Hesses, p. 146.

30 *Ibid.*, p. 147.

31 L. Fürst (1938), 'Deutschlands repräsentativster Film. Gedanken vor Leni Riefen-stahls Olympia-Film', *Der deutsche Film*, Vol. 2, No. 9, March, 249.

32 BA R 4606/2693, p. 67. On Schelkes cf. D. van der Vat (1997), *The Good Nazi: The Life and Lies of Albert Speer*. London: Weidenfeld and Nicholson, pp. 43, 71ff.

33 *Oberbaurrat* Hans Stephan was a head of section in Speer's GBI; cf. van der Vat (1997), p. 71.

34 BA R 4606/2693, pp. 64, 65. Leni Riefenstahl does not mention the project in her memoirs. She does, however, describe and date a conversation with Speer. 'My records indicate that my conversation with Speer took place in mid-August 1939 – just two weeks before war broke out' (*Memoiren I*, p. 344). According to Riefenstahl, Speer showed her the model of his plans for Berlin, and tried to persuade her to direct a film about the model buildings. She refused on account of *Penthesilea* and

suggested instead that her own production company make the film, with Arnold Fanck as director.

35 Riefenstahl names another architect – 'Hans Ostler, an architect from Garmisch' – whom she claims she commissioned together with his partner, Max Otte. However, cf. H. J. Zechlin (1939), *Landhäuser*. Berlin: Wasmuth, pp. 154–5, which clearly shows that Petersen designed the building.

36 At this time it was also noted that the situation regarding land ownership remained to be resolved. BA R 4606/2693, p. 59.

37 *Ibid.*, p. 58.

38 *Ibid.*, p. 53.

39 *Ibid.*, p. 51.

40 *Ibid.*, pp. 46, 47.

41 'Professors Kreis and Breker are each to have a state studio built for them, so that they can carry out the large commissions with which they have been entrusted for the redevelopment of the Reich capital. The construction site lies in the vicinity of Kronprinzenallee, and is also under Prussian ownership. Unfortunately, the normal land price there of RM20 is so high that the necessary mortgage would jeopardize the project. I, however, am very keen that it should go ahead; two professors' work and their tie to Berlin depend upon it. Given the special circumstances surrounding these cases, I therefore ask you, in the interests of art, to reduce the price by half', *ibid.*

42 20 July 1939; BA R 4606/2693, p. 43.

43 *Ibid.*, pp. 36, 37.

44 *Ibid.*, pp. 29, 30, 31.

45 12 August 1939, BA R 4606/2693, p. 25.

46 29 August 1939, R 4606/2693, p. 23.

47 7 August 1942, R 4606/2693, p. 1.

8 A Partial Retreat: *Tiefland*

1 The press first mentions *Penthesilea* in 1935; cf. *Film-Kurier*, 12 September 1939. From then on, there are regular references to the project.

2 From a Riefenstahl manuscript entitled 'Warum verfilme ich Penthesilea?' (1939), quoted in H. Weigel (1972), 'Randbemerkungen zum Thema', *Filmkritik*, Vol. 16, No. 8, August, 430. An English translation also appeared: L. Riefenstahl (1973a), 'Why I am filming Penthesilea', *Film Culture*, No. 56–7, 192–215.

3 L. Riefenstahl (1972), 'Notizen zu Penthesilea', *Filmkritik*, Vol. 16, No. 8, 423.

4 *Ibid.*, 424.

5 *Ibid.*, pp. 416–17.

6 'The classical temples notwithstanding, the whole city must have a wild, natural, primitive character; partly cave dwellings. I think the temples, the Queen's palace and the houses inhabited by the Amazons should be quite different from one another. The latter should be very primitive.' *Ibid.*, 422.

7 T. Koebner (1997), 'Der unversehrbare Körper. Anmerkungen zu Filmen Leni Riefenstahls', in T. Koebner (ed.), *Lehrjahre im Kino. Schriften zum Film*. St Augustin: Gardez, p. 224: 'The hymnic, unbridled elements in the *Penthesilea* project would have demanded of Riefenstahl a more "obsessive" dramatic form and pictorial language than she ever allowed herself in other cinematic and photographic work.'

8 *Memoiren I*, p. 341.

9 E. von Manstein (1978), *Verlorene Siege*. Munich: Bernhard und Graefe, p. 43. Manstein also describes the director's appearance: 'Otherwise, she looked nice and daring, a bit like an elegant partisan who might have obtained her outfit from the rue de Rivoli in Paris. Her beautiful hair swirled around her interesting face with its

close-set eyes like a blazing mane. She was wearing a kind of tunic, breeches and soft, high boots. A pistol hung from the leather belt which was slung around her hips. Her close-combat gear was completed by a knife, stuck into her boot-leg, Bavarian style. I must admit that the staff were a little perplexed by this unusual phenomenon.'

10 Cf. the section entitled 'The Massacre at Konskie' in the next chapter.

11 Cf. A. Bodek (n.d.), 'Die ohnmächtige Leni?', MS, n.p. (I am grateful to the author for making this unpublished manuscript available to me.) Cf. also H. Krausnick (1993), *Hitlers Einsatzgruppen. Die Truppen des Weltanschauungskrieges 1938–1942*. Frankfurt am Main: Fischer.

12 The director's lengthy illness had forced filming in Spain to be broken off.

13 K. Sabel (1940), 'Die eigenwillige Gestaltung des "Tiefland"-Stoffes', *Film-Kurier*, No. 258, 2 November.

14 'They are making the most of all the resources available today in terms of optical aids, film material and filters', *ibid*.

15 The marquis, Don Sebastian, denies water to the village of Roccabruna because he wants it for his fighting bulls. He dismisses the villagers' objections high-handedly. He takes the gypsy girl, Martha, back to his castle after falling in love with her when he saw her dancing. The affair provokes the local mayor, who wants his daughter to marry the heavily indebted marquis. He buys up all Don Sebastian's debts in order to exert pressure on him. Martha wants to help the villagers, and gives them the diadem she had received as a gift from Don Sebastian. Her offer, however, is haughtily rejected, and Don Sebastian beats Martha when he hears what she has done. She flees to the mountains, where the shepherd, Pedro – who is also in love with her – takes care of her in his hut. The marquis's men track her down, however, and drag her back to the castle. At his steward's instigation, Don Sebastian agrees to marry the mayor's daughter; to keep up appearances, Martha is to marry Pedro at the same time. When Martha realizes that Pedro knows nothing of the intrigue, her hostility towards him is transformed into affection. Pedro kills the marquis in their struggle, strangling him just as he had strangled the wolf which had threatened his herd.

16 Koebner (1997), p. 222.

17 All the problems meant that the film burned up a total of at least RM 4.3 million by 1945. This was the figure Riefenstahl mentioned in the legal action against *Revue*. Cf. *Illustrierte Filmwoche*, 10 December 1949. Even that amount was enough to make *Tiefland* one of the most expensive films ever made under Nazi rule, probably rivalled only by Ufa's anniversary film, *Münchhausen* (directed by Josef von Baky, 1943), and *Kolberg* (a *Durchhaltefilm* – endurance film – directed by Veit Harlan, 1945).

18 Riefenstahl's use of internees as extras is scandalous even if it is true that she did not actually visit the Maxglan camp herself to select them. Certainly, her later remarks concerning the 'good treatment' the internees received during the filming do not betray the slightest hint of self-reproach. The memoirs contain the claim: 'The gypsies – adults and children alike – were our favourites. After the war we saw nearly all of them again' (*Memoiren I*, p. 361). Harald Reinl was director's assistant to Riefenstahl at the time; she claimed that it had been he who had selected the extras at the camp. In the court case against Nina Gladitz (see below), Reinl claimed that one of the surviving extras told him in 1949 that she would prefer 'two more years at Auschwitz to being liberated by the Russians again', U. Enzensberger (1985b), '"Lieber noch zwei Jahre Auschwitz als noch einmal von den Russen befreit werden."', *die tageszeitung*, 9 March. There is no evidence that Riefenstahl has ever distanced herself from either Reinl's remark or her own.

19 H. Weigel (1972a), 'Interview mit Leni Riefenstahl', *Filmkritik*, Vol. 16, No. 8, August, 407. Riefenstahl has always taken a very critical attitude towards *Tiefland*, which

evidently failed to meet her aesthetic demands. After the premiere, those reviewers who desisted from simply dismissing the showing of the film as a scandal praised the quality of the photography, although they were more sceptical about the story and the actors.

20 Riefenstahl claims (*Memoiren I*, p. 364) that Goebbels obstructed the shooting of the film, that complete sets had to be demolished in order to vacate the studio 'for "Ohm Krüger" and "Der alte und der junge König", films important to the war effort'. (Here she is almost certainly confusing the latter with *Der grosse König*, which Riefenstahl also refers to in the Weigel interview (1972a, p. 408.) There is, however, no evidence that those films were ever filmed in Babelsberg. Cf. J. Schöning, 'Filmographie', in Stiftung Deutsche Kinemathek (ed.), (1992), *Babelsberg 1912–1992. Ein Filmstudio*. Berlin: Argon, pp. 339 ff. Both films were Tobis productions and were filmed in the company studios, beginning on 21 October 1940 in the case of *Ohm Krüger* (at Tobis-Grunewald and Efa-Cicerostrasse) and on 27 December 1940 in the case of *Der grosse König* (Tobis-Johannistal). Cf. K. Kanzog (1994), '*Staatspolitisch besonders wertvoll.' Ein Handbuch zu 30 deutschen Spielfilmen der Jahre 1934 bis 1945*. Munich: Schaudig und Ledig (= *diskurs film*, Vol. 6, pp. 253 and 297).

21 Ufa management meeting, 22 January 1941 (BA R 109 I/1034a, p. 60). Nevertheless, on 13 November 1941, Ufa refused an application for two sound stages (for periods of six and a half and five and a half weeks) and the large *Mittelhalle* (11 weeks) 'since we and Terra [Film] have already suffered losses of ca. RM500,000 on account of this company's use of our studios' (BA R 109 I/1034b, p. 43). The studio was required for a Ufa or Terra film in each case.

22 Letter to *Reichsminister* Lammers, 2 August 1942, BA R 43/II 810b, p. 81. In this case Riefenstahl was probably unaware of Bormann's involvement. Groskopf wrote that she was not informed 'due to the delicate final stage of shooting and due to her extremely precarious state of health' (*ibid.*, p. 83).

23 Letter from Bormann to *Reichsminister* Lammers, 9 May 1943 (BA R 43/810b, p. 93).

24 At the time, this appears to have been widely believed. U. Enzensberger (1985a), 'KZ Zigeuner tanz mit mir', in *konkret*, No. 2, quotes a letter from the Tobis files: 'The capital for the film was apparently made available unofficially by the NSDAP treasurer, and allegedly originated from the Führer's own resources.'

25 'There is a general consensus that the secretary to the Führer quite frequently represented casual remarks Hitler had made over dinner, or his own, uncharted initiatives – which always furthered his personal, selfish aspirations – as Hitler's concrete instructions.' J. C. Fest (1965), *Das Gesicht des Dritten Reiches*. Frankfurt am Main, Vienna, Zürich: Büchergilde pp. 183–4.

26 For more on Max Winkler, the *éminence grise* of the film world under National Socialism, cf. H.-M. Bock and M. Töteberg (eds) (1992), *Das Ufa-Buch*. Fraunkfurt am Main: Zweitausendeins, pp. 388 ff.

27 Letter from Riefenstahl to Dr h.c. Max Winkler, 18 June 1944 (BA R 109 III/16).

28 Letter from Dr Müller-Goerne to Riefenstahl, 3 July 1944: 'May I take the liberty of drawing your attention to the fact that this decision represents a considerable sacrifice, as it prevents the production of a colour film by Terra. Overall, therefore, one less film can be made' (BA RKK/BDC, Riefenstahl file).

29 Inquiry from Müller-Goerne, 7 August 1944, BA RKK/BDC Riefenstahl file.

30 There is a handwritten note on the letter of 7 February 1945 which Müller-Goerne received from Riefenstahl Film: 'under *no* circumstances *can* we *continue* to help the F. couple – H.' (*ibid.*).

31 *Memoiren I*, p. 405: 'In these last, desolate days of the war, we were still trying feverishly to dub our film. This work became a race against time; we wanted to complete "Tiefland" before the end of the war at any price.'

32 Cf. letter from Jean Arnaud, Directeur de l'Information, 31 July 1946, to the Chef de la Section Cinéma (BA RKK/BDC Riefenstahl file).

33 H. H. Prinzler (1995), *Chronik des deutschen Films 1895–1994*. Stuttgart, Weimar: Metzler, p. 200: 'In 1954 it is not possible to view a Riefenstahl film impartially. The reviews are malicious.' In fact the reaction is not so unanimous, but the frequent praise for the photography and shot composition is generally accompanied by criticism of the story and the actors.

34 H. Sanders-Brahms, (1990), 'Tyrannenmord', in H. H. Prinzler (ed.), *Das Jahr 1945. Filme aus fünfzehn Ländern*. Berlin: Stiftung Deutsche Kinemathek, pp. 173, 176; R. von Dassanowsky (1995), '"Wherever you may run, you cannot escape him." Leni Riefenstahl's Self-Reflection and Romantic Transcendence of Nazism in "Tiefland"', *Camera Obscura*, No. 35, 107–28.

35 Sanders-Brahms (1990), p. 173. That desire was a hitherto unsuspected one, and the symbolic decoding of the film involves some assumptions which are difficult to justify.

36 *Ibid.*, pp. 175–6.

37 Von Dassanowsky (1995), p. 117, even considers that Minetti looks like Hitler, 'complete with Hitler-like poses and gestures', and that the ride through the town is a quotation from Hitler's drive through Nuremberg.

38 Cf. H. Pöttker (1990), '"Leni" verzeihen? Am Ende der Nachkriegszeit eine Retrospektive auf ihren Anfang', *Medium*, Vol. 20, No. 2, 15. In his polemical review, Pöttker refers to the 'duel between two members of the master race over the "female" – as she is actually termed'.

39 Robert von Dassanowsky, in particular, takes his interpretation of the film as a basis for interpreting the life story.

40 Outside the film, Riefenstahl cannot be said to have disassociated herself. This point has often been made by quoting her congratulatory telegram to Hitler following the capitulation of France: 'With indescribable joy, deeply moved and filled with ardent gratitude we share with you, my Führer, in your and Germany's greatest triumph: the entry of German troops into Paris. You go beyond anything the human imagination has the power to conceive, achieving deeds without like in the history of humanity; how can we possibly thank you? Expressing my congratulations is an inadequate way of showing you the feelings which move me' (BA RKK/BDC, Riefenstahl file).

41 Von Dassanowsky (1995), p. 120.

42 Sanders-Brahms (1990), p. 176. It is a matter of record that Riefenstahl has never claimed any such thing. Indeed, there is a remarkable consistency in her admissions that her doubts about Hitler emerged only at a very late stage.

43 Weigel (interview, 1972a), p. 408.

9 The Return of the Outcast

1 The report concerning her interrogation is reprinted in *Film Culture*, No. 77, 1992, 35–8: 'American Intelligence Report on Leni Riefenstahl – 30 May 1945'. By the time the interrogation took place, according to the report, she had already prepared substantial parts of her legend, including her version of her arrival in the United States in 1938. The report concludes as follows: 'If her statements are sincere, she has never grasped, and still does not grasp, the fact that she, by dedicating her life to art, has given expression to a gruesome regime and contributed to its glorification.'

2 L. Riefenstahl (1995), *Memoiren 1945–1987*. Frankfurt am Main, Berlin: Ullstein (henceforth cited as *Memoiren II*), pp. 15, 21, 24, 25.

3 In 1954 Riefenstahl told the *Mannheimer Morgen* (16 January) that approval for the release of *Tiefland*, having been granted, was withdrawn when the forged 'diary of

Eva Braun' appeared. 'I began to become emotionally disturbed and suffer from persecution mania. For four months I lay in Professor Beringer's Psychiatric Clinic in Freiburg.' The memoirs, by contrast, refer to the French forces of occupation forcibly admitting her to the secure unit of the psychiatric clinic in Freiburg due to her depressed condition (*Memoiren II*, p. 19). Here, as in many other cases, it is virtually impossible to determine which version is closer to the truth.

4 Publications in the United States, even before 1945, included the entirely spurious article, 'Is Hitler in Love with a Jewess?' (by Princess Catherine Radziwill, in *Liberty*, 16 July 1938), and the ten instalments of Ernst Jaeger's 'How Leni Riefenstahl became Hitler's Girlfriend' (*Hollywood Tribune*, 28 April to 17 July 1939; also on microfiche in *Historical Journal of Film, Radio and Television*, Vol. 13, No. 4, 1993). The latter oscillated somewhat irresponsibly between pure invention, free interpretation of the facts and accuracy. 'Nazi Pin up Girl', by Budd Schulberg, which appeared in the *Saturday Evening Post* (30 March 1946) received more attention and was much better written (if not necessarily more reliable). Schulberg was one of the organizers of the campaign against Riefenstahl and *Olympia*; the title of his article defined a prejudice which was not without influence, at least in the short term.

5 The ruling against the magazine was issued on 10 September 1948 by the regional court at Munich (Landgericht München I, 9. Zivilkammer).

6 Cf. F. Knilli (2000), *Ich war Jud Süss. Die Geschichte des Filmstars Ferdinand Marian*. Berlin: Henschel. 'Jew Süss' was the central character in the eponymous, notoriously anti-Semitic film.

7 'I must inform you that there are grave reservations here about the retrospective nomination of the film *Tiefland*, which does not seem suitable in any way to represent filmmaking in the Federal Republic of Germany abroad. I therefore regret, esteemed Mr President, that I cannot accede to your request', *Memoiren II*, p. 115.

8 The text of the telegram (*Die Welt*, 23 January 1949) is certainly very strange: 'A congratulation given to me by my Führer is fulfilment possible: that is why my heart has moved me to give thanks. Today I embrace the roses, which are as red as the surrounding mountains caressed by the last of the sun. Thus I look up to the rose garden, to its gleaming towers and walls, and stroke the red flowers with my hands and know only that I am inexpressibly happy. Your Leni Riefenstahl.' Peradifassa (Italy) is specified as the telegram's place of origin; it was sent on 24 August and collected on '25/8 0038'. Riefenstahl's objection was that she was not in or near Peradifassa in August 1938. '0038', however, probably refers to the time rather than the year.

9 See above. Schünemann presented his view of the affair in a letter to the editor published in *Die Welt* (25 January 1949): 'I would like to point out that, at the time, I told Leni Riefenstahl's secretary it would be beneath my dignity to make propaganda films of that sort. Since that cast a very dark cloud over me, I followed the advice of Herr Alberti, who was then the chief of the cultural department and Herr Auen's superior, and made an amendment to the effect that it was beneath my dignity to work under Leni Riefenstahl. Riefenstahl received a villa in Dahlem as a present from her Führer. She also boasted that she could come and go around her Führer without any prior notice. At the time in question, she would have liked to hand me over to the Gestapo, had Herr Alberti not protected me.'

10 After 1945, the way Riefenstahl was defined consistently depended on how her past was interpreted. The debate always took the same form: she repeated the basic message she had been repeating since her interrogation by the US army, whilst the doubters quoted sources which contradicted her version.

11 More facts emerged after 1949, and were presented in Riefenstahl's lawsuits (in 1983 and 1987) against Nina Gladitz (see below).

12 *Die Welt* (24 November 1949) refers to a 'fierce dispute between the plaintiff and the defence. Frau Riefenstahl never allowed the defendant to finish a full sentence, urging the lawyer on with vehement gestures.' Another description also mentions that the proceedings were 'very fierce' (*Abend*, 24 November 1949). Elsewhere there is a photograph of 'a fierce dispute' between the plaintiff and the defence (*Hamburger Abendblatt*, 25 November 1949), and a reference to 'duels of words as sharp as knives' (*Sozialdemokrat*, 29 November 1949).

13 *Hamburger Abendblatt*, 24 November 1949; *Sozialdemokrat*, 29 November 1949; *Der Spiegel*, 1 December 1949; *Hannoversche Allgemeine Zeitung*, 2 December 1949. The only markedly malicious comment was the one in *Tribüne* (3 December 1949), the newspaper of East Germany's general trade union (FDGB).

14 *Hannoversche Allgemeine Zeitung*, 2 December 1949.

15 A. Polgar (1982), *Kleine Schriften*, Vol. 1. Reinbek: Rowohlt, p. 246. The text originally appeared in *Aufbau*, Vol. 15, No. 52 (30 December 1949), p. 5.

16 *Tribüne* (3 December 1949) treated the trial as a symptom of the 'illicit state'. At the end of his article, Polgar clearly highlights continuities between the 'Third Reich' and West Germany.

17 *Die Welt*, 22 November 1949.

18 *Memoiren I*, p. 361.

19 *Revue*, No. 16, 19 April 1949, 6–7.

20 Leni Riefenstahl claimed that the events happened on 9 September (*Memoiren I*, p. 350). H. Krausnick (1993), p. 48, indicates on the basis of source material that the massacre took place on 12 September. *Revue* quoted a witness's statement specifying 5 September. The original spelling of 'Konskie' (variously Końskie, Końsky, Końskiew) has not been altered in the quotations from contemporary reports in the present volume.

21 'When the grave was deep enough, the Jews had to climb out and were made to cross to a house on the other side of Końsky's market square. As they did so, an air-force lieutenant ordered shots to be fired at the cobblestones, so that only ricochets actually hit the Jews. The result was that 31 Jews were killed . . . During the bloodbath, Leni Riefenstahl fainted' (*Revue*, No. 16, 19 April 1952, p. 7). *Die Tat* (3 December 1949) had already alleged that Riefenstahl was present at the massacre: 'In the vicinity of Warsaw, she was accorded the opportunity to witness a mass shooting of Polish Jews, of men, women, children and old men.'

22 *Memoiren I*, p. 351.

23 Quoted after *Memoiren II*, p. 98.

24 *Stern*, No. 19, 11 May 1952, p. 10.

25 *Memoiren I*, pp. 350–1.

26 'I wanted to avoid a further lawsuit against the "Revue". I felt too weak to defend myself successfully against such a potentially strong opponent.' Eventually a settlement was reached, involving a compensation payment of DM10,000. Cf. *Memoiren II*, pp. 97 and 109.

27 *Der Tagesspiegel*, 22 April 1952.

28 *Die Welt*, 20 December 1949. This was the trial, by a British military court, of one of the most senior German officers, and was regarded by reporters at the time as the 'last' war-criminal trial.

29 *Die Welt*, 2 November 1949.

30 *Die Welt*, 4 November 1949.

31 Manstein (1978), p. 44.

32 BA, Zentralnachweisstelle Aachen, file: Geschäftsstelle des Gerichts A.O.K. 6.

33 Thesis by Wolfgang Benz, in H.-G. Thiele (ed.) (1997), *Die Wehrmachtsausstellung. Dokumentation einer Kontroverse*. Bonn: Bundeszentrale für politische Bildung.

34 Greater interest in the events might have helped clarify several issues even at that time. It appears, for instance, that the German soldiers fell whilst fighting Polish troops (cf. Krausnick (1993), p. 38) and bore no visible signs of mutilation. Between 40 and 50 Jews were forced to excavate the grave near the church and were severely maltreated as they did so. When they were driven off, suffering further beatings in the process, a newly arrived lieutenant provoked an outburst of shooting by firing his pistol. Other soldiers then fired at the fleeing Jews. (Cf. Bodek (n.d.), pp. 8–9).

35 M. Mitscherlich (1987), 'Triumph der Verdrängung', *Stern*, No. 42, 8 October.

10 Projects

1 'Wie ein deutscher Film-Welterfolg entstand', *Star* 3/1952. In this interview, Riefenstahl deliberately sets her film apart. It appeared just before the film's German premiere, as did an article in *Film und Mode Revue* (No. 22, 1952: 'Kunst ist niemals "Reprise". Leni Riefenstahls Film "Das blaue Licht" – ein Markstein in der Geschichte des Kinos' (Art is Never 'Reprise'. Leni Riefenstahl's Film 'Das Blaue Licht' – a Milestone in Cinema History)). The magazine followed Riefenstahl's lead, welcoming the project 'with genuine enthusiasm, at a time when the fashionable phenomenon of out and out realism is already past its best'.

2 Cf. *Memoiren II*, p. 95, suggesting that the showing in Rome took place on 21 November 1951, although the cutting from *Die Tat* in the Deutsches Filminstitut is dated 9 March 1952. The article may have appeared at this late date to mark the imminent premiere of the film in Germany.

3 '*Das blaue Licht* will probably again be a popular success, as romanticism enjoys a considerable following – even if the artistic arbiters describe it as outmoded', *Der neue Film*, No. 31, 21 April 1952.

4 'Leni Riefenstahl, actress, author, director – in fact one of the most versatile women in the history of German cinema – has finally achieved her goal. In *Tiefland*, once again, she both acted and directed. Splendid Films Inc., New York, has already acquired the American rights for the film. And the press in England promises "Leni" a "great comeback." ' *Bild*, 10 December 1953. There were detailed advance reports in *Abendpost*, Beilage Filmillustrierte, No. 1, 1954 (' "Tiefland". Die Odysse eines Opernfilms'); *Mannheimer Morgen*, 16 January 1954 ('Zwanzig Jahre "Tiefland" '); *General-Anzeiger*, 28 January 1954 ('Riefenstahl-Film wird starten').

5 *Memoiren II*, p. 113.

6 *Die Filmwoche*, 6 February 1954.

7 'Leni Riefenstahl . . . may not be a particularly strong actress – but as a director, she has made a film that remains a timeless document full of valid beauty, despite the changes in its directorial and cutting techniques', *Film-Echo*, 13 February 1954.

8 *Der Neue Film*, 22 February 1954.

9 Riefenstahl received very little support, and her dancing was also criticized. Edmund Luft termed her a 'completely unerotic dancer' (*Filmbeobachter*, No. 6, 1954). The *Stuttgarter Zeitung* considered that 'Leni Riefenstahl did her film no favour by selecting herself for the main role of the beggar-dancer, Martha' (28 May 1954). The *Stuttgarter Nachrichten* (13 February 1954) referred to a 'wrong choice'; Ulrich Seelmann-Eggebert concluded: 'When one sees her dancing here, one suspects that the world of ballet was only too happy to lose her to the world of film; when one sees her act, one concludes that in fact she should have stuck to ballet' ('Die Dreifaltigkeit der Leni Riefenstahl', *Mannheimer Morgen*, 13 February 1964). Yet even the latter critic concludes that it is 'an interesting film. In fact it is the most interesting German-made film to have appeared at all for at least ten years.'

10 Thus Prinzler (1995), p. 200, on the reception received by the film. There were unfavourable reviews in, for example, *Evangelischer Filmbeobachter*, Vol. 6, 1954 ('an uncomfortable half-way house, as this film is very good in some ways, but very bad in others', pp. 112–13); *Stuttgarter Nachrichten*, 13 February 1952 (Dieter Raabe: 'Virtuosic Monotony'); *Süddeutsche Zeitung*, 20 April 1954 ('The way it is stylized to achieve a romantic, statuesque effect seems outmoded and unintentionally funny.'); *Deutsche Zeitung und Wirtschaftszeitung*, 17 February 1954 ('Bosoms which surge operatically and mists which surge realistically do not belong together.')

11 *Film-Echo*, 13 February 1954.

12 *Neue Ruhr-Zeitung*, 19 February 1954. There was more pronounced criticism in: *Fränkische Tagespost*, 27 March 1954; *Neue Volkszeitung Essen*, 19 June 1954; *Welt der Arbeit*, 26 February 1954.

13 'This is the time, as her *Tiefland* film opens in Germany, to get rid of the false prejudices concerning her personality', *Heidelberger Tageblatt*, 29 January 1954. Cf., in very similar vein, *Kasseler Post*, 15 May 1954.

14 'Das Unbehagen an Leni Riefenstahl' – the title of an article marking the premiere of *Olympia* at the Bremen Filmclub (*Weser-Kurier*, 29 November 1957).

15 *Der Tag*, 6 December 1957.

16 Lenssen (1999), p. 112.

17 *Memoiren II*, p. 78.

18 *Film-Kurier*, 1 April 1930.

19 The first reference to it appeared on 22 October 1950 in the *Essener Tageblatt*. This concerns a film to be shot during the Olympic Games, entitled *Hymnus auf das Leben* (Hymn to Life), in which 'Kleist's drama, *Penthesilea* . . . is to be transformed into a modern sports story. *Penthesilea* is a top skier who yields to the man she loves even though she can outdo him in sporting terms.' This might fairly be described as a typical Riefenstahl idea. Other early references to the combination of a ski film and *Penthesilea* appeared in *Echo der Woche* (17 November 1950) and *Frankenpost* (30 November 1950).

20 'Lenis "Rote Teufel". Ein Gespräch mit Frau Riefenstahl', interview in *Hamburger Abendblatt*, 25/26 April 1953. See also *Memoiren II*, p. 108.

21 *Memoiren II*, p. 120.

22 *Ibid.*, p. 169.

23 *Ibid.*, p. 207.

24 *Ibid.*, p. 199.

25 *Ibid.*, pp. 133 and 215.

26 In fact Kordofan was by then identified on all the better large-scale maps, and an encyclopaedia would have provided at least a rough indication of where the Nuba Hills were.

27 *Memoiren II*, p. 227.

28 J. C. Faris (1993), 'Leni Riefenstahl and the Nuba Peoples of Kordofan Province, Sudan', *Historical Journal of Film, Radio and Television*, Vol. 13, No. 1, 97. Faris visited the Nuba in the early 1970s and published a book about them in 1972. He is probably right to argue that the Nuba were neither as isolated nor as hard to reach as Riefenstahl suggested. He also suspects: 'Riefenstahl came to the south-east Nuba because of my own publications' (96) – a reference to the south-eastern tribes which Riefenstahl calls the 'Nuba of Kau', and which she visited only after Faris. Cf. also O. Iten (1977), 'Bilder und Zerrbilder der Nuba', *Tagesanzeiger Magazin*, No. 50, 17 December, 6–45. The criticism of Riefenstahl for contributing to the destruction of Nuba culture through her sensational photographs, however, cuts both ways. Any report of an expedition to peoples 'still untouched by civilization' helps to publicize those peoples and may turn them into a tourist attraction. Faris and Iten are also at

odds with Riefenstahl over the issue of who allegedly paid for photographs and exploited the Nuba.

29 *Memoiren II*, p. 229.

30 Cf. *ibid.*, p. 247.

31 *Ibid.*, pp. 243, 254, 260.

32 *Ibid.*, p. 343.

33 Faris (1993), p. 96, denies that the government attempted to Islamize the Nuba.

34 *Memoiren II*, p. 389.

35 L. Riefenstahl (1976), *Die Nuba von Kau*. Munich, Rheda-Wiedenbrück: Bertelsmann Club, p. 6. The book was also published in English (1976) as *The People of Kau*. New York: Harper Row and London: William Collins. Riefenstahl's previous volume of Nuba photographs was published in English (1974) as *The Last of the Nuba*. New York: Harper Row and (1976) in London: William Collins.

36 A total of 35 crates, according to *Memoiren II*, p. 411; about 1.5 tonnes according to I. Walk (1999), 'Bildproduktion und Weltmodell', in Filmmuseum Potsdam (ed.), *Leni Riefenstahl*. Berlin: Henschel, p. 163.

37 Walk (1999). Riefenstahl provides two tellingly different versions. In *Memoiren II* (p. 417) she writes: 'I had often seen a particularly beautiful girl among the rocks, in front of a hut, but I had never managed to photograph her. I had brought beads with me as a lure. I indicated my camera; she understood and posed in front of the door, as rigid as a puppet, just as I had anticipated. She was truly beautiful – the figure of an Amazon, with a defiant, wild expression. The effort was worthwhile. After I had taken a few photographs she received the bag [of beads].' In *Die Nuba von Kau* (1976) (p. 211) she describes her powers of persuasion as follows: 'This time I had brought a bag of beads with me, as a lure. As always, she ran into the hut when she saw me coming up . . . Suddenly a woman – not yet very old – spoke to me excitedly. I could not understand a word. I took the plastic bag containing the beads from my camera apron and held them up in front of the woman's face. She wanted to grab the bag immediately, but I pulled it away from her. The beads must have worked miraculously: she quickly realized whom they were meant for. She called loudly: "Jamila – Jamila". The girl came hesitantly through the narrow entrance on the other side of the hut.'

38 *Memoiren II*, p. 465. The same passage also refers to the treatment of sick people, which the present author does not mean to question. The point is that Riefenstahl regards payment in kind or by small amounts of cash – insofar as she is involved – as quite different from a financial transaction.

39 *Ibid.*, p. 394.

40 *Ibid.*, p. 285.

41 Faris (1993), p. 96, refers to a BBC film in which some of the Nuba allegedly stated that Riefenstahl had paid for shots of 'cicatrization' and 'bracelet sport combats' – 'she "paid for blood"' (as it was clearly expressed by local people interviewed in the BBC TV production)'.

42 Walk (1999), p. 162.

43 *Ibid.*, p. 163.

44 *Memoiren II*, p. 464.

45 W. Bittorf (1976), 'Blut und Hoden', *Der Spiegel*, No. 44, 25 October, 228.

46 *Ibid.*, 230. Susan Sontag (1980) 'Fascinating Fascism', in S. Sontag, *Under the Sign of Saturn*. New York: Farrar, Straus, Giroux, p. 88, expressed a similar view: 'Although the Nuba are black, not Aryan, Riefenstahl's portrait of them evokes some of the larger themes of Nazi ideology: the contrast between the clean and the impure, the incorruptible and the defiled, the physical and the mental, the joyful and the critical.' In this, the reprinted article, several serious mistakes have been eliminated from the original version, which appeared in the *New York Times*. Nevertheless, in the passage

quoted here, Sontag discusses Riefenstahl as though she really meant Harlan. The *confrontation* between such opposites has never, except in *Tiefland*, been Riefenstahl's primary interest: rather, it is the main interest of the melodrama.

11 Legal Questions and the Question of Tact

1 Cf. the description of the production process in the present book and also Barkhausen (1974a), 'A Footnote to the History of Riefenstahl's "Olympia"', *Film Quarterly*, Vol. 28, No. 1, 8–12; P. Nowotny (1981), *Leni Riefenstahls 'Triumph des Willens'. Zur Kritik dokumentarischer filmarbeit im NS-Faschismus.* Dortmund: Arbeitshefte zur Medientheorie und Medienpraxis, Vol. 3.; M. Loiperdinger (1987a), *Rituale der Mobilmachung.* Opladen: Leske und Budrich; C.C. Graham (1986), *Leni Riefenstahl and Olympia.* Metuchen, N.J. and London: Scarecrow Press.

2 *Die Welt*, 10 March 1954.

3 *Memoiren II*, p. 195.

4 *Berliner Zeitung*, 9 December 1960; likewise a report in *Welt der Arbeit* (27 January 1961).

5 *Düsseldorfer Nachrichten*, 10 December 1960. The 'substantial sum' referred to DM35,000, paid to Leni Riefenstahl by Neue Film-Verleih to reach their settlement. Cf. *Der Spiegel*, No. 3, 1961, p. 55. In her memoirs, Leni Riefenstahl gives a breakdown of the sum: DM30,000 represented the licence fee for West Germany and DM5,000 the one for Austria: *Memoiren II*, p. 194.

6 Riefenstahl claims that, on the advice of her lawyer, 'I met my debts by ceding all other demands arising from screenings of this film outside Germany and Austria to my main creditor, the producer Friedrich A. Mainz. I did not want to go on burdening myself with legal wrangles' *Memoiren II*, p. 195.

7 *Der Spiegel*, No. 3, 1961, p. 55.

8 Federal Supreme Court judgment in the legal dispute between film producer Friedrich A. Mainz (plaintiff) and the Minerva company (defendant), pronounced on 10 January 1969, IZR 48/67.

9 *Der Abend* (10 December 1960); *Berliner Morgenpost* (11 December 1960); *Stuttgarter Zeitung* (12 December 1960); *Frankfurter Rundschau* (13 December 1960); *Der Tagesspiegel* (14 December 1960); *Welt der Arbeit* (27 January 1961).

10 *Berliner Zeitung* (9 and 12 December 1960); *Neuer Tag* (14 December 1960); *Norddeutsche Zeitung* (4 February 1961).

11 *Berliner Morgenpost*, 11 December 1960; the *Frankfurter Rundschau* (13 December 1969) took a similar view, regretting that when Riefenstahl saw *Mein Kampf*, a 'cinematic document . . . which provides an invaluable insight into the character and consequences of the Third Reich, she was moved by only one feeling: This is a chance for Leni Riefenstahl to make some money! . . . Could one expect the "not affected" grand dame of Reich cinema to show some inhibitions, or even some tact? Could one assume that she – like many young people – would cover her face with her hands in shame at the scenes in the film "Mein Kampf" and take the chance to support its message? No, she simply demanded her "rights" – her money. She is eager to trouble the courts again, but no court can acquit her of this lack of political and moral instinct.'

12 *Der Tagesspiegel*, 14 December 1960. This article, signed 'V.B.' (probably Volker Baer), is one of the few to mention the 'fee' Riefenstahl received, thereby alluding to her position within the production.

13 In East Germany the verdict at the Munich regional court was seen as evidence of the resurgence of former Nazis and was occasionally cited as a typical symptom of the condition of West German society (*Norddeutsche Zeitung*, 4 February 1961).

14 A report in *Bella* magazine (issue 26/1957) notes: 'Leni Riefenstahl had to break off her convalescence in Madrid to attend a revival of her Olympia film organized by film clubs in Hamburg, Bremen and Berlin. The clubs also called on Leni Riefenstahl to say something about her film, and she could not bring herself to disappoint her cinematic friends, although she does continue to fear the aggression of the press.' In her memoirs she gives her point of view and concludes: 'The success was overwhelming in all three cities, not just among the audiences, but also in the press' *Memoiren II*, p. 174.

15 L. Riefenstahl (1958): 'Begründung des Einspruchs gegen die Entscheidung des Bewertungsausschusses vom 30. Januar 1958.' MS, 19 April; Archiv des Deutschen Filminstituts, Frankfurt-am-Main.

16 Leni Riefenstahl compiled a brochure containing press reactions to accompany *Olympia*, not dissimilar to the one dedicated to her performances as a dancer. Unsurprisingly, she only included positive comments. It does appear, however, that the reactions at the relatively few, carefully selected events at which the film was shown were largely positive.

17 'Notiz des Referates 202', 9 January 1956, Foreign Ministry political archive (Politisches Archiv des AA), 'Referat 605', vol. 473, case no. 4207, 'Olympia-Film'.

18 Letters from Leni Riefenstahl Production to the Foreign Ministry, 1 and 20 August, 19 December 1957 (*ibid.*).

19 Letters of 27 May and 7 June 1958 (*ibid.*).

20 The author was told of Riefenstahl's opposition in the course of a conversation with Hans Brecht on 24 September 1999, in Hamburg. Riefenstahl herself mentioned the broadcast when she appeared on the chat show *Je später der Abend . . .*, saying that she had been unable to prevent it.

21 The only press reactions found so far were those in the following newspapers: *Der Tagesspiegel* (1 October 1974); *Die Welt* (1 October 1974) – both relating to the first broadcast on 29 September 1974 ('Nordkette' and HR III); the second broadcast on 4 September 1976 ('Nordkette' and HR III again, also SWF III) produced an advance report in the *Frankfurter Rundschau* (4 September 1976) and commentaries in *Mannheimer Morgen* (6 September 1976); *Frankfurter Abendpost* (7 September 1976); *Berliner Allgemeine Jüdische Wochenzeitung* (10 September 1976). The reactions to the second broadcast were more critical; the magazine *Frauen und Film* specifically referred to it in the foreword to its Riefenstahl issue (No. 14, December 1977), in which it registered its opposition to the filmmaker's 'renaissance' (p. 2). The editor responsible for the broadcasts, Hans Brecht, and Joachim C. Fest, who provided the commentary which followed the film on each occasion, have both told the author that there were no debates concerning the programme either before or after its transmission.

22 The sources cited for the OLG verdict in the Munich decision included the *Protokoll* of the Ufa board meeting (28 August 1934), the report of the Ufa auditor (31 May 1935) and the censor card for the 16mm copy of the film. For its part, the Supreme Court demanded an expert report from the Federal Justice Ministry.

23 *Memoiren II*, pp. 355 ff.

24 Federal Supreme Court judgment of 10 January 1969, p. 2.

25 *Memoiren II*, p. 356. In fact the description is typed in the *Protokoll* for the Ufa annual report of 10 August 1934 (BA R 109 I/2420).

26 Copies in BA R 109 I/2163.

27 In her usual, melodramatic style she terms Raether her 'chief enemy', claiming that his opposition to her was so persistent that 'he was even briefly imprisoned'. (*Memoiren II*, p. 357). If Raether really was ever imprisoned, it was certainly not on account of his aversion to Riefenstahl (although that aversion is undeniable). Even

during the filming of *Triumph des Willens*, he remained in the propaganda ministry; when he was expelled it was, according to Goebbels in his diary, on suspicion of corruption.

28 Quoted after Leni Riefenstahl, *Memoiren II*, p. 358.

29 'This document is unchallengeable in any court of law. I desisted from legal action against Herr Leiser. It is enough for me to have in my hands such an important token in support of my case.' *Memoiren II*, p. 359.

30 'Transit Filmvertrieb GmbH' – a public limited company – plays a part in the complicated and chequered history of the administration of the Ufi assets after 1945. In 1960, the company's manager, Dr Söhnel, sketched out the background. The company, he said, emerged from the original Transit Film company, which 'until the end of the war had the task of importing and exporting films which did not derive from productions of the Ufi/Ufa concern (Cinematic Arts).' On 1 January 1954, the company was re-founded, this time with the task of exploiting the film rights belonging to former state companies abroad and securing the assets of the former Reich film industry, also abroad. Within Germany, it was the Ufi Filmvertrieb GmbH distribution company which dealt with such matters. 'In the interests of simplification and consistency, the two companies – Transit Film and Ufi GmbH Filmvertrieb, were merged to form a single company called Transit Filmvertrieb GmbH with effect from 1 January 1957' BA R 109 I/ 2992. Letter from Söhnel of 15 February 1960.

31 The parties to the contract were represented by the abbreviations LR and Transit.

32 BA R 109 I/2163. Agreement between Transit-Filmvertrieb GmbH and Leni Riefenstahl of 16 January 1964.

33 BA R 109 I/2163, letter of 17 January 1968.

34 The articles of association for Transit Film GmbH were concluded on 18 January 1966. The sole shareholder is the West German state, whose representatives formed the supervisory board.

35 Letter of 29 March 1968 to Ufa Film GmbH i.L., on the subject of *Triumph des Willens*. In the course of the correspondence it became apparent that Transit's interest was by no means confined to that film alone.

36 BA R 109 I/2163, letter from Ufa Film GmbH i.L. to Transit Film GmbH of 1 April 1968.

37 BA R 109 I/2163, letter of 4 October 1968.

38 'According to the Interior Minister's statement of 25.3.1969, the two Olympia films specified above are subject to the decision of 1.4.1960, which stipulates that, being documentary films, they are to be transferred to the Federation. At the time, it was explained that even full-length films without a dramatic plot were to be regarded as documentary films. Herr Dr Michel explicitly specified that such films are subject to the decision of 1.4.1960. May we respectfully request that you inform us of your position' Letter of 14 April 1969, BA R 109 I/2163 (which also includes the reply of 15 April 1969).

39 BA R 109 I/2163, draft contract of 17 March 1969.

40 The 38th meeting of the Ufi liquidation committee addressed these matters on 1 April 1960. The following decision was formulated about the attitude to be adopted regarding the rights to wartime weekly newsreels: '1. The rights to the photographs taken by PK film reporters and the film material shall be released from administration by the liquidator of Ufa Film GmbH and transferred to the Federation. 2. The film rights and the film material of the former Deutsche Wochenschau GmbH i.L. [the German weekly newsreel company] shall be transferred to the Federation. 3. There shall be no charge for the transfer: the liquidation committee is assuming that there will be no further evaluations of past income and expenditure, i.e., that they are cancelled out. 4. The transfer is conditional

on the Federation declaring that it is ready to return any such rights and any such material which turns out not to fall under § 7, clause 2 of the Ufi liquidation legislation' (R 109 I/2986). The committee passed the motion with eight votes in favour, three abstentions and one vote against. The *Protokoll* for the meeting makes it clear that the discussions really did take account only of wartime weekly newsreels.

41 Information from Transit Film GmbH.

42 Oral information provided to the present author by the person responsible at the time in the Interior Ministry.

43 *Berliner Allgemeine Jüdische Wochenzeitung* (26 October 1979).

44 Today, *Triumph des Willens* is not always used with Transit's consent. Apart from illegal copies, Transit also seems to have overlooked the Italian magazine *L'Espresso*'s spectacular offer of a video of *Triumph des Willens* in its 'Riefenstahl edition' (for 9,900 Lire).

12 A Renaissance – But No Rehabilitation

1 *Memoiren II*, p. 467.

2 H. E. Holthusen (1975), 'Leni Riefenstahl in Amerika', *Merkur*, Vol. 29, No. 325, June, 569–78.

3 *Film-Echo*, 17 May 1972. The 'Evangelical Aid Society for former Victims of Racial Persecution' had written to the West Berlin minister for internal affairs, informing him that the premiere was to be 'used to pay homage to Frau Riefenstahl, who is known as a Nazi'. Cf. press reports, for example those in *Die Welt* and *Der Tagesspiegel*, both 6 May 1972.

4 The transmission on 16 April 1974 was followed by a commentary by Joachim C. Fest. The first part of the film, *Fest der Völker*, had already been shown by NDR on 7 December 1968. Riefenstahl is wrong to claim that 'in Germany the Olympic films had never been shown on television, despite their topicality when the Games came to Munich. Not a single German broadcaster had expressed any interest' *Memoiren II*, p. 371.

5 *Film-Echo*, 17 May 1972 and *Münchener Merkur*, 25 July 1972.

6 W. Limmer (1972), 'Körper-Kunst. Leni Riefenstahls Olympia-Film von 1936 im Arri-Kino', *Süddeutsche Zeitung*, 28 July. A few days later (1 August 1972) the same newspaper also published a vehemently critical piece: 'Euthanasia in film form. Everything ordinary or relative has been filtered away or cut out. An idealized projection of what was being prepared . . . A symphony of horror.'

7 W. Donner (1972), 'Politik hat sie nie interessiert. Leni Riefenstahls Comeback', *Die Zeit*, 18 August.

8 V. Polcuch (1972), 'Leni Riefenstahls Weg führte vom "Heiligen Berg" zum "Triumph des Willens"', *Die Welt*, 21 August.

9 R. Ganz (1972), 'Leni Riefenstahls fragwürdige Renaissance', *Frankfurter Rundschau*, 25 August: 'Even today it has not yet been generally understood that Leni Riefenstahl's liaison with the brown regime was not coincidental. In fact, irrespective of her subjective political views, she was a representative of a purely fascist aesthetic.'

10 K. Kreimeier (1972), 'Schöne gefährliche Bilder. Kritische Anmerkungen zu Leni Riefenstahl', *Stuttgarter Zeitung*, 25 August: 'Fascism produced no "art" or "aesthetic" of its own, but it found enough apolitical artists and aesthetes prepared to accept its norms blindly. "Triumph des Willens" is a political eulogy to the point of excess; its ornamentation is a cinematic hymn to fascism's murderous contempt for the masses.' Kreimeier also makes reference to the film's aesthetic principles: 'This pattern was made to measure for the flood of images. The aim is to make the

optical impressions flow as smoothly and agreeably as possible, avoiding any conflict.'

11 In addition to the pieces by Donner, Ganz, Kreimeier, Limmer and Polcuch cited above, cf. also S. Haffner (1972), 'Man glaubt Goebbels zu hören. Leni Riefenstahls Olympia-Film von 1936', *Deutsches Allgemeines Sonntagsblatt*, 20 August; H. R. Blum (1972), 'Die Riefenstahl im Streit der Meinungen', *Bremer Nachrichten*, 21 August; U. Greiner (1972), 'Das unaufhaltsame Comeback der Leni Riefenstahl', *Frankfurter Allgemeine Zeitung*, 1 September.

12 *Bild*, 1 November 1976. Tabloid journalism has its own set of rules, and on 11 November 1976 *Bild* published a story by Franz Josef Wagner entitled 'Was ist aus ihnen geworden? Leni Riefenstahl' (What Became of Them? Leni Riefenstahl). Leni Riefenstahl was particularly annoyed by this article, and it is one case in which one can only sympathize with her. The chat show produced an extraordinary reaction; cf.: J. Bönk (1976) 'Leni-Riefenstahl-Show' (*Bonner Rundschau*, 1 November); R. Rostow (1976), 'Je später der Abend' (*Die Welt*, 1 November); K. O. Saur (1976), 'Ausgewogenheit pervers' (Perverted Balance) (*Süddeutsche Zeitung*, 2 November); M. Stone (1976), 'Kurz angemerkt' (*Der Tagesspiegel*, 2 November); Momos (i.e. Walter Jens, 1976), 'Eine papierne Paarung' (A Wooden Combination) (*Die Zeit*, 5 November); H. von Nussbaum (1976), 'Leni Riefenstahl oder die Banalität des Verführers' (Leni Riefenstahl or the Banality of the Seducer) (*epd/Kirche und Rundfunk*, 6 November); W. Hellmuth (1976), 'Die Riefenstahl rief pfui' (Riefenstahl Shouted Boo!) (*Welt am Sonntag*, 7 November).

13 *Hör zu*, the main television magazine at the time, published selected letters on the subject on 20 November 1976 (No. 47) and 27 November 1976 (No. 48). According to its editors, 90 per cent of the reactions it received were in Riefenstahl's favour.

14 *AZ* (Munich), 3 November 1976.

15 'Wir halten zu Leni Riefenstahl!', *Das Neue Blatt*; in the cuttings collection of the Stiftung Deutsche Kinemathek it is dated simply 1976. It probably appeared at the end of November or beginning of December, certainly after issue number 47.

16 She did not, however, make many television appearances. After her chat show experience, Riefenstahl only accepted selected one-to-one interviews: *Ich habe nicht darüber nachgedacht* (I Did Not Think About It) by Fritz Schindler (ARD, 19 August 1977); *Lebensläufe* by Hermann Schreiber (ARD, 22 August 1980); *Berliner Begegnungen* by Engelbert Sauter (11 March 1999).

17 In her old age, she was indeed compared to Dietrich. Cf. the radio play by Thea Dorn, *Preussische Diven blond wie Stahl* (Prussian Divas Blonde as Steel, SFB/ORB) and E. Bronfen (2000), 'Leni Riefenstahl und Marlene Dietrich: Zwei deutsche Stars', in W. Jacobsen, H. H. Prinzler and W. Sudendorf (eds), *Filmmuseum Berlin. Katalog*. Berlin: Nicolai, pp. 169–90. I am grateful to Wolfgang Jacobsen for drawing my attention to the latter article.

18 'We have left a terrible legacy. I owe a debt. Guilt remains; one can call it by that name' *Die Welt*, 8 May 2000.

19 H. G. Rodek (1999), 'Geburt von Leni Riefenstar', *Die Welt*, 8 February. Cf. other references to uncharacteristically indulgent journalists in: A Mihan (1999), 'Abtauchen ist ihre Sache nicht' (*Märkische Allgemeine*, 8 February); B. Werneburg (1999), 'Der Besuch der alten Dame' (*die tageszeitung*, 8 February); H. Martenstein (1999), 'Und immer an das Gute glauben' (*Der Tagesspiegel*, 7 February).

20 The documents appear in: Dokumentationsarchiv des österreichischen Widerstands (ed.) (n.d.), *Widerstand und Verfolgung in Salzburg 1933–1945. Eine Dokumentation*. Vienna: Österreichischer Bundesverlag, pp. 511 and 504.

21 E. Thurner (n.d.), 'Die nationalsozialistische Zigeunerverfolgung am Beispiel des Zigeunerlagers Salzburg-Maxglan', in Magistratsabteilung II/Kultur und Schulver-

waltung Salzburg (ed.), *Salzburg. Ein Beitrag zum 40jährigen Bestehen der Zweiten Republik.* Salzburg, p. 31.

22 *Memoiren II*, p. 64.

23 H. Kühnert. (1987), 'Wenn Juristen Vergangenheit klären', *Die Zeit*, 27 March.

24 Mitscherlich (1987). For other comments regarding the memoirs cf.: W. Ross (1987), 'Zwischen Edelmenschen und Schurken' (Between Nobility and Villainy) (*Frankfurter Allgemeine Zeitung*, 6 October); F. J. Raddatz (1987), 'Hitler lobte Helenes Apfelstrudel' (Hitler Praised Helene's Apfelstrudel) (*Die Zeit*, No. 42, 9 October); H. Klunker (1987), 'Das Schicksal musste nicht Hitler heissen' (Fate Did not Have to Mean Hitler) (*Deutsches Allgemeines Sonntagsblatt Magazin*, No. 41, 11 October); V. Baer (1987), 'Dokumente des Unbetroffenseins' (Records of Being Unaffected) (*Der Tagesspiegel*, 1 November); C. Riess (1987), 'Suchen nach der verlorenen Unschuld' (Searching for Lost Innocence) (*Die Welt*, 28 November).

25 Ross (1987). After reading the memoirs, Fritz J. Raddatz (1987) asked himself 'whether the lady might perhaps be rather stupid?'

26 Cf. the interview with *L'Espresso*'s sales director, Guido Ferrantelli, who puts sales of *Triumph des Willens* at between 130,000 and 150,000: *die tageszeitung*, 22 April 1997.

27 Cf. R. Schnell (1992), 'Triumph des Überlebenswillens', *Frankfurter Rundschau*, 7 January and itt. (i.e. Uwe Schmitt), 'Lenismus', *Frankfurter Allgemeine Zeitung*, 20 January 1992.

28 Schnell (1992). The German public was able to view parts of the exhibition at first hand: the extra-large prints of the Nuba photographs which were produced for Tokyo were also shown at the Galerie Schlüter in Hamburg and the Filmmuseum Potsdam.

29 The *Frankfurter Allgemeine Zeitung* (7 August 1996) noted that 'Italy has the courage to show the first Riefenstahl retrospective' (Italien traut sich und zeigt die erste Leni-Riefenstahl-Retrospektive')!

30 Filmmuseum Potsdam (ed.) (1999), *Leni Riefenstahl*. Berlin: Henschel.

31 'Keine Hommage an Leni Riefenstahl. Interview mit Regisseur Ray Müller', *Frankfurter Rundschau*, 26 March 1994.

32 S. Reinecke (1994), 'Die trübe Macht der Bilder', *Wochenpost*, No. 2, 5 January. 'Since no admission of guilt was forthcoming from the older woman, a belated reconciliation seems to have been put on the agenda. Formerly, the subjectivity of the younger woman barricaded itself behind accusatory gestures and naked facts; the new approach is benign and slightly melancholy and it is no longer necessary to be quite so pedantic about the facts.'

33 J. Schmidt (1996), 'Küsst die Faschisten, wo ihr sie trefft' (Kiss the Fascists Wherever You Can), *Frankfurter Allgemeine Zeitung*, 4 November.

34 M. Peters (1996), 'Die Hommage', *Das Sonntagsblatt*, 8 November.

35 K. Umbach (1996), 'Schaf im Wolfspelz' (A Sheep in Wolf's Clothing), *Der Spiegel*, No. 45, 4 November. The 'visit of the old lady' is a reference to Dürrenmatt's play – *Der Besuch der alten Dame* (translated as 'The Visit').

36 Thea Dorn (1998) 'Marleni. Preussische Diven blond wie Stahl' (SFB/ORB – later also produced as a stage play).

37 Cf. Klunker (1987).

38 Riefenstahl (1937), p. 283. The text continues as follows: 'Arthur Grimm took the stills. The photographs of work in progress are by Arthur Grimm and Rolf Lantin. Guzzi Lantschner selected the pictures from the film footage. Enlargements and preparation of the photographs: Gertrud Sieburg and Rolf Lantin.'

13 In Conclusion: A Change of Persona

1 M. Mund (1999), 'Riefenstahl und die anderen', *Neues Deutschland*, 13 January.
2 G. Seesslen (1994b), 'Die Ästhetik des Barbarischen', *Die Woche*, 14 April.
3 Cf. O. Bulgakowa (1999), 'Riefenstein – Demontage eines Klischees', in Filmmuseum Potsdam (ed.), *Leni Riefenstahl*. Berlin: Henschel, pp. 132 ff.

Appendices

Chronology

22.8.1902	Helene Bertha Amalie Riefenstahl is born in Berlin. She is the first child of Alfred and Bertha Ida.
1918	Leni Riefenstahl takes dancing lessons at the Grimm-Reiter school, later also with Jutta Klamt, Eugenie Eduardova and Mary Wigman.
21.2.1921	First performance by Leni Riefenstahl as a dance student in a Grimm-Reiter school production.
23.10.1923	First solo performance as a dancer at the Tonhalle in Munich.
27.10.1923	Solo performance at the Blüthner-Saal in Berlin, followed by a tour which includes performances in Zürich, Prague, Innsbruck, Breslau, Braunschweig, Cologne and elsewhere.
8-9.11.1923	Popular uprising, led by Adolf Hitler, against the Reich authorities in Munich.
16.11.1923	Introduction of the 'Rentenmark' achieves currency stabilization; end of inflation.
May 1924	A knee injury forces Riefenstahl to interrupt her career.
20.1.1926	Riefenstahl makes her brief comeback as a dancer with another performance at the Blüthner-Saal in Berlin.
17.12.1926	Premiere of *Der heilige Berg* at the Ufa-Palast am Zoo, Berlin.
20.12.1927	Premiere of *Der grosse Sprung* at the Ufa-Palast am Zoo.

11-19.2.1928	Winter Olympics in St Moritz; Riefenstahl is there as a visitor.
16.11.1928	Hitler's first speech at the Sportpalast in Berlin.
15.11.1929	Premiere of *Die weisse Hölle vom Piz Palü* at the Ufa-Palast am Zoo.
25.12.1930	Premiere of *Stürme über dem Montblanc* in Dresden and Frankfurt am Main.
10.12.1931	Premiere of *Der weisse Rausch* at the Ufa-Palast am Zoo.
24.3.1932	Premiere of *Das blaue Licht* at the Ufa-Palast am Zoo.
May 1932	Riefenstahl meets Hitler for the first time.
28.9.1932	She returns from shooting *S.O.S. Eisberg* in Greenland.
30.1.1933	Hitler appointed as Reich Chancellor.
1.4.1933	The NSDAP organizes a boycott of businesses belonging to Jews throughout the Reich.
7.4.1933	The opposition and Jewish officials lose their jobs in the restructuring of the civil service following the 'Gesetz zur Wiederherstellung des Berufsbeamtentums' (bill to restore a professional civil service).
10.5.1933	Book burning at the Opernplatz in Berlin.
17.5.1933	Goebbels discusses a 'Hitler film' with Riefenstahl.
23.8.1933	Riefenstahl's appointment as artistic director of the Party Rally film is made public.
30.8-3.9.1933	NSDAP Party Rally in Nuremberg.
30.8.1933	Premiere of *S.O.S. Eisberg* at the Ufa-Palast am Zoo.
2.12.1933	Premiere of *Sieg des Glaubens*, Ufa-Palast am Zoo.
25.4.1934	Riefenstahl leaves for a short lecture tour of England. She speaks about her film work in Oxford, London and Cambridge.
June 1934	Riefenstahl is taken ill while filming *Tiefland* in Spain. The project has to be broken off.
30.6.1934	In a surprise move, Ernst Röhm is arrested and then, on 1 July, shot. Other opposition figures are also murdered, along with some individuals

	who were not involved. The propaganda refers to the 'Röhm Putsch'.
2.8.1934	Death of the President of Germany, Paul von Hindenburg. Hitler succeeds him.
20.8.1934	Riefenstahl and Hitler inspect the preparations for the NSDAP Reich Party Rally.
4-10.9.1934	NSDAP Reich Party Rally in Nuremberg.
7.12.1934	Hitler visits the Geyer processing laboratories, where he and Riefenstahl watch parts of *Triumph des Willens*.
25.3.1935	Riefenstahl holds a press conference in the Schinkel-Saal at the Propaganda Ministry and talks about *Triumph des Willens*.
28.3.1935	Premiere of *Triumph des Willens*, Ufa-Palast am Zoo.
1.5.1935	German National Film Prize awarded to *Triumph des Willens*.
10-16.9.1935	NSDAP Party Rally. Riefenstahl films material for the 'Reich Party Rally Film Archive' and for the '*Wehrmacht* Film'.
15.9.1935	During the Party Rally, the Nuremberg Laws, depriving Jewish citizens of their rights, are passed: the 'Reichsbürgergesetz' (The Reich Citizenship Law) and the 'Gesetz zum Schutze des Deutschen Blutes und der Deutschen Ehre' (Law for the Protection of German Blood and German Honour).
17.9.1935	*Triumph des Willens* wins prize for the best documentary film at the Venice Film Festival.
9.12.1935	Foundation of the company 'Olympia Film GmbH'; preparations for *Olympia* begin.
10.12.1935	Official announcement that Goebbels has appointed Riefenstahl to make *Olympia*.
19.12.1935	Press preview of *Tag der Freiheit*.
30.12.1935	Premiere of *Tag der Freiheit*, Ufa-Palast am Zoo.
26.1.1936	Mussolini receives Riefenstahl in Rome for a meeting.
6-12.2.1936	Winter Olympics at Garmisch-Partenkirchen; Riefenstahl is present as a visitor.

7.3.1936	German troops march into the demilitarized Rhineland.
17.7.1936	Riefenstahl leaves for Greece to film the journey of the Olympic torch.
1-16.8.1936	Summer Olympics in Berlin.
8-14.9.1936	NSDAP Party Rally in Nuremberg.
26.4.1937	The German 'Condor Legion' devastates the Basque city of Guernica in a bombing raid.
24.5.1937	Opening of the World Fair in Paris.
3.7.1937	Premiere of *Triumph des Willens* in Paris; the film is awarded a 'Grand Prix' at the World Exhibition.
18.7.1937	Hitler opens the 'House for German Art' in Munich.
19.7.1937	The 'Degenerate Art' exhibition opens in Munich.
25.9.1937	Benito Mussolini arrives in Berlin for a state visit.
12.3.1938	German troops march into Austria.
10.4.1938	Plebiscite in Austria and Germany on the issue of the *Anschluss*. Cinema artists including Leni Riefenstahl campaign in print in the *Film-Kurier*.
20.4.1938	Premiere of *Olympia*, Ufa-Palast am Zoo.
1.5.1938	German Film Prize for *Olympia*.
10.5.1938	First showing of *Olympia* abroad, in Zürich.
3.6.1938	Martin Bormann is appointed as one of Hitler's adjutants; the Adolf Hitler's 'Privatkanzlei' (private office), led by Bormann, is integrated into the NSDAP.
31.8.1938	*Olympia* wins the prize for the best film at the Venice Film Festival.
27.9.1938	Re-premiere of *Das blaue Licht*.
30.9.1938	The German Reich, France, Great Britain and Italy sign the Munich Agreement. The four powers agree to cede the Sudeten German territories to the Reich, without listening to the Czech government. The decision represents a further attempt to avoid war by making concessions to Hitler.
5.10.1938	The passports of German Jews lose their validity.

From now on their papers have to be stamped with a 'J'.

4.11.1938	Riefenstahl arrives in New York aboard the *Europa*.
9.11.1938	SA troops all over Germany organize the destruction of synagogues, businesses and community centres. 91 Jewish citizens are killed, 21,000 arrested.
24.11.1938	Riefenstahl's arrival in Hollywood.
9.1.1939	Completion of the new Reich Chancellery building designed by Albert Speer.
16.3.1939	German troops occupy Bohemia, Moravia and parts of western Slovakia. The establishment of the 'Reich Protectorate' signifies the end of Czechoslovakia.
22.5.1939	The treaty of friendship between Italy and Germany ('Steel Pact') is renewed in Berlin during the state visit by Italian foreign minister Galeazzo Ciano.
23.8.1939	German foreign minister Joachim von Ribbentrop and his opposite number Vyacheslav Molotov sign the German–Soviet non-aggression pact.
1.9.1939	German armed forces invade Poland. Start of World War II.
12.9.1939	Riefenstahl witnesses atrocities committed by German soldiers against Polish civilians in the course of her work as a war reporter. She subsequently resigns from her position.
6.10.1939	Surrender of the Polish army.
8.11.1939	Hitler is fortunate to escape a bomb attack planned by Georg Elser in Munich's Bürgerbräu-Keller.
January 1940	Foundation of the Riefenstahl GmbH company.
22.6.1940	Signing of the armistice with France at Compiègne; Riefenstahl sends a telegram to Hitler, congratulating him.
6.8.1940	Filming of *Tiefland* begins.
23.9.1940	A list of 'gypsies allocated to work for

	Riefenstahl-Film GmbH' names 19 individuals, 15 of them children.
10.5.1941	The 'Führer's deputy', Rudolf Hess, flies to England, allegedly to negotiate a ceasefire. Hitler declares him to be 'mad'; Martin Bormann takes over Hess's position.
22.6.1941	Germany attacks the Soviet Union.
1.9.1941	Jews in the German Reich are obliged to wear the yellow star.
17.11.1941	Ernst Udet – General Director of Aircraft at the Air Ministry since 1938 – commits suicide.
7.12.1941	Japanese aircraft bomb the American naval base of Pearl Harbor on Hawaii. The USA goes to war with Japan.
11.12.1941	The German Reich declares war on the USA.
13.12.1941	Hitler takes over supreme command of the army.
20.1.1942	The 'Wannsee Conference' resolves to systematically murder all European Jews.
8.2.1942	Fritz Todt dies in an air crash. Albert Speer is appointed to succeed him as minister for armaments and munitions.
2.2.1943	Final destruction of the remnants of the Sixth Army at Stalingrad.
18.2.1943	Goebbels declares 'total war' in a speech at Berlin's Sportpalast.
Summer 1943	Riefenstahl in Spain to film *Tiefland*.
8.9.1943	Italy surrenders after allied troops land in Sicily and the mainland.
12.9.1943	German paratroopers liberate Benito Mussolini from his incarceration.
November 1943	Riefenstahl moves to Kitzbühel and establishes her film company there.
21.3.1944	Riefenstahl marries Peter Jacob.
30.3.1944	Riefenstahl and her husband visit Hitler at the Berghof, Obersalzberg; this is to be her last meeting with him.
6.6.1944	Allied landings in Normandy.
July 1944	Riefenstahl's father Alfred dies and her brother Heinz falls on the Eastern Front.

20.7.1944	The attempt by Graf von Stauffenberg's resistance group to assassinate Hitler fails.
25.8.1944	Allied troops liberate Paris.
September 1944	Final scenes of *Tiefland* are shot at the Barrandov Studios in Prague.
16.10.1944	The Red Army reaches East Prussia.
21.10.1944	US troops occupy Aachen.
27.1.1945	The Red Army liberates the Auschwitz extermination camp.
19.3.1945	Hitler issues the order for the blanket destruction of roads, bridges, industry, etc. in order to impede the Allied advance (the 'Nero Order').
29.3.1945	The US army takes Frankfurt am Main.
30.4.1945	Hitler commits suicide.
2.5.1945	Surrender of Berlin.
7-8.5.1945	Unconditional surrender of the German Reich.
6.6.1945	Leni Riefenstahl, having been arrested for interrogation, is released by the US Seventh Army.
20.11.1945	The war crimes trials in Nuremberg begin.
June 1947	Riefenstahl is referred to a psychiatric clinic in Freiburg.
Summer 1947	Divorce from Peter Jacob.
1.12.1948	First denazification trial in Villingen: Riefenstahl is categorized as 'nicht betroffen' (not affected).
1948	After a delay caused by the war, *Olympia* receives a Gold Medal from the International Olympic Committee.
1.5.1949	*Revue* publishes an article attacking Riefenstahl's conduct during the filming of *Tiefland*.
6.7.1949	Second denazification trial in Freiburg; Leni Riefenstahl is again categorized as 'nicht betroffen'.
23.11.1949	Civil trial concerning the allegations in *Revue* about the filming of *Tiefland*.
Early 1950	Riefenstahl is categorized as a 'Mitläufer' (follower or fellow traveller).
September 1950	Riefenstahl works on a film project in Italy (*Die roten Teufel*).

21.11.1951	Premiere of *Das blaue Licht* (new version – re-edited and with a new soundtrack) in Rome.
6.4.1952	German premiere of the new version of *Das blaue Licht*.
19.4.1952	*Revue* reports on the Konskie massacre.
21.4.1952	Denazification trial in Berlin
11.2.1954	Premiere of *Tiefland* in Stuttgart.
July 1955	Riefenstahl in Spain, where she seeks partners for new film projects.
April 1956	Riefenstahl leaves for her first trip to Africa and is involved in a serious car crash.
November 1957	*Olympia* shown for the first time since the war in Hamburg and Bremen.
August 1959	Retrospective of Riefenstahl's films at the Biennale in Venice.
10.1.1960	Following public protests, the British Film Institute withdraws its invitation for Riefenstahl to give a talk about her filmmaking on 10.4.1960.
31.8.1960	Riefenstahl receives DM35,000 from the distributors of the film *Mein Kampf* for the use of excerpts from *Triumph des Willens*.
14.12.1960	Riefenstahl holds a 'tearful press conference' (*Frankfurter Allgemeine Zeitung*) in London in order to advance the cause of a remake of *Das blaue Licht*.
December 1962	Riefenstahl visits the Nuba in Sudan for the first time.
8.8.1963	She returns from her trip to Africa.
December 1964	Riefenstahl's second stay among the Nuba.
14.1.1965	Death of Riefenstahl's mother; Riefenstahl breaks off her African expedition.
December 1966	Riefenstahl's third trip to the Nuba.
December 1968	Riefenstahl sets off on her fourth journey to the Nuba, shortly after getting to know Horst Kettner.
10.1.1969	The West German Federal Supreme Court verdict on the use of excerpts from *Triumph des Willens* in Erwin Leiser's film, *Mein Kampf* goes in favour of the Swedish production company.

November 1970	Riefenstahl goes on a photographic safari in East Africa.
5.5.1972	Planned matinee showings of *Olympia* in Berlin's Zoo-Palast are cancelled following protests.
26.8-11.9.1972	Summer Olympics in Munich. Riefenstahl employed as a photographer for the *Sunday Times*.
1973	The book of photographs, *Die Nuba – Menschen wie von einem anderen Stern* is published (in English as *The Last of the Nuba* in the same year).
December 1974	Second expedition to the Nuba of Kau.
1974	First diving expeditions (Indian Ocean, Maldives).
April 1976	The Art Directors Club of Germany awards Leni Riefenstahl its gold medal for the best photographic work of 1975.
17.7.-1.8.1976	Summer Olympics in Montreal: Riefenstahl is a guest of honour.
October 1976	The book of photographs *Die Nuba von Kau* is published (in English as *People of Kau* in the same year).
30.10.1976	Riefenstahl appears on the television chat show *Je später der Abend* . . .
18.8.1977	Germany's top three magazines, *Stern*, *Bunte* and *Quick* publish articles marking Riefenstahl's 75th birthday.
November 1978	The book of photographs *Korallengärten* is published (in English as *Coral Gardens* in the same year).
1982	*Mein Afrika* is published (in English as *Leni Riefenstahl's Africa* in the same year).
6.12.1982	German television broadcaster WDR shows Nina Gladitz's film *Zeit des Schweigens und der Dunkelheit* on its third channel.
March 1987	Verdict in the second court case involving Nina Gladitz.
August 1987	Riefenstahl's memoirs are published in German.
November 1990	The book of photographs *Wunder unter Wasser* is published.

December 1991	Exhibition entitled *Leni Riefenstahl – Life* in Tokyo.
7.10.1993	German television broadcaster Arte shows Ray Müller's documentary, *Die Macht der Bilder*, for the first time (English title: *The Wonderful, Horrible Life of Leni Riefenstahl*).
October 1995	Retrospective of Riefenstahl's films at the documentary film festival in Leipzig.
July-Oct. 1996	Photographic exhibition in Milan, Palazzo della Ragione.
November 1996	Johann Kresnik stages and choreographs *Riefenstahl* at Cologne's Schauspielhaus.
April 1997	Photographic exhibition in Rome, Palazzo delle Esposizioni.
April 1997	*L'Espresso* launches a Riefenstahl video edition, including *Triumph des Willens*.
15.8-14.9.1997	Photographic exhibition at the Galerie Schlüter, Hamburg.
September 1997	Riefenstahl receives a life-achievement award from the Cinecon film association in Los Angeles.
3.3.1998	*Time* magazine celebrates its 75th anniversary in New York; Riefenstahl is one of the guests (each of whom appears on the cover of the magazine).
October 1998	The rock group Rammstein releases its video *Stripped*, in which the music is accompanied by a montage of images from *Olympia*.
3.12.1998	Opening of the exhibition *Leni Riefenstahl* at the Film Museum in Potsdam (closes 28.2.1999).
1.12.1999	Jodie Foster's production company Egg Pictures announces plans for a Riefenstahl film with Foster in the leading role.
February-March 2000	Riefenstahl in the Sudan, filming with Ray Müller. She suffers severe injuries in a helicopter crash.
5.5.2000	Opening of the exhibition featuring photographs from *Olympia* in the Camera Work gallery, Berlin.

Filmography

Film Credits

Abbreviations

D: Director; Ass-D: Assistant-director; Sc: Script; C: Camera; C-Ass: Camera assistant; SC: Special camera, special effects; Ph: Stills photographer; M: Music; Ed: Editing; Sd-Ed: Sound editing; Sd: Sound; Sd-Eng: Sound engineer; Set: Set design; Cos: Costumes; MU: Make-up; Con: Consultants; Cast; P: Production; Pr: Producer; PM: Production Manager; Ass-PM: Assistant production managers; Dis: Distribution; Prem: Premiere; CD: Censor date; Cert: Certificate/rating; Prz: Prizes, awards; Stu: Studio; Loc: On-location scenes; Shot: Shooting dates; L: Length; F: Format

Translator's note: This filmography includes a courtesy translation for each film title; this should not be taken to denote an official English-language version of that film. Reference is made to such versions in the text where relevant.

The information given under 'CD' relates to the data on the censor's card: the censorship date(s), the censorship number(s) preceded by a letter indicating which censor's office examined the film ('B' denotes the Berlin office), the length of film examined (in metres) and the number of 'acts'. 'Jv.' stands for 'Jugendverbot' – banned for young people. 'Jf.' stands for 'Jugendfrei' – approved for young people.

Der heilige Berg (The Holy Mountain)
'Ein Heldenlied aus ragender Höhenwelt' (A heroic song from among the soaring peaks, 1925/26)

D: Arnold Fanck; Sc: Arnold Fanck, Hans Schneeberger; C: Sepp Allgeier, Helmar Lerski, Hans Schneeberger; in nature: Arnold Fanck and the Freiburger Schule; C-Ass: Albert Benitz, Kurt Neubert; M: Edmund Meisel; Ed: Arnold Fanck; Set: Leopold Blonder; Sculptor: Karl Böhm; Cast: Leni Riefenstahl, Luis Trenker, Ernst Petersen, Hannes Schneider, Friedrich Schneider, Frida Richard, Edmund Meisel; P: Universum-Film AG (Ufa), Kulturabteilung (Department of Culture), Berlin; Dis: Parufamet; Transit-Film, Munich; Prem: 17.12.1926, Ufa-Palast am Zoo, Berlin; CD: 25.1.1933; 17.10.1935, B. 32938, 1128 m, 9 acts (16mm); Shot: October 1925 (studio); L: 3100 m, 9 acts, 90 min.; F: 35 mm, b/w, 1:1.33, silent.

Der grosse Sprung (The Great Leap)
'Eine unwahrscheinliche, aber bewegte Geschichte' (An improbable but eventful story, 1927)

   D: Arnold Fanck; Sc: Arnold Fanck; C: Sepp Allgeier, Hans Schneeberger, Albert Benitz, Richard Angst, Kurt Neubert; Ph: Hans Casparius; M: Werner Richard Heymann; Ed: Arnold Fanck; Set: Erich Czerwonski; Cast: Leni Riefenstahl, Luis Trenker, Hans Schneeberger, Paul Graetz; P: Universum-Film AG (Ufa), Berlin; PM: Ernst Krieger; Dis: Parufamet; Prem: 20.12.1927, Ufa-Palast am Zoo, Berlin; CD: B. 17658; 14.1.1928, B. 17914, 2671 m; Loc: Dolomites, Arlberg ski slopes; Shot: May to November 1927; L: 2931 m, 7 acts; F: 35 mm, b/w, 1:1.33, silent.

Das Schicksal derer von Habsburg (The Fate of the House of Hapsburg)
'Die Tragödie eines Kaiserreiches' (The Tragedy of an Empire, 1928)

   D: Rudolf Raffé; Ass-D: Rolf Eckbauer; Sc: Max Ferner; C: Marius Holdt; Set: Arthur Berger; Cast: Fritz Spira, Erna Morena, Maly Delschaft, Leni Riefenstahl, Alson Fryland, Franz Kammauf, Willi Hubert, Ernst Recniczek, Albert Kersten, Paul Askonas, Ferry Lukacs, Irene Kraus, Carmen Cartellieri, Alice Roberte, Minje van Gooten; P: Essem-Film Produktion GmbH, Berlin; PM: Leo Meyer; Dis: Berlin-East: Star Film GmbH, Berlin; Rhineland, Westphalia, Saar region: Rheinische Film-GmbH, Cologne; central Germany: Siegel Monopolfilm, Dresden; Southern Germany: Leofilm AG Munich; Northern Germany: Nordfilm GmbH, Hamburg; Prem: 16.11.1928, Waterloo-Theater, Hamburg; CD: 22.10.1928.

Die weisse Hölle vom Piz Palü (The White Hell of Piz Palü, 1929)
D: Arnold Fanck, Georg Wilhelm Pabst; Ass-D: Mark Sorkin; Sc: Arnold Fanck, Ladislaus Vajda; after an idea by Arnold Fanck; C: Sepp Allgeier, Richard Angst, Hans Schneeberger; Ph: Hans Casparius; M: Willy Schmidt-Gentner (silent version), Giuseppe Becce (sound version); Ed: Arnold Fanck, Hermann Haller; Set: Ernö Metzner; Cast: Leni Riefenstahl, Gustav Diessl, Ernst Petersen, Ernst Udet, Mizzi Götzel, Christian Klucker; P: H. R. Sokal-Film GmbH, Berlin; Pr: Henry R. Sokal; PM: Henry R. Sokal; Ass-PM: Heinz Landsmann; Dis: Aafa Film AG, special distribu-

tion for Berlin; Goldeck; Prem: Silent film: 11.10.1929, various cinemas in Vienna; 22.10.1929 Universum-Lichtspiele, Mannheim; 15.11.1929, Ufa-Palast am Zoo, Berlin; Sound film: 23.12.1935 Ufa Pavillon am Nollendorfplatz, Berlin; CD: Silent film: 18.10.1929, B. 23880, 3330 m; 7 acts; Jf.; 1.11.1929, B. 24062, 93 m (opening credits); Sound film: 15.11.1935, B. 40690, 2509 m; 11.12.1935, B. 40926, 114 m (opening credits); Cert: Educational film and artistic; Stu: Grunewald studio, Berlin; Loc: Bernina massif; Shot: January to June 1929; L: silent version: 3330 m, 7 acts; F: 35 mm, b/w, 1:1.33, sound version: 2509 m, Tobis-Tonsystem (sound system).

Stürme über dem Montblanc (Storms Over Mont Blanc, 1930)
D: Arnold Fanck; Sc: Arnold Fanck; Dr: Carl Mayer; C: Hans Schneeberger, Richard Angst, Sepp Allgeier; Pilot of the aeroplane used for aerial photography: Claus von Suchotzky; M: Paul Dessau, Otto Firl (not credited), Edmund Meisel (not credited); Welte organ: W. A. Harnisch; Electronic Music: "Trautonium"; Ed: Arnold Fanck; Sd-Ed: Alwin Elling; Sd-Eng: Emil Specht, Hans Grimm, Erich Lange; Set: Leopold Blonder; Con: Phonetic advice: Herbert Kuchenbuch; Dramatic collaboration: Carl Mayer; Cast: Leni Riefenstahl, Sepp Rist, Ernst Udet, Mathias Wieman, Friedrich Kayssler, Alfred Beierle, Ernst Petersen; P: Aafa-Film AG of Tobis; PM: Henry R. Sokal; Ass-PM: Karl Buchholz; Dis: Aafa-Film-AG, Berlin; Prem: 25.12.1930, Prinzess-Theater, Dresden; Ufa-Theater Schwan, Frankfurt am Main; 2.2.1931, Ufa-Palast am Zoo, Berlin; 19.1.1931, Vienna; CD: 24.12.1930, 16.10.1935, B. 27775, 2964 m; 7 acts, Jv.; 24.1.1931, B. 28038, 179 m (opening credits); Cert: LK 2726/30 Educational film and artistic; 22.2.1933, Not approved for Good Friday; Stu: Ufa studios, Berlin-Tempelhof; Loc: Arosa, Mont Blanc, Vallot observatory, Bernina Pass, Babelsberg observatory; Shot: 12.8/30.8.1930; L: 2964 m, 110 min.; F: 35 mm, b/w, 1:1.33, Tobis Klangfilm (sound film).

Der weisse Rausch (The White Rapture)
'Neue Wunder des Schneeschuhs' (New miracles of the snow-shoe, 1931)
D: Arnold Fanck; Sc: Arnold Fanck; C: Richard Angst, Kurt Neubert (external), Hans Karl Gottschalk (studio); C-Ass: Robert Dahlmeier; M: Paul Dessau (director), Fritz Goldschmidt (assis-

tant); Ed: Arnold Fanck; Sd-Ed: Fritz Seeger; Sd: Hans Bittmann, Emil Specht; Set: Leopold Blonder; Cast: Leni Riefenstahl, Hannes Schneider, Guzzi Lantschner, Walter Riml, Rudi Matt, Lothar Ebersberg, Luggi Föger, Josef Gumboldt, Hans Kogler, Benno Leubner, Otto Leubner, Harald Reinl (not credited); P: H. R. Sokal-Film GmbH, Berlin, for Aafa-FilmAG, Berlin; Pr: Henry Richard Sokal; PM: Arnold Fanck; Ass-PM: Walter Tost; Dis: Aafa-Film-AG, Berlin; Goldeck; Prem: 10.12.1931, Ufa-Palast am Zoo, Berlin; CD: 9.12.1931, B.30600, 2565 m; 28.11.1931, B.30512, 137 m (opening credits); Cert: Artistic, educational film; Stu: Jofa studios, Berlin-Johannisthal; Loc: St Anton and Zürs am Arlberg; L: 2565 m, 5 acts, 94 min.; F: 35 mm, b/w, 1:1.33, Tobis-Klangfilm (sound film).

Das blaue Licht (The Blue Light)
'Eine Berglegende aus den Dolomiten' (A Mountain Legend from the Dolomites, 1932)

  D: Leni Riefenstahl; Sc: Béla Balázs, Leni Riefenstahl, Carl Mayer (not credited), Hans Schneeberger; C: Hans Schneeberger; C-Ass: Heinz von Jaworsky; Ph: Walter Riml; M: Giuseppe Becce; Ed: Leni Riefenstahl; Sd-Ed: Hanne Kuyt; Sd: Hans Bittmann; Set: Leopold Blonder; Cast: Leni Riefenstahl, Mathias Wieman, Beni Führer, Max Holzboer, Franz Maldacea, Martha Mair, farmers from the Sarntal; P: Leni Riefenstahl Studio-Film GmbH of H. R. Sokal-Film GmbH, Berlin; Pr: Leni Riefenstahl, Henry Richard Sokal (not credited); PM: Walter Traut; Ass-PM: Karl Buchholz; Dis: Aafa-Film AG, Berlin (special distribution); Degeto-Kulturfilm GmbH, Berlin (from 1938); National (after 1945); Taurus (Video); Prem: 24.3.1932, Ufa-Palast am Zoo, Berlin; New prem: 27.9.1938, Kurbel, Berlin; CD: 21.3.1932, B. 31261 (opening credits of film); 22.3.1932, B. 31261; Jv.; 22.3.1932, B. 31269 (double inspection); 5.10.1939, B. 52357, 931 m (16mm sound film); Cert: artistically valuable, authorized for young people and holidays; Prz: Silver Medallion of the International Festival of Cinematic Art 1932 in Venice (Biennale); Loc: Sarentino in the Sarntal, the ruined castle of Runkelstein, Crozzon in the Brenta range (Dolomites), Tessin Valley; Shot: July to September 1931; L: 2344 m, 9 acts, 86 min.; F: SW, 35 mm, 1:1.33, Tobis-Klangfilm (sound film).

Sieg des Glaubens (Victory of Faith)
'Der Film vom Reichsparteitag der NSDAP' (The film of the NSDAP Reich Party Rally, 1933)

D: Leni Riefenstahl; C: Sepp Allgeier, Franz Weihmayr, Walter Frentz, R. Quaas, Paul Tesch; M: Herbert Windt; Ed: Leni Riefenstahl, Waldemar Gaede; Sd-Ed: Waldemar Gaede; Sd: Siegfried Schulze; Sd-Eng: Siegfried Schulze; P: NSDAP Reichs-propagandaleitung (Propaganda Administration), Division IV (Film), Berlin; PM: Arnold Raether; Ass-PM: tech. dir.: R. Quaas; Dis: Ufa, NSDAP regional film offices; Prem: 1.12.1933, Ufa-Palast am Zoo, Berlin; Shot: September 1933; L: 1756 m, 64 min.; F: 35 mm, b/w, 1:1.33, Tobis-Klangfilm (sound film).

S.O.S. Eisberg (S.O.S. Iceberg, 1933)
D: Arnold Fanck; Ass-D: Werner Klingler; Dialogues-D: Hans Hinrich; Sc: Arnold Fanck, Fritz Löwe (not credited), Ernst Sorge (not credited), Hans Hinrich; Dialogues: Edwin E. Knopf; Collaboration: Friedrich Wolf; Adaptation: Tom Reed; C: Richard Angst, Hans Schneeberger; SC: Aerial shots: Hans Schneeberger; Flight shots: Ernst Udet, Franz Schrieck; C-Ass: Walter Traut, Fritz von Friedl, Heinz von Jaworski, Luggi Föger; Ph: Ferdinand Vogel; M: Paul Dessau; Ed: Hermann Haller, Arnold Fanck; Sd-Ed: Alice Ludwig; Sd: Zoltan Kegl, Erich Lange, Werner Klingler, Charles Metain; Set: Fritz Maurischat, Ernst Petersen, Arno Richter; MU: Paul Dannenberg; Scientific Con: Fritz Loewe, Ernst Sorge (not credited), Emmy Langberg; Cast: Leni Riefenstahl, Gustav Diessl, Ernst Udet, Gibson Gowland, Sepp Rist, Max Holzboer, Walter Riml, Arthur Grosse, Tommy Thomas; Mountain guides: David Zogg, Fritz Steuri, Hans Ertl; P: Deutsche Universal-Film AG Berlin; Pr: Paul Kohner (not credited); PM: Alfred Stern; Ass-PM: Karl Buchholz; Rudolf Fichtner; Heinz Landsmann; Dis: Deutsche Universal-Film AG Berlin; Ring; Ufa (Video); Prem: 30.8.1933, Ufa-Palast am Zoo, Berlin; CD: 28.8.1933, B. 34373, 2592 m; 28.8.1933, B. 34373, 2596 m; Cert: artistic; Stu: Jofa studios, Berlin-Johannisthal; Loc: Greenland, Bernina Pass, Berlin; Shot: June to November 1932 in Greenland; L: 2827 m, 6 acts, 103 min.; F: 35 mm, b/w, 1:1.33, Tobis Klangfilm (sound film).

Triumph des Willens (Triumph of the Will, 1935)
D: Leni Riefenstahl; Ass-D: Erna Peters, Guzzi Lantschner, Otto Lantschner, Walter Prager; Sc: Leni Riefenstahl; C: Sepp Allgeier, Karl Attenberger, Werner Bohne, Walter Frentz, Hans Gottschalk, Werner Hundhausen, Herbert Kebelmann, Albert Kling, Franz Koch, Herbert Kutschbach, Paul Lieberenz, Richard Nickel, Walter Riml, Arthur von Schwertführer, Karl Vass, Franz Weihmayr, Siegfried Weinmann, Karl Wellert; SC: Aerial shots: Albert Kling; Special effects: Arbeitsgemeinschaft Svend Noldan, Fritz Brunsch, Hans Noack; Ph: Rolf Lantin; Image Processing: Gisela Lindeck-Schneeberger; M: Herbert Windt; Post-synchronization of the march music: band of the SS-Leibstandarte Adolf Hitler; Ed: Leni Riefenstahl; Sd-Ed: Bruno Hartwich, Alice Ludwig; Sd: Siegfried Schulz, Ernst Schütz; Set: Albert Speer; Technical set construction for the film: City Councillor Brugmann, Architect Seegy; P: Reich Party Rally Film division of L. R. Studio-Film, Berlin; NSDAP, Office for the Reich Party Rally Film; PM: Leni Riefenstahl; Ass-PM: Arthur Kiekebusch; Footage from weekly newsreels: Ufa, Deulig, Tobis-Melo, Fox, Paramount; Dis: Ufa-Filmverleih GmbH; Prem: 28.3.1935, Ufa-Palast am Zoo, Berlin; CD: 26.3.1935; 12.9.1935, B. 40072, 1232 m (16mm sound film); Cert: Of special national political and artistic value, educational for the people; Prz: National Film Prize 1934/35; Venice International Film Festival 1935: Coppa dell'Istituto Nazionale LUCE (Best Foreign Documentary Film); Gold Medallion and Grand Prix of France 1937; L: 3109 m, 114 min.; F: 35 mm, b/w, 1:1.33, sound film.

Tag der Freiheit. Unsere Wehrmacht (Day of Freedom – Our Army, 1935)
D: Leni Riefenstahl; C: Willy Zielke, Guzzi Lantschner, Walter Frentz, Hans Ertl, Kurt Neubert, Albert Kling; M: Peter Kreuder; Ed: Leni Riefenstahl; P: Reichsparteitagfilm for L. R. Studio-Film, Berlin; PM: Leni Riefenstahl; Dis: Ufa-Filmverleih GmbH; Prem: 30.12.1935, Ufa-Palast am Zoo; CD: 26.11.1936; B. 44096, 302 m (16mm sound film); Cert: of artistic value, educational for the people, of national political value, approved for young people; L: 755 m, 28 min.; F: 35 mm, b/w. 1:1.33, Tobis Klangfilm (sound film).

Olympia (1938): *Fest der Völker* (Festival of the People: Part 1); *Fest der Schönheit* (Festival of Beauty: Part 2)

D: Leni Riefenstahl; C: Hans Ertl, Walter Frentz, Guzzi Lantschner, Kurt Neubert; Hans Scheib; Andor von Barsy, Wilfried Basse, Josef Dietze, Edmund Epkens, Fritz von Friedl, Hans Gottschalk, Richard Groschopp. Wilhelm Hameister, Wolf Hart, Hasso Hartnagel, Walter Hege, Eberhard von der Heyden, Albert Hächt, Paul Holzki, Werner Hundhausen, Heinz von Jaworsky, Hugo von Kaweczynski, Herbert Kebelmann, Sepp Ketterer, Wolfgang Kiepenheuer, Albert Kling; Ernst Kunstmann, Leo de Laforgue, Alexander von Lagorio, Eduard Lamberti, Otto Lantschner, Waldemar Lemke, Georg Lemki, C. A. Linke, Erich Nitzschmann, Albert Schattmann. Wilhelm Schmid, Hugo Otto Schulze, Leo Schwedler, Alfred Siegert, Wilhelm Georg Siem, Ernst Sorge, Hellmuth von Stvolinski, Karl Vass; SC: Torch relay – animated shots: Arbeitsgemeinschaft Svend Noldan; Ph: Rolf Lantin; M: Herbert Windt, Walter Gronostay; Ed: Leni Riefenstahl, Max Michel, Johannes Lüdke, Arnfried Heyne, Guzzi Lantschner; Ass: Wolfgang Brüning, Otto Lantschner; Sd-Ed: Max Michel, Johannes Lüdke, Arnfried Heyne, Guzzi Lantschner, Wolfgang Brüning, Otto Lantschner; Sd: Hermann Storr; Sd-Eng: Siegfried Schulze; Set: Robert Herlth; P: Olympia-Film GmbH, Berlin; Pr: Leni Riefenstahl; PM: Walter Traut, Walter Grosskopf; Ass-PM: Arthur Kiekebusch, Rudolf Fichtner, Konstantin Boenisch; Technical collaboration/ organization: Rudolf Schaad; Narrators: Paul Laven, Rolf Wernicke, Henri Nannen, Johannes Pagels; Footage from weekly newsreels: Fox, Paramount, Tobis-Melo, Ufa; Dis: Tobis, Müller, Taurus (Video); Prem: 20.4.1938, Ufa-Palast am Zoo, Berlin; CD: 9.5.1938, B. 4307, 80 m (opening credits of film); 30.10.1939, B. 52580, 1340 m (part 1); 31.10.1939, B. 52581, 1111 m (part 2); (both parts 16mm sound film); Cert: of national political value, of artistic value, educational for the people, approved for young people, approved for all holidays, approved as an educational film in school classes; Prz: National Film Prize 1937/38; Venice International Film Festival 1938: Coppa Mussolini (Best Film); Porla Prize, Sweden 1938; International Lausanne Film Festival 1948: Olympic Diploma for the Olympic Gold Medal from the Comitée International Olympique; 1938: Greek Sport Prize; Shot: July/August 1936/37; L: 3429 m, 126 min. (part 1); 2722 m, 100 min. (part 2); F: 35 mm, b/w, 1:1.33.

Tiefland (The Lowlands, 1940/54)
D: Leni Riefenstahl; Georg Wilhelm Pabst (not credited); Ass-D: Harald Reinl; Sc: Leni Riefenstahl, Harald Reinl after the opera by Eugen d'Albert; C: Albert Benitz; Ph: Rolf Lantin; M: Giuseppe Becce (as originally planned); 1954: Herbert Windt, using melodies from the d'Albert opera; Ed: Leni Riefenstahl; Sd: Rudolf Kaiser, Herbert Janeczka; Set: Erich Grave; Isabella Ploberger; Interior props: Paul Prätel; External props: Fritz Bollenhagen; Cos: Gustav Jäger, Elisabeth Massary; MU: Paul Lange, Franz Siebert; Con: D-cons.: Georg Wilhelm Pabst, Arthur Maria Rabenalt, Veit Harlan; Artistic collaboration: Mathias Wieman; Cast: Leni Riefenstahl, Franz Eichberger, Bernhard Minetti, Aribert Wäscher, Maria Koppenhöfer (voice: Til Klock), Luise Rainer, Frida Richard, Karl Skraup, Max Holzboer, Bekuch Hamid, Charlotte Komp, Hans Lackner; P: Riefenstahl-Film GmbH, Berlin for Tobis Filmkunst GmbH, Berlin (to 1945) Plesner-Film GmbH; Pr: Leni Riefenstahl, Josef Plesner; PM: Max Hüske; Walter Traut; Ass-PM: Rudolf Fichtner; Hugo Lehner; Dis: Allianz Verleih; Deutsche Cosmopol, Taurus (Video); Prem: 11.2.1954, EM-Theater, Stuttgart; Stu: Ufa studios Babelsberg; Prag-Film; Loc: Krün/Mittenwald, Karwendel mountains, in the Dolomites, Spain; Shot: 1940 to 1944; L: 2695 m, 99 min.; F: b/w, 35 mm, 1:1.33; Completed 1953.

Films Officially Produced by Leni Riefenstahl

Osterskitour In Tirol (Easter Ski Tour in the Tyrol, 1939)
D: Guzzi Lantschner, Harald Reinl; M: Otto Schubert; Cast: Heli Lantschner, Trude Lechle, Dori Neu; P: Olympia-Film GmbH; Dis: Bavaria; CD: 20.12.1939, B. 52941, jf.; Cert: of artistic value, educational for the people; L: 578 m.

Der Wurf im Sport (The Discus in Sport)
'Betrachtungen für Freunde des Sports' (Observations for Friends of Sport, 1939)
   D/Sc/Ed: Joachim Bartsch; P: Olympia-Film GmbH; Dis: Tobis; CD: 13.3.1939, B. 50973, jf.; 27.1.1943, B. 58317, 355 m; Cert: educational for the people, educational film; L: 375 m; Overall supervisor: Dr Eckhardt; leftover footage from the Olympic Games, 1936; Narrator: Willi Dohm.

Kraft und Schwung, die Grundelemente des Turnens (Strength and Energy, the Basics of Gymnastics, 1940)

Ed: Otto Lantschner; P: Olympia-Film GmbH; CD: 1940, B. 58335, 317 m, jf.; Narrator: Rolf Wernicke.

Laufen (Running, 1940)
D: Joachim Bartsch; P: Tobis-Filmkunst GmbH.

Der Sprung (Vaulting, 1940)
D: Joachim Bartsch; P: Tobis-Filmkunst GmbH; CD: 16.8.1940, B. 54121, 363 m, jf.; 16.2.1943, B. 58365, 224 m (9 min.), jf.; Cert: educational for the people, approved as an educational film in school classes; L: 363 m.

Bergbauern (Mountain Farmers, 1940)
D: Guzzì Lantschner; Ass-D: (collaboration) Harald Reinl, Otto Lantschner; M: Otto Schubert; P: Olympia-Film GmbH; CD: 27.3.1940, B. 53255, 464 m; Cert: of artistic value, educational for the people, approved as an educational film in school classes; L: 464 m.

Wildwasser (Torrent, 1942)
D: Guzzi Lantschner; Ass-D: (collaboration) Harald Reinl; Sc: Guzzi Lantschner; M: Herbert Windt; Ed: (collaboration) Harald Reinl; Cast: Peter, Xaverl, Fee, Ulli, Rolf, Erwin; P: Olympia-Film GmbH; CD: 10.12.1942, B. 57860, 850 m; Cert: of artistic value, educational for the people, approved as an educational film in school classes; Loc: Karst region along the River Enz; Shot: Summer 1939; L: 850 m (835 m/CineGraph), 32 min. (30 min./CineGraph); F: 35 mm, b/w, 1:1. 33; also as a 16mm sound film: 3.3.1942, B. 56723, 334 m, jf.; Cert: educational for the people; 16mm: 10.12.1942, B. 58127, 318 m, jf.; Cert: educational for the people; Adapted for the National Socialist's Reichsbund für Leibesübungen (National League for Gymnastics): Herbert Kühne; Applicant on the censor card: IG Farbenindustrie Aktiengesellschaft (industrial union for the paint industry, joint stock company), Frankfurt am Main.

Schwimmen und Springen (Swimming and Diving, 1943)
D: Joachim Bartsch; P: Olympia-Film GmbH; CD: 1.2.1943, B. 58362,

374 m, jf.; Cert: educational for the people, approved as an educational film in school classes; L: 374 m, 14 min.

Höchstes Glück der Erde auf dem Rücken der Pferde (The Greatest Happiness in the World on Horseback, 1943)

D: Joachim Bartsch; P: Olympia-Film GmbH; CD: 6.1.1943, B. 58346, 428 m; 14.9.1939, B. 52221, 429 m; Cert: of artistic value, educational for the people, approved as an educational film in school classes; L: 428 m, 16 min.; Banned by the Allies after 1945.

Josef Thorak, Werkstatt und Werk (Josef Thorak, Workshop and Work, 1943)

D: Arnold Fanck, Hans Cürlis; C: Walter Riml, Otto Cürlis, Arnold Fanck; P: Kulturfilm-Institut GmbH (Riefenstahl-Film GmbH); CD: 23.12.1943, B. 59773, 388 m; L: 388 m, 14 min.; F: 35 mm, b/w, 1:1.33; Banned after 1945; Film footage used in the Deutsche Wochenschau (German Weekly Newsreel) No. 538.

Arno Breker (1944)

D: Dr Arnold Fanck; Sc: Dr Hans Cürlis; C: Walter Riml, Dr Arnold Fanck; M: Rudolf Perak; Ed: Dr Hans Cürlis; P: Riefenstahl-Film GmbH/Kulturfilm-Institut GmbH; Pr: Leni Riefenstahl; PM: Walter Traut; CD: 18.10.1944, B. 60674, 359 m, jf.; Cert: of cultural value, educational for the people; L: 359 m, 14 min.; F: 35 mm, b/w, 1:1.33; Narrator: Hans Cürlis.

The filmography is based on data from the volume published by the Filmmuseum Potsdam in 1999 about the life and work of Leni Riefenstahl.

Bibliography

Quotations from files (such as those in the Bundesarchiv, German Foreign Ministry or the Stiftung Dokumentationszentrum des österreichischen Widerstands) are detailed in the notes to the main text. 'BA' denotes files from the Bundesarchiv (Germany's national archive), and is followed by the relevant shelf-mark and page number. Other archival sources are identified by name in the notes.

To save space, the bibliography only includes newspaper articles attributed to a particular author. Anonymous articles and those merely initialled are identified in the notes, with details of the newspaper and date of publication.

English translations of major works are mentioned in the text and notes where relevant.

Publications by Leni Riefenstahl

Texts

Riefenstahl, L. (1927), 'In Fels, Wasser und Schnee auf die Fensterltürme', *Film-Kurier*, No. 301, 21 December.

— (1928), 'Die weisse Arena', *Film-Kurier*, No. 67, 17 March.

— (1929), 'Fünf Monate über den Wolken', *Film-Kurier*, No. 262, 4 November.

— (1930a), 'Als Filmstar im Flugzeug über dem Montblanc', *Film-Kurier*, No. 125, 27 May.

— (1930b), '. . . und Leni Riefenstahl', *Film-Kurier*, No. 167, 17 July.

— (1931), 'Ohne Atelier und Filmstatisten', *Film-Kurier*, No. 172, 25 July.

— (1933), *Kampf in Schnee und Eis*. Leipzig: Hesse und Becker.

— (1935a), *Hinter den Kulissen des Reichsparteitags-Films*. Munich: Eher.

— (1935b), 'Freiheit des Künstlers', *Film-Kurier*, No. 96, 25 April.

— (1935c), 'Wie der neue Wehrmachtsfilm entstand', *Filmwelt*, 29 December.

— (1937), *Schönheit im olympischen Kampf*. Berlin: Deutscher Verlag.

— (1938a), 'Schönheit und Kampf in herrlicher Harmonie', *Licht-Bild-Bühne*, No. 88, 13 April.

— (1938b), 'Zum 10. April', *Film-Kurier*, No. 84, 9 April.

— (1938c), 'Olympia', *Das Magazin*, No. 168, August.

— (1940/41), 'Über Wesen und Gestaltung des dokumentarischen Films', in *Der deutsche Film. Zeitschrift für Filmkunst und Filmwirtschaft. Sonderausgabe*. Berlin: Max Hesses, pp. 146–7.

— (n.d. (1958)), *Über die Herstellung der Olympia-Filme (Falsche Behauptungen und ihre Widerlegung)*. N.p.

— (1967), 'Statement on Sarris/Gessner Quarrel about Olympia', *Film Comment*, Vol. 4, No. 2–3, 126.

— (1972), 'Notizen zu Penthesilea', *Filmkritik*, Vol. 16, No. 8, 416–25.

— (1973a), 'Why I am filming Penthesilea', *Film Culture*, No. 56–7, 192–215.

— (1973b), 'The production of the Olympia Films. Incorrect statements, their refutations', *Film Culture*, No. 56–7, 170–4.

— (1973c), 'A Letter to Gordon Hitchens, 11 June 1972', *Film Culture*, No. 56–7, 217–19.

— (1973d), *Die Nuba. Menschen wie von einem anderen Stern*, Munich: List.

— (1976), *Die Nuba von Kau*. Munich, Rheda-Wiedenbrück: Bertelsmann Club (first edition published in the same year in Munich by Paul List).

— (1978), *Korallengärten*. Munich: Paul List.

— (1982), *Mein Afrika*. Munich: Paul List.

— (1990), *Wunder unter Wasser*. Munich: Herbig.

— (1994), *Olympia*. New York: St Martin's Press.

— (1995), *Memoiren 1945–1987*. Frankfurt am Main, Berlin: Ullstein (2nd paperback edition; first edition 1987).

— (1996), *Memoiren 1902–1945*. Frankfurt am Main, Berlin: Ullstein (3rd paperback edition; first edition 1987).

Interviews

(1935) ' "Noch nie in der Welt hat sich ein Staat derartig für einen Film eingesetzt." Unterredung mit Leni Riefenstahl', *Hakenkreuzbanner*, No. 37, 22 January.

(1938) 'So entstand das "Blaue Licht". Gespräch mit Leni Riefenstahl', *Film-Kurier*, No. 224, 24 September.

(1939) 'Interview mit Leni Riefenstahl', *Film-Kurier*, No. 27, 1 February.

(1952) 'Wie ein deutscher Film-Welterfolg entstand', *Star*, 3.

(1953) 'Lenis "Rote Teufel". Ein Gespräch mit Frau Riefenstahl', *Hamburger Abendblatt*, 25/26 April.

(1997) ' "Mir kam nichts obskur vor." ' *Die Woche*, 22 August.

Delahaye, M. (1965), 'Entretien avec Leni Riefenstahl', *Cahiers du cinéma*, No. 170, September.

Dr F. (1926), 'Leni Riefenstahl', *Film-Kurier*, No. 171, 24 July.

Flot, Y. (1972), 'Entretien avec Leni Riefenstahl', *Ecran* 72, No. 9, November.

Hitchens, G. (1965): 'Interview with a Legend', *Film Comment*, Vol. 4, Winter, 4–11.

— (1973), 'Leni Riefenstahl interviewed by G. Hitchens, 11 October 1971, Munich', *Film Culture*, No. 56–57, 94–121.

Weigel, H. (1972a), 'Interview mit Leni Riefenstahl', *Filmkritik*, Vol. 16, No. 8, August, 395–410.

Reif, A. (1988), 'Eine besessene Filmschaffende. SHZ-Gespräch mit Leni Riefenstahl', *Schweizerische Handels-Zeitung*, No. 38, 22 September, 69.

Rower, J. (1997), ' "Wie viele Leben haben Sie gelebt, Frau Riefenstahl?" ', *Die Zeit*: 'Magazin', No. 36, 29 August, 10–13.

Schreiber, M. and Weingarten, S. (1997), ' "Realität interessiert mich nicht", Spiegel-Interview mit Leni Riefenstahl', *Der Spiegel*, No. 34, 18 August, 202–5.

Other literature

(1992), 'American Intelligence Report on Leni Riefenstahl. May 30th, 1945', *Film Culture*, No. 77, 34–8.

Aitken, W. (1976), 'La grande dame blonde aux petits gents blancs', *Take One*, Vol. 5, No. 1, October, 15.

Albrecht, G. (ed.) (1979), *Film im Dritten Reich*. Karlsruhe: Schauburg.

Alkemeyer, T. (1996), *Körper, Kult und Politik. Von der 'Muskelreligion' Pierre de Coubertins zur Inszenierung von Macht in den Olympischen Spielen von 1936*. Frankfurt, New York: Campus.

Andrews, R. (1974), 'Hitler's Favorite Filmmaker Honored at Colorado Film Festival', *New York Times*, 15 September.

Baer, V. (1987), 'Dokumente des Unbetroffenseins', *Der Tagesspiegel*, 1 November.

Balázs, B. (ed.) (1984), *Schriften zum Film*, Vol. 2. Berlin: Henschel.

Barkhausen, H. (1973), 'War auch Walter Ruttmann politisch blind?', *Neue Zürcher Zeitung*, 18 August.

— (1974a), 'Footnote to the History of Riefenstahl's "Olympia" ', *Film Quarterly*, Vol. 28, No. 1, 8–12.

— (1974b), ' "Auf Veranlassung des Reiches". Leni Riefenstahl und die Olympia-Filme 1936', *Neue Zürcher Zeitung*, No. 367, 10 August.

Barsam, R. M. (1973), 'Leni Riefenstahl. Artifice and Truth in a World Apart', *Film Comment*, Vol. 9, No. 6, 32–7.

— (1975), *Filmguide to "Triumph of the Will"*. Bloomington: Indiana University Press.

Behrenbeck, S. (1996), *Der Kult um die toten Helden. Nationalsozialistische Mythen, Riten und Symbole*. Vierow: SH-Verlag.

Benjamin, W. (1978), *Das Kunstwerk im Zeitalter seiner technischen Reproduzierbarkeit*, in W. Benjamin, *Gesammelte Schriften*, Vol 1. Frankfurt am Main: Suhrkamp.

— (1985), *Moskauer Tagebuch*, in W. Benjamin, *Gesammelte Schriften*, Vol. 6. Frankfurt am Main: Suhrkamp.

Berg-Pan, R. (1980), *Leni Riefenstahl*. Boston: Twayne.

Bernstein, S.; MacMillan, M. (1977), 'Leni Riefenstahl: a Selected Annotated Bibliography', *Quarterly Review of Films Studies*, Vol. 2, No. 4, 439–57.

Berson, A. (1965), 'The Truth about Leni Riefenstahl', *Films and Filming* (London), Vol. 11, No. 7, 15–19.

Bittorf, W. (1976), 'Blut und Hoden', *Der Spiegel*, No. 44, 25 October.

Blum, H. R. (1972), 'Die Riefenstahl im Streit der Meinungen', *Bremer Nachrichten*, 21 August.

Bock, H. (ed.) (1984 ff.), *CineGraph. Lexikon zum deutschsprachigen Film*. Munich: edition text und kritik.

Bock, H.-M. and Töteberg, M. (eds) (1992), *Das Ufa-Buch*. Frankfurt am Main: Zweitausendeins.

Bodek, A. (n.d.), 'Die ohnmächtige Leni?', MS, n.p.

Bönk, J. (1976), 'Leni-Riefenstahl-Show', *Bonner Rundschau*, 1 November.

Brandlmeier, T. (1997), 'Sinnzeichen und Gedankenbilder', in J. C. Horak (ed.), *Berge, Licht und Traum. Dr Arnold Fanck und der deutsche Bergfilm*. Munich: Bruckmann.

Brandt, H.-J. (1986), 'Walter Ruttmann: Vom Expressionismus zum Faschismus. 3. Teil', *Filmfaust*, No. 51, 42–54.

— (1987), *NS-Filmtheorie und dokumentarische Praxis*. Tübingen: Niemeyer.

Bronfen, E. (2000), 'Leni Riefenstahl und Marlene Dietrich: Zwei deutsche Stars', in W. Jacobsen, H. H. Prinzler and W. Sudendorf (eds), *Filmmuseum Berlin. Katalog*. Berlin: Nicolai, pp. 169–90.

Brownlow, K. (1966), 'Leni Riefenstahl', *Film*, Winter.

Bulgakowa, O. (1999), 'Riefenstein – Demontage eines Klischees', in Filmmuseum Potsdam (ed.), *Leni Riefenstahl*. Berlin: Henschel, pp. 132–43.

Cocteau, J. (1973), 'Four Letters by Jean Cocteau to Leni Riefenstahl', *Film Culture*, No. 56–7, 90–3.

Corliss, R. (1969), 'Leni Riefenstahl: A Bibliography', *Film Heritage*, Vol. 5, No. 1, 27–36.

Culbert, D. (1993), 'Leni Riefenstahl and the Diary of Joseph Goebbels', *Historical Journal of Film, Radio and Television*, Vol. 13, No. 1, 85–93.

Culbert, D. and Loiperdinger, M. (1992), 'Leni Riefenstahl's "Tag der Freiheit": the 1935 Nazi Party Rally Film', *Historical Journal of Film, Radio and Television*, Vol. 12, No. 1, 3–40.

Dassanowsky, R. von (1995), ' "Wherever you may run, you cannot escape him." Leni Riefenstahl's Self-Reflection and Romantic Transcendence of Nazism in "Tiefland" ', *Camera Obscura*, No. 35, 107–28.

Demandowski, E. von (1935), 'Das grösste Filmwerk, das wir je gesehen haben', *Der Filmbeobachter*. Supplement to the *Völkischer Beobachter*, 30 March.

Dokumentationsarchiv des österreichischen Widerstands (ed.) (n.d.), *Widerstand und Verfolgung in Salzburg 1933–1945. Eine Dokumentation*. Vienna: Österreichischer Bundesverlag.

Dolezel, S. and Loiperdinger, M. (1995), 'Hitler in Parteitagsfilm und Wochenschau', in M. Loiperdinger, R. Herz and U. Polhmann, *Führerbilder. Hitler, Mussolini, Roosevelt, Stalin in Fotografie und Film*. Munich, Zürich: Piper.

Donner, W. (1972), 'Politik hat sie nie interessiert. Leni Riefenstahls Comeback', *Die Zeit*, 18 August.

Dorn, T. (1998), *Preussische Diven blond wie Stahl*. Berlin: MS.

Downing, T. (1992), *Olympia*. London: BFI.

Elsaesser, T. (1993), 'Leni Riefenstahl: the Body Beautiful, Art Cinema and Fascist Aesthetics', in P. Cook and P. Dodd (eds), *Women on Film. A Sight and Sound Reader*. London: Scarlet Press, pp. 186–97.

— (1994), 'Portrait of the Young Artist as a Young Woman', *Sight and Sound*, Vol. 3, No. 2, 14–18.

Enzensberger, U. (1985a), 'KZ Zigeuner tanz mit mir', *konkret*, No. 2.

— (1985b), ' "Lieber noch zwei Jahre Auschwitz als noch einmal von den Russen befreit werden" ', *die tageszeitung*, 9 March.

Erens, P. (1979), *The World of Women in Film*. New York: Horizon Press.

Esderts, H. (1974), 'Vom Himmel herab naht er', *Bremer Nachrichten*, 24 August.

Fanck, A. (1973), *Er führte Regie mit Gletschern, Stürmen und Lawinen*. Munich: Nymphenburger.

Faris, J. C. (1993), 'Leni Riefenstahl and the Nuba Peoples of Kordofan Province, Sudan', *Historical Journal of Film, Radio and Television*, Vol. 13, No. 1, 95–7.

Ferber, C. (ed.) (1981), *Der Querschnitt*. Berlin: Ullstein.

Fest, J. C. (1965), *Das Gesicht des Dritten Reiches*. Frankfurt am Main, Vienna, Zürich: Büchergilde.

— (1973), *Hitler. Eine Biographie*. Frankfurt am Main, Berlin: Ullstein.

Filmmuseum Potsdam (ed.) (1999), *Leni Riefenstahl*. Berlin: Henschel.

Fischer, W. (1995), 'Mit Kanonen auf Spatzen geschossen', *Film & TV Kameramann*, Vol. 44, 143.

Ford, C. (1982), *Leni Riefenstahl*. Munich: Heyne.

Fraser, J. (1982), 'An Ambassador for Nazi Germany', *Films and Filming*, Vol. 2, No. 5, 12–14.

Fröhlich, E. (ed.) (1987), *Die Tagebücher von Joseph Goebbels*, Munich, London, New York, Oxford, Paris: K. G. Saur.

Fromm, B. (1993), *Als Hitler mir die Hand küsste*. Reinbek: Rowohlt.

Fulks, B. A. (n.d. (1989)), 'Walter Ruttmann, der Avantgardefilm und die Nazimoderne', in J. Goergen (ed.), *Walter Ruttmann. Eine Dokumentation*. Berlin: Freunde der Deutschen Kinemathek, pp. 67–71.

Fürst, L. (1937), ' "Woran liegt es?" Von der Problematik des Filmschaffens', *Der deutsche Film*, Vol. 2, No. 5, November, 125–8.

— (1938), 'Deutschlands repräsentativster Film. Gedanken vor Leni Riefenstahls Olympia-Film', *Der deutsche Film*, Vol. 2, No. 9, March, 247–9.

Gabel, B. (1992), 'Der ewige Traum', *Film und Kritik*, No. 1, June, 39–52.

Ganz, R. (1972), 'Leni Riefenstahls fragwürdige Renaissance', *Frankfurter Rundschau*, 25 August.

Gardner, R. (1965), 'Can the Will Triumph?', *Film Comment*, Vol. 3, No. 1, 28–31.

Gensert, H.-H. (1938), 'Die neue Kunstanschauung und ihr Ausdruck', *Der deutsche Film*, Vol. 2, No. 12, June, 323–6.

Goergen, J. (n.d. (1989)), 'Walter Ruttmann – Ein Porträt', in J. Goergen (ed.), *Walter Ruttmann. Eine Dokumentation*. Berlin: Freunde der Deutschen Kinemathek.

Grafe, F. (1985), 'Leni Riefenstahl. Falsche Bauern, falsche Soldaten und was für ein Volk', in F. Grafe, *Beschriebener Film: Die Republik*, Nos 72–5.

Graham, C. C. (1986), *Leni Riefenstahl and Olympia*. Metuchen, N.J., and London: Scarecrow Press.

— (1993), '"Olympia" in America, 1938: Leni Riefenstahl, Hollywood, and the Kristallnacht', *Historical Journal of Film, Radio and Television*, Vol. 13, No. 4, 433–50.

Gregor, U. (1965), 'A come back for Riefenstahl?', *Film Comment*, Vol. 3, No. 1, 24–5.

Greiner, U. (1972), 'Das unaufhaltsame Comeback der Leni Riefenstahl', *Frankfurter Allgemeine Zeitung*, 1 September.

Gressieker, H. (1936), 'Leni Riefenstahl', *Der deutsche Film*, Vol. 1, No. 2, August, 40–1.

Gruel-Wemper, H. (1935), 'Pensionserlebnisse mit Leni Riefenstahl', *Filmwelt*, 19 May.

Gunston, D. (1960), 'Leni Riefenstahl', *Film Quarterly*, Vol. 13, No. 1, 4–19.

Haffner, S. (1972), 'Man glaubt Goebbels zu hören. Leni Riefenstahls Olympia-Film von 1936', *Deutsches Allgemeines Sonntagsblatt*, 20 August.

Hagen, P. (1933), '"Der Sieg des Glaubens". Die Welturaufführung des Films vom Reichsparteitag', *Angriff*, 2 December.

Hanfstaengl, E. (1970), *Zwischen weissem und braunem Haus*. Munich: Piper.

Hattendorf, M. (1994), *Dokumentarfilm und Authentizität*. Constance: Ölschläger.

Hattendorf, M. (ed., 1995), *Perspektiven des Dokumentarfilms*. Munich: Schaudig und Ledig (= *diskurs Film*, Vol. 7).

Heck-Rabi, L. (1984), *Women Filmmakers. A Critical Reception*. Metuchen, N. J., London: Scarecrow Press.

Hellmuth, W. (1976), 'Die Riefenstahl rief pfui', *Welt am Sonntag*, 7 November.

Henke, J. (1977), 'Die Reichsparteitage der NSDAP in Nürnberg 1933–1938 – Planung, Organisation, Propaganda', in H. Boberach and H. Booms (eds), *Aus der Arbeit des Bundesarchivs*. Boppard: Boldt.

Hickethier, K., Müller, E. and Rother, R. (eds) (1997), *Der Film in der Geschichte*. Berlin: Edition Sigma.

Hildebrandt, F. (1925), *Tageblätter*, Vol. 1 1923/4. Berlin: Landsberg-Verlag.

Hinton, D. B. (1975), '"Triumph of the Will": Document or Artifice?', *Cinema Journal*, Vol. 15, No. 1, 48–57.

— (1978), *The Films of Leni Riefenstahl*. Metuchen, N.J., London: Scarecrow Press.

Hitchens, G. (1996), 'Recent Riefenstahl Activities and a Commentary on Nazi Propaganda Filmmaking', *Film Culture*, No. 79, 35–47.

Hitchens, G. (ed.) (1973), ' "Olympiad 1936". Andrew Sarris and Dick Schaap discuss Riefenstahl Film', *Film Culture*, No. 56–7, 175–92.

Hitchens, G., Bond, K. and Hanhardt, J. (1973), 'Henry Jaworsky, Cameraman for Leni Riefenstahl interviewed', *Film Culture*, No. 56–7, 122–61.

Hoffmann, H. (1988), *'Und die Fahne führt uns in die Ewigkeit'. Propaganda im NS-Film*, Vol. 1. Frankfurt am Main: Fischer.

— (1993), *Mythos Olympia. Autonomie und Unterwerfung von Sport und Kultur*. Berlin: Aufbau.

Hohenberger, E. (1997), 'Ohne Scham und Schuld. Leni Riefenstahl wird 95', *filmdienst*, No. 17, 19 August, 4–7.

Holloway, D. and Holloway, R. (1993), 'The Power of Images: Leni Riefenstahl', *Kino/German Film*, No. 52, 9–10.

Holthusen, H. E. (1975), 'Leni Riefenstahl in Amerika', *Merkur*, Vol. 29, No. 325, June, 569–78.

Horak, J. C. (ed.) (1997a), *Berge, Licht und Traum. Dr. Arnold Fanck und der deutsche Bergfilm*. Munich: Bruckmann.

Horak, J. C. (1997b), 'Dr. Arnold Fanck: Träume vom Wolkenmeer und einer guten Stube', in J. C. Horak (ed.) (1997a), *Berge, Licht und Traum. Dr Arnold Fanck und der deutsche Bergfilm*. Munich: Bruckmann.

Horton, W. G. (1984), 'Capturing the Olympics', *American Cinematographer*, Vol. 65, No. 7, 42–8.

Hull, D. S. (1969), *Film in the Third Reich. A Study of the German Cinema 1933–1945*. Berkeley, Los Angeles: University of California Press.

Hüser, R. (1993), 'Arena Abenteuer', *filmwärts*, No. 27, September, 35.

Infield, G. B. (1976), *Leni Riefenstahl: the Fallen Film Goddess*. New York: Crowell.

Iten, O. (1977), 'Bilder und Zerrbilder der Nuba', *Tagesanzeiger Magazin*, No. 50, 17 December, 6–45.

Jacobs, T. (1992), 'Visuelle Traditionen des deutschen Bergfilms: Von Fidus zu Friedrich oder Das Ende der bürgerlichen Fluchtbewegungen im Faschismus', *Film und Kritik*, No.1, June, 28–38.

Jacobsen, W. (1989), *Erich Pommer. Ein Produzent macht Filmgeschichte*. Berlin: Argon.

Jacobsen, W. (ed.) (1997), *G. W. Pabst*. Berlin: Argon.

Jacobsen, W., Kaes, A. and Prinzler, H. H. (1993), *Geschichte des deutschen Films*. Stuttgart/Weimar: Metzler.

Jaeger, E. (1939), 'How Leni Riefenstahl became Hitler's Girlfriend', *Hollywood Tribune*, 28 April–17 July (also on microfiche: *Historical Journal of Film, Radio and Television*, Vol. 13, No. 4, 1993).

Kanzog, K. (1994), *'Staatspolitisch besonders wertvoll.' Ein Handbuch zu 30 deutschen Spielfilmen der Jahre 1934 bis 1945*. Munich: Schaudig und Ledig (= *diskurs film*, Vol. 6.)

— (1995), 'Der Dokumentarfilm als politischer Katechismus', in M. Hattendorf (ed.), *Perspektiven des Dokumentarfilms*. Munich: Schaudig und Ledig (= *diskurs Film*, Vol. 7), pp. 57–84.

Kelman. K. (1973), 'Propaganda as Vision – Triumph of the Will', *Film Culture*, No. 56–7, 162–9.

Keiper, J. (1992), 'Alpträume in Weiss', *Film und Kritik*, No. 1, June, 53–70.

Klunker, H. (1987), 'Das Schicksal musste nicht Hitler heissen', *Deutsches Allgemeines Sonntagsblatt Magazin*, No. 41, 11 October.

Knilli, F. (2000), *Ich war Jud Süss. Die Geschichte des Filmstars Ferdinand Marian*. Berlin: Henschel.

Koebner, T. (1995), 'Olympia', in T. Koebner (ed.), *Filmklassiker*, Vol. 1. Stuttgart: Reclam, pp. 370–4.

— (1997), 'Der unversehrbare Körper. Anmerkungen zu Filmen Leni Riefenstahls', in T. Koebner (ed.), *Lehrjahre im Kino. Schriften zum Film*. St Augustin: Gardez, pp. 212–40.

Konlechner, P. and Kubelka, P. (eds) (1972), *Propaganda und Gegenpropaganda im Film 1933–1945*. Vienna: Österreichisches Filmmuseum.

Kracauer, S. (1947), *From Caligari to Hitler. A Psychological History of the German Film*. Princeton, N.J.: Princeton University Press.

Krausnick, H. (1993), *Hitlers Einsatzgruppen. Die Truppen des Weltanschauungskrieges 1938–1942*. Frankfurt am Main: Fischer.

Kreimeier, K. (1972), 'Schöne gefährliche Bilder. Kritische Anmerkungen zu Leni Riefenstahl', *Stuttgarter Zeitung*, 25 August.

— (1992), *Die Ufa-Story*. Munich, Vienna: Hanser.

Kühnert, H. (1987), 'Wenn Juristen Vergangenheit klären', *Die Zeit*, 27 March.

Laugstien, T. (1980), 'Die Organisation des Ideologischen im Reichsparteitags-Film', *Das Argument*, Sonderband 62, 307–36.

Leiser, E. (1973), 'Dans les coulisses d'"Olympia"', *Ecran*, No. 19, November, 13–14.

— (1989), *'Deutschland erwache'. Propaganda im Film des Dritten Reiches*. Reinbek: Rowohlt.

Lenssen, C. (1996), 'Die fünf Karrieren der Leni Riefenstahl', *epd Film*, No. 1, 27–31.

— (1999), 'Leben und Werk', in Filmmuseum Potsdam (ed.), *Leni Riefenstahl*. Berlin: Henschel, pp. 12–117.

— (2000), 'Unterworfene Gefühle. Nationalsozialistische Mobilisierung und emotionale Manipulation der Massen in der Parteitagsfilmen Leni Riefenstahls', in C. Benthien, A. Fleig and I. Kasten (eds) *Emotionalität. Zur Geschichte der Gefühle*. Cologne, Weimar, Vienna: Böhlau, pp. 198–211.

Lewis, M. (1965), 'Triumph des Willens', *Film Comment*, Vol. 3, No. 1, 22–3.

Limmer, W. (1972), 'Körper-Kunst. Leni Riefenstahls Olympia-Film von 1936 im Arri-Kino', *Süddeutsche Zeitung*, 28 July.

Loewy, H. (1999), 'Medium und Initiation. Béla Balázs: Märchen, Ästhetik, Kino'. Frankfurt am Main: MS (diss.).

Loiperdinger, M. (1980), *'Triumph des Willens'. Einstellungsprotokoll*. Frankfurt am Main: Institut für Historisch-Sozialwissenschaftliche Analysen (= Arbeitspapier, No. 12).

— (1987a), *Rituale der Mobilmachung*. Opladen: Leske und Budrich.

— (1987b), 'Faschistische Gelöbnisrituale im Parteitagsfilm ''Triumph des Willens'' ', in J. Schissler and D. Berg-Schlosser (eds): 'Politische Kultur in Deutschland – Facetten einer dramatischen Entwicklung' = *Sonderheft 18 der Politischen Vierteljahresschrift*, 159–62.

— (1988), 'Halb Dokument, halb Fälschung. Zur Inszenierung der Eröffnungsfeier in Leni Riefenstahls Olympia-Film ''Fest der Völker'' ', *Medium*, Vol. 18, No. 3, 42–6.

— (1993), *'Sieg des Glaubens*. Ein gelungenes Experiment nationalsozialistischer Filmpropaganda', in U. Herrmann and U. Nassen (eds), *Formative Ästhetik im Nationalsozialismus*. Weinheim and Basel: *Zeitschrift für Pädagogik*, Supplement 31, pp. 35–48.

Loiperdinger, M. and Culbert, D. (1988), 'Leni Riefenstahl, the SA and the Nazi Party Rally Films, Nuremberg 1933–1934. ''Sieg des Glaubens'' and ''Triumph des Willens'' ', *Historical Journal of Film, Radio and Television*, Vol. 8, No. 1, 3–38.

Luft, E. (1954), 'Tiefland', in *Filmbeobachter*, No. 6.

Luft, H. G. (1973), 'The Screen as a Propaganda Weapon', *Journal of the Producers Guild of America*, Vol. 15, No. 2, June, 11–14.

Mandell, R. D. (1971), *The Nazi Olympics*. New York: Macmillan.

Manstein, E. von (1978), *Verlorene Siege*. Munich: Bernhard und Graefe.

Maraun, F. (1938), 'Der wichtigste Film des Monats. Triumph des Dokumentarfilms', *Der deutsche Film*, Vol. 2, No. 11, May, 317.

— (1939), 'Warum sieht man das nie im Spielfilm?', *Der deutsche Film*, Vol. 3, No. 8, February, 211–14.

— (1940a), 'Deutscher Sozialismus im Film', *Der deutsche Film*, Vol. 4, No. 11, 205–9.

— (1940b), 'Unsere Wehrmacht im Film', *Der deutsche Film*, Vol. 4, No. 12, 227–32.

Martenstein, H. (1999), 'Und immer an das Gute glauben', *Der Tagesspiegel*, 7 February.

Martineau, B. H. (1975), 'Paris – Chicago. Women's Film Festivals 1974', *Women and Film*, Vol. 2, No. 7, 10–27.

Matzka, D. (1995), 'Sie hat es geschafft oder die Wiedergeburt einer ewigen Gestrigen?', *Film & TV Kameramann*, Vol. 44, February, 116–22.

Melichar, A. (1937), 'Entstofflichung des Films', *Der deutsche Film*, Vol. 2, No. 1, July, 13–15.

Mihan, A. (1999), 'Abtauchen ist ihre Sache nicht', *Märkische Allgemeine*, 8 February.

Mitscherlich, M. (1987), 'Triumph der Verdrängung', *Stern*, No. 42, 8 October.

— (1994), *Über die Mühsal der Emanzipation*. Frankfurt am Main: Fischer.

Moeller, F. (1998), *Der Filmminister*. Berlin: Henschel.

— (1999), 'Die einzige von all den Stars, die uns versteht', in Filmmuseum Potsdam (ed.), *Leni Riefenstahl*. Berlin: Henschel, pp. 144–58.

Momos (i.e. Walter Jens) (1976), 'Eine papierne Paarung', *Die Zeit*, 5 November.

Monaco, J. (1985), *American Film Now: the People, the Power, the Money, the Movies*. New York: Oxford University Press (revised edition: 2000).

Müller, A. and Pottmeier, G., 'Faschismus und Avantgarde. Leni Riefenstahls "Triumph des Willens"', *Augenblick*, Vol. 22, 39–58.

Mund, M. (1999), 'Riefenstahl und die anderen', *Neues Deutschland*, 13 January.

Naughton, L. (1996), 'Leni Riefenstahl. A Wonderful Life in an Horrible World', *Metro*, No. 106, August, 22–7.

Neale, S. (1979), '"Triumph of the Will". Notes on Documentary and Spectacle', *Screen* (London), Vol. 20, No. 1, 63–86.

Netzeband, G. (1984), 'Kritik der Unvernunft', *Film und Fernsehen*, Vol. 12, No. 6, 25–9.

Nowotny, P. (1981), *Leni Riefenstahls 'Triumph des Willens'. Zur Kritik dokumentarischer Filmarbeit im NS-Faschismus*. Dortmund: Arbeitshefte zur Medientheorie und Medienpraxis, Vol. 3.

Nussbaum, H. von (1976), 'Leni Riefenstahl oder die Banalität des Verführers', *epd / Kirche und Rundfunk*, 6 November.

Peters, M. (1996), 'Die Hommage', *Das Sonntagsblatt*, 8 November.

Polcuch, V. (1972), 'Leni Riefenstahls Weg führte vom "Heiligen Berg" zum "Triumph des Willens"', *Die Welt*, 21 August.

Polgar, A. (1982), *Kleine Schriften*, Vol. 1. Reinbek: Rowohlt.

Pöttker, H. (1990), '"Leni" verzeihen? Am Ende der Nachkriegszeit eine Retrospektive auf ihren Anfang', *Medium*, Vol. 20, No. 2, 12–17.

Prinzler, H. H. (1995), *Chronik des deutschen Films 1895–1994*. Stuttgart, Weimar: Metzler.

Prinzler, H. H. (ed.) (1990), *Das Jahr 1945. Filme aus fünfzehn Ländern*. Berlin: Stiftung Deutsche Kinemathek.

Pyros, J., 'Notes on Women Directors', *Take One*, Vol. 3, No. 2, 7–9.

Raabe, D. (1952), 'Virtuose Langeweile', *Stuttgarter Nachrichten*, 13 February.

Raddatz, F. J. (1987), 'Hitler lobte Helenes Apfelstrudel', *Die Zeit*, No. 42, 9 October.

Radziwill, C. (1938), 'Is Hitler in Love with a Jewess?', *Liberty*, July 16.

Raether, A. (1943), 'Die Entwicklung des nationalsozialistischen Filmschaffens', *Der deutsche Film*, Vol. 7, No. 7, 6.

Rapp, C. (1997), *Höhenrausch. Der deutsche Bergfilm*. Vienna: Sonderzahl.

Rathkolb, O. (1991), *Führertreu und gottbegnadet. Künstlereliten im Dritten Reich*. Vienna: Österreichischer Bundesverlag.

Reeves, J. (1997), 'Cinema, Spectatorship and Propaganda. "Battle of the Somme" (1926) and its Contemporary Audience', *Historical Journal for Film, Radio and Television*, Vol. 19, No. 1, 5–28.

Regel, H. (1970), 'Triumph des Willens', *Filmkritik*, Vol. 14, No. 5, 249–51.

Reichel, P. (1991), *Der schöne Schein des Dritten Reiches. Faszination und Gewalt des Faschismus*. Munich: Hanser.

Reimers, K. F. (1979), 'Der Reichsparteitag als Instrument totaler Propaganda', *Zeitschrift für Volkskunde*, Vol. 75, 216–28.

Reinecke, S. (1994), 'Die trübe Macht der Bilder', *Wochenpost*, No. 2, 5 January.

Reisz, K. and Millar, G. (1988), *Geschichte und Technik der Filmmontage*. Munich: Filmland Presse.

Renker, G. (n.d.), *Bergkristall*. Gütersloh: Bertelsmann.

Rentschler, E. (1989), 'Fatal Attraction: Leni Riefenstahl's "The Blue Light"', *October*, No. 48, 46–68.

— (1992a), 'Hochgebirge und Moderne. Eine Standortbestimmung des Bergfilms', *Film und Kritik*, No.1, June, 8–27.

— (1992b), 'Home sweet Heimat. Luis Trenker, the Prodigal Son', *Filmexil*, No. 1, 13–27.

— (1996), *The Ministry of Illusion. Nazi Cinema and its Afterlife*. Cambridge, Mass., London: Harvard University Press.

Reuth R. G. (ed.) (1992), *Joseph Goebbels. Tagebücher*, 5 Vols. Munich: Piper.

Riess, C. (1987), 'Suchen nach der verlorenen Unschuld', *Die Welt*, 28 November.

Rodek, H. G. (1999), 'Geburt von Leni Riefenstar', *Die Welt*, 8 February.

Ross, W. (1987), 'Zwischen Edelmenschen und Schurken', *Frankfurter Allgemeine Zeitung*, 6 October.

Rostow, R. (1976), 'Je später der Abend', *Die Welt*, 1 November.

Rother, R. (1990), 'Die Form der Abbildung und die Struktur der Erzählung', *filmwärts*, No. 17, 34–9.

— (1996), 'Der Olympia-Film 1936', *Magazin. Mitteilungen des Deutschen Historischen Museums*, No. 18, Vol. 6, 34–6.

— (1998), *Mythen der Nationen. Völker im Film*. Munich, Berlin: Koehler und Amelang.

Rother, R. (ed.) (1992), *Das deutsche Bilderimperium. Die Ufa 1917–1945*. Berlin: Deutsches Historisches Museum/Stiftung Deutsche Kinemathek.

Sabel, K. (1940), 'Die eigenwillige Gestaltung des "Tiefland"-Stoffes', *Film-Kurier*, No. 258, 2 November.

Salkeld, A. (1996), *A Portrait of Leni Riefenstahl*. London: Jonathan Cape.

Sanders-Brahms, H. (1990), 'Tyrannenmord', in H. H. Prinzler (ed.), *Das Jahr 1945. Filme aus fünfzehn Ländern*. Berlin: Stiftung Deutsche Kinemathek.

Saur, K. O. (1976), 'Ausgewogenheit pervers', *Süddeutsche Zeitung*, 2 November.

Schenk, I. (1997), 'Zu Vorstellungen der Wirkung von NS-(Propaganda-) Filmen in der Filmgeschichtsschreibung. Eine überfällige, weil verdrängte "Polemik" ', in K. Hickethier, E. Müller and R. Rother (eds), *Der Film in der Geschichte*. Berlin: Edition Sigma, pp. 167–77.

Schikowski, J. (1923a), 'Animalisches und seelisches Temperament', *Vorwärts*, 31 October.

— (1923b), 'Mit der Wünschelrute', *Vorwärts*, 16 November.

Schille, P. (1977), 'Lenis blühende Träume', *Stern*, No. 35, 18 August, 34–43.

Schlüpmann, H. (1988), 'Faschistische Trugbilder weiblicher Autonomie', *Frauen und Film*, Nos 44–5, 44–66.

Schmidt, J. (1996), 'Küsst die Faschisten, wo ihr sie trefft', *Frankfurter Allgemeine Zeitung*, 4 November.

Schneider, A. (1940), 'Der Film als Dokument', *Filmwelt*, No. 19, 10 May.

Schnell, R. (1992), 'Triumph des Überlebenswillens', *Frankfurter Rundschau*, 7 January.

— (2000), *Medienästhetik. Zur Geschichte und Theorie audiovisueller Wahrnehmungsformen*. Stuttgart, Weimar: Metzler.

Schulberg, B. (1946), 'Nazi Pin up Girl', *Saturday Evening Post*, 30 March.

Schwarzer, A. (1999), 'Leni Riefenstahl. Propagandistin oder Künstlerin?', *Emma*, No. 1, 39–47.

Seel, M. (1992), 'Arnold Fanck oder die Verfilmbarkeit von Landschaft', *Film und Kritik*, No. 1, June, 71–82.

Seelmann-Eggebert, U. (1964), 'Die Dreifaltigkeit der Leni Riefenstahl', *Mannheimer Morgen*, 13 February.

Seesslen, G. (1993), 'Die Krieger, der Tanz. das Mädchen und der Führer', *Blimp*, No. 22/3, 20–8.

— (1994a), *Tanz den Adolf Hitler*. Berlin: Klaus Bittermann.

— (1994b), 'Die Ästhetik des Barbarischen', *Die Woche*, 14 April.

Segebrecht, H. (1999), 'Hitler und Riefenstahl', in K. Hickethier (ed.), *Schauspieler und Montage*. St Augustin: Gardez, pp. 31–45.

Seltzer, A. (1985), 'Bildbanditen', *Merkur*, Vol. 39, No. 7, 621–5.

Servaes, F. (1923), 'Eine neue Tänzerin', *Der Tag*, 29 October.

Short, K. R. M. and Dolezel, S. (1988), *Hitler's Fall. The Newsreel Witness*. London, New York, Sidney: Croom Helm.

Sinsheimer, H. (1933), 'Zwei Legenden', *Berliner Tageblatt*, 26 March.

Sklar, R. (1994), 'The Devil's Director', *Cineaste*, Vol. 20, No. 3, 18–23.

Sokal, H. R. (1979), ' "Lebt wohl, Leidenschaften" ', *Stau!*, No. 8/9, 37–41.

Sokolowsky, K. (1999), 'Die neue Rechte', *Konkret*, No. 3, 12–17.

Sontag, S. (1980), 'Fascinating Fascism', in S. Sontag, *Under the Sign of Saturn*. New York: Farrar, Straus, Giroux, pp. 71–105.

Soussloff, C. and Nichols, B. (1996), 'Leni Riefenstahl: The Power of Image', *Discourse*, Vol. 19, No. 3, 20–44.

Speer, A. (1969), *Erinnerungen*. Frankfurt am Main, Berlin, Vienna: Ullstein.

Spielhofer, H. (1939), 'Filmstil und Stilbruch', *Der deutsche Film*, Vol. 3, No. 8, February, 214–17.

Spiker, J. (1975), *Film und Kapital. Der Weg der deutschen Filmwirtschaft zum nationalsozialistischen Einheitskonzern*. Berlin: Volker Spiess.

Stiftung Deutsche Kinemathek (ed.) (1992), *Babelsberg 1912–1992. Ein Filmstudio*. Berlin: Argon.

Stone, M. (1976), 'Kurz angemerkt', *Der Tagesspiegel*, 2 November.

Stutterheim, K. D. (2000), *Okkulte Weltvorstellungen im Hintergrund dokumentarischer Filme des "Dritten Reiches"*. Berlin: Weissensee.

Sudendorf, W. (1994), 'Nicht zur Veröffenlichung. Zur Biographie des Filmjournalisten Ernst (Ejott) Jäger', *Filmexil*, No. 5, December, 61–6.

Taylor, J. F. (1983), 'Directors of the Decade: the Thirties: Leni Riefenstahl', *Films and Filming*, No. 342, March, 14–15.

Teichler, H. J. (1996), 'Die Olympischen Spiele Berlin 1936 – eine Bilanz nach 60 Jahren', *Aus Politik und Zeitgeschichte*: supplement to the weekly newspaper *Das Parlament*, 12 July, 13–22.

Thiele, H.-G. (ed.) (1997), *Die Wehrmachtsausstellung. Dokumentation einer Kontroverse*. Bonn: Bundeszentrale für politische Bildung.

Thurner, E. (n.d.), 'Die nationalsozialistische Zigeunerverfolgung am Beispiel des Zigeunerlagers Salzburg-Maxglan', in Magistratsabteilung II/Kultur und Schulverwaltung Salzburg (ed.), *Salzburg. Ein Beitrag zum 40jährigen Bestehen der Zweiten Republik*. Salzburg, pp. 29–35.

Tobis Filmkunst-GmbH, Olympia-Pressedienst (Olympic press service, 1936), *Olympia. Fest der Völker. Erster Film von den Olympischen Spielen*. Berlin.

Trimborn, J. (1998), 'Gletscher, Schnee und Eis', *Plakat-Journal*, No. 4, 14–19.

Ulbrich, P. (1978), 'Lenis blühende Träume', *Film und Fernsehen*, Vol. 6, No. 5, 32–8.

Umbach, K. (1996), 'Schaf im Wolfspelz', *Der Spiegel*, No. 45, 4 November.

Uricchio, W. (n.d. (1989)), 'Ruttmann nach 1933', in J. Goergen (ed.), *Walter Ruttmann. Eine Dokumentation*. Berlin: Freunde der Deutschen Kinemathek, pp. 59–65.

Vat, D. van der (1997), *The Good Nazi: The Life and Lies of Albert Speer*. London: Weidenfeld and Nicholson.

Vaughan, Dai (1977), 'Berlin versus Tokyo', *Sight and Sound*, Vol. 46, No. 4, 210–15.

Wagner, F. J. (1976), 'Was ist aus ihnen geworden? Leni Riefenstahl', *Bild*, 11 November.

Walk, I. (1999), 'Bildproduktion und Weltmodell', in Filmmuseum Potsdam (ed.), *Leni Riefenstahl*. Berlin: Henschel, pp. 160–8.

Wallace, P. (1974), 'The Most Important Factor was the "Spirit": Leni Riefenstahl during the Filming of "The Blue Light"', *Image*, Vol. 17, No. 1, 16–28.

— (1975), 'An Historical Study of the Career of Leni Riefenstahl from 1923 to 1933'. MS (diss.).

Warneke, P. (1998), 'Recherche für die Ausstellung "Leni Riefenstahl"'. N.p. (Potsdam): MS.

Weigel, H. (1972), 'Randbemerkungen zum Thema', *Filmkritik*, Vol. 16, No. 8, August, 426–41.

Weiss, W. (1935), 'Der Film der Bewegung', *Völkischer Beobachter*, 30 March.

Welch, D. (1983), *Propaganda and the German Cinema 1933–1945*. Oxford: Clarendon Press.

Werneburg, B. (1999), 'Der Besuch der alten Dame', *die tageszeitung*, 8 February.

Wildmann, D. (1998), *Begehrte Körper. Konstruktion und Inszenierung des 'arischen' Männerkörpers im 'Dritten Reich'*. Würzburg: Königshausen und Neumann.

Winston, B. (1981), 'Reconsidering "Triumph of the Will": was Hitler there?', *Sight and Sound*, Vol. 50, No. 2, 102–7.

Witte, K. (1995), *Lachende Erben, Toller Tag. Filmkomödie im Dritten Reich*. Berlin: Vorwerk 8.

Wulf, J. (1989), *Kultur im Dritten Reich. Eine Dokumentation* (= *Theater und Film im Dritten Reich*, Vol. 4). Frankfurt am Main, Berlin: Ullstein.

Wysocki, G. von (1980), *Die Fröste der Freiheit. Aufbruchphantasien*. Frankfurt am Main: Syndikat.

Zechlin, H. J. (1939), *Landhäuser*. Berlin: Wasmuth.

Ziesel, K. (1935), 'Ein Walzer mit Leni Riefenstahl', *Preussische Zeitung*, 6 April.

Index

Note: The abbreviation LR has been used for Leni Riefenstahl. Films Riefenstahl directed are indicated in *bold italic*; those in which she acted are *underlined in italic*. The following abbreviations have been used for the names of films - *DbL* for *Das blaue Licht*, *DhB* for *Der heilige Berg*, *SdG* for *Sieg des Glaubens*, *TdF* for *Tag der Freiheit* and *TdW* for *Triumph des Willens*.

actors and actresses
  De Sica, Vittorio 137, 140
  Dietrich, Marlene 168, 174–5
  Koppenhöffer, Maria 115
  Marian, Ferdinand 123
  Minetti, Bernhard 112, 115
  Mir, Martha 38
  Petersen, Ernst 23, 25, 30, 100
  Richards, Frida 23
  Trenker, Luis 23, 25, 26, 27
  Udet, Ernst 140
  Wieman, Mathias 36
  see also Riefenstahl, Leni: careers,
    acting
aesthetics
  advertising 173, 177
  fascist 84–5, 147, 170, 181
  film/photography 3, 29, 60, 65–6, 139
    LR's influence on 95, 121, 136,
      164, 178, 180
    DbL 43, 146
    mass participation imagery
      and 77, 182
    Nuba photographs 163
    and *Olympia* 89, 162
    propaganda films 177, 182
    structure in *TdW* 64
  picturesque 74, 110
  romantic 107
Africa 141–7, 160
Aktiengesellschaft für Filmverwaltung i.l.
  (Joint-stock Company for Film
  Administration [In
  Liquidation]) 154, 156, 157

anti-fascism 133
  Tiefland as 115–17
Anti-Nazi League 93
anti-realism 24
anti-semitism 84, 91, 94, 96, 123
archive material 76, 103, 154
  Bundesarchiv 153, 155, 156
art, LR's life as 174–6
auteur, LR as 31–41, 52, 73–4, 107
  of Nazi films 59–76, 180
    TdW 60–1, 63, 72–6
avant-garde 3, 96

Balázs, Béla 33, 37, 146
Benjamin, Walter 3–4
bergfilme (mountain films) generally 22,
  24, 28, 32
  compared with
    DbL 35–6
    TdW 64–5
  and party rally films 163
  see also films (generally);
    documentaries; Party Rally films;
    sports films
Böhmer, Anton 170
Bormann, Martin 99, 100, 102, 112–13,
  114
Breker, Arno 2, 3, 101
Bundesarchive (West German state
  archive) 153, 155, 156

camera technique 30, 36, 55–6, 66, 79, 87
  close-ups 70, 75
  filters 36, 110